W9-CHE-134

THE WITCH HUNTS

A HISTORY OF THE WITCH PERSECUTIONS IN EUROPE AND NORTH AMERICA

A REVISED EDITION OF
WITCH, WICCE, MOTHER GOOSE

ROBERT W. THURSTON

PEARSON
Longman

Harlow, England • London • New York • Boston • San Francisco • Toronto
Sydney • Tokyo • Singapore • Hong Kong • Seoul • Taipei • New Delhi
Cape Town • Madrid • Mexico City • Amsterdam • Munich • Paris • Milan

Pearson Education Limited

Edinburgh Gate
Harlow CM20 2JE
United Kingdom
Tel: +44 (0)1279 623623
Fax: +44 (0)1279 431059
Website: www.pearsoned.co.uk

First published in Great Britain in 2001 as *Witch, Wicce, Mother Goose*
This edition published in 2007

© Pearson Education Limited 2001, 2007

The right of Robert W. Thurston to be identified as author
of this work has been asserted by him in accordance
with the Copyright, Designs and Patents Act 1988.

ISBN-13: 978-1-4058-4083-5
ISBN-10: 1-4058-4083-8

British Library Cataloguing in Publication Data
A CIP catalogue record for this book can be obtained from the British Library

Library of Congress Cataloging in Publication Data
Thurston, Robert W.
The witch hunts : a history of the witch persecutions in Europe and North America /
Robert W. Thurston.
p. cm.
Rev. ed. of: Witch, wicce, Mother Goose. 2001.
Includes bibliographical references and index.
ISBN-13: 978-1-4058-4083-5 (pbk.)
ISBN-10: 1-4058-4083-8 (pbk.)
1. Witchcraft—Europe—History.   2. Witchcraft—United States—History.   3. Trials
(Witchcraft)—Europe—History.   4. Trials (Witchcraft)—United States—History.   I.
Thurston, Robert W. Witch, wicce, Mother Goose.   II. Title.

BF1584.E9T48 2006
133.4'3094—dc22

2006050686

10   9   8   7   6   5   4   3   2   1
10   09   08   07

Set by 35 in 11/13.5pt Garamond MT
Printed and bound in Great Britain by Clays Ltd., Bungay, Suffolk

The Publisher's policy is to use paper manufactured from sustainable forests.

THE WITCH HUNTS

for Lara,
bewitching
(in the very best sense of the word)
and bemusing

CONTENTS

ILLUSTRATIONS

1. The devil presenting the demon pact to Theophilus. Illumination of *c.*1210 from the Psalter of Queen Ingeborg of Denmark in the Musée Condé, Chantilly. © 2005 TopFoto/Fortean Picture Library, UK.
2. Knights Templar: Jacques de Molay burned at the stake with Geoffrey de Charney, 14 March 1314. © 2005 TopFoto/Fortean Picture Library, UK.
3. Limbourg Brothers, Hell, from *Les Très Riches Heures du Duc de Berry*, *c.*1413. Musée Condé, Paris. The Ancient Art & Architecture Collection.
4. 'The Four Witches' with a demon. Engraving by Albrecht Dürer, 1497. © 2005 TopFoto/Fortean Picture Library, UK.
5. Four English women hanged as witches – original caption begins 'many poor women imprisoned'. © Bettmann/Corbis.
6. 'Witches' Sabbat' by Hans Baldung Grien, 1510. Note the pseudo-Hebrew letters on the witches' pot, once again making the link between various enemies of Christianity and humanity. © Bettmann/Corbis.
7. Anonymous drawing of witches at work from Johann Geiler von Kaysersberg, *Die Emeis*, 1517. Cornell University Library.
8. Pieter Brueghel's *Dulle Griet (Mad Meg)*, (*c.*1515–69). (GIR325) Museum Mayer van der Berg, Antwerp, Belgium. The Bridgeman

Arts Library, London/Getty Images. Meg, powerful and un-feeling, has emerged from hell bearing her loot. Other women wait for a demon to scoop money to them from his behind.

9. Lucas Cranach the Elder, *Melencolia*, 1528 (furious horde in the upper left). Columbus, Ohio Museum of Art. © Christie's images/Corbis.

10. A witch feeding her 'familiars' (imps). © 2004 TopFoto/Fortean Picture Library, UK.

11. Man being prepared for the strappado. © 2005 TopFoto/Fortean Picture Library, UK.

12. The North Berwick coven, 1591: members drink in the cellar, one takes down the words of the devil preaching from the pulpit, others boil up a cauldron to create a storm and sink a ship at sea. The large figure of a man reclining in two places is surely meant to represent the Earl of Bothwell. © 2005 TopFoto/Fortean Picture Library, UK.

13. Frans Francken (II the Younger), *The Witches' Sabbath*, 1606, Victoria & Albert Museum. © Stapleton Collection/Corbis.

14. The witch house at Bamberg. © 2003 Charles Walker/TopFoto.co.uk.

15. Artemis/Diana with her bow and arrow. The Furious Horde is no longer to be seen. From Tooke's *Pantheon*, 1659, p. 208. Mary Evans Picture Library, London.

16. The witches' sabbat. A typical image from the period of the hunts, although a bit late in their history. Note the ritual kiss of the devil's posterior, here depicted as a goat. From Gottlief Spisseln, *Die Gebrochne Macht der Finsternuss*, 1687. © TopFoto/Fortean Picture Library, UK.

MAPS

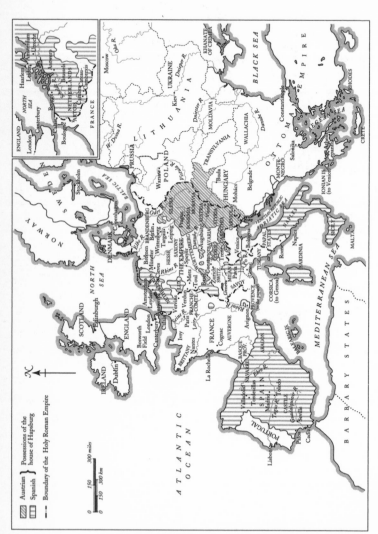

Map 1 Europe in the 16th Century.

Map 2 Western Europe under Attack, 8th–10th Centuries.

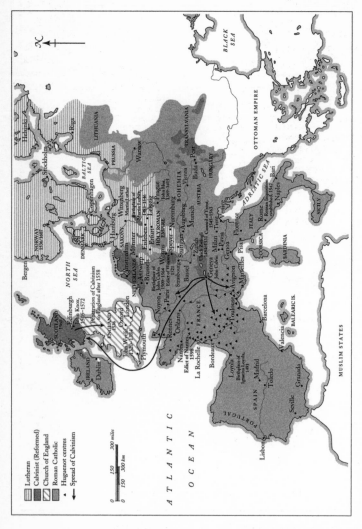

Map 3 Religious divisions in Western Europe in the 17th Century. The Huguenots were French Protestants.

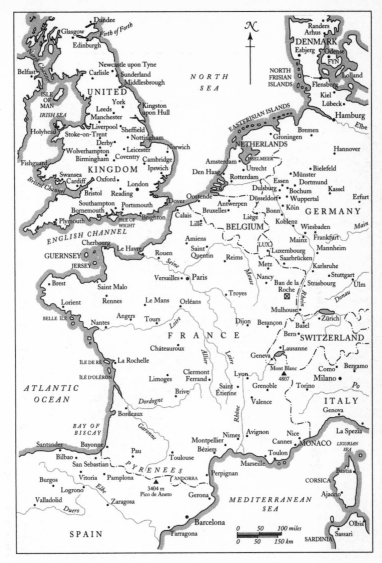

Map 4 Seventeenth-Century France. Ban de la Roche is at the right-centre of the map, between Nancy and Strasbourg.

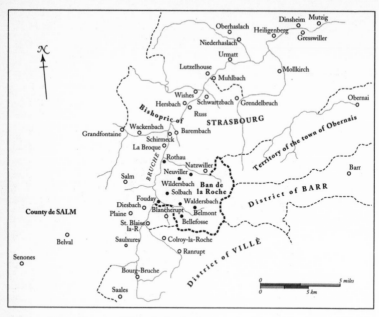

Map 5 The villages of Ban de la Roche.

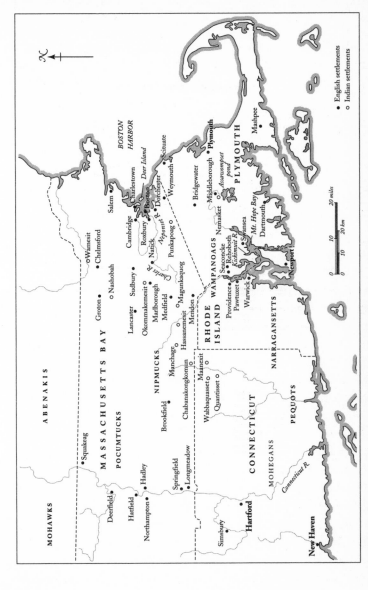

Map 6 Indian and English settlements in Seventeenth-Century Massachusetts.

PREFACE TO THE REVISED EDITION

It is not often that we get an opportunity to take back a word said, change an action performed. I am grateful to Pearson Education for giving me the chance to write a second edition of a book on the European and North American witch hunts.

In general, I believe, the first edition has held up well. For example, other writers have now come closer to the estimate offered there of the total number executed – a figure, I should say, that I derived in the first place from educated guesses by some specialists. The first edition argued against the view that state-building or rebellion was an essential factor at work behind the witch hunts, and recently published material appears to support my contention more than undermine it.

It is the new studies – a great flood of them, constantly increasing – that call for a revision of my first effort. A magnificent new *Encyclopedia of Witchcraft*, in particular, sums up the state of enquiries into the persecutions and virtually demands a new broad exploration of them. Other, specialized studies on the meaning and goals of demonology, the vast contemporary literature on witchcraft produced in Europe from the early fifteenth century into the eighteenth, require a rethinking of that topic. We seem closer than ever to unravelling the question of why women were so often the victims of the hunts. The role of the Protestant and Catholic Reformations seems clearer now than several years ago, and the issue of how often the folk magicians, the 'wise' or 'cunning' people, ended on the gallows or the stake is better focused.

While the first edition was deemed clear and readable by virtually all who commented on it, I hope to make certain ideas even more accessible in this try. In particular, were the witch hunts 'functional'? That is, did they have the primary aim or the secondary outcome of disciplining people and scaring them into the behaviour desired by the elite? My answer here is still no, but I shall make the reasons for that conclusion sharper.

What did not work in the first edition was its title, *Witch, Wicce, Mother Goose*. The point of that phrase, besides the obvious goal of catching potential readers' attention, was to show that a change in European terms for certain women summed up the whole course of the witch hunts. Although I tried in the text to explain what I had in mind, apparently only I and my original editor understood what I was attempting to get at. 'Wicce', the first of my three words chronologically, is an old Anglo-Saxon term that might be rendered in modern English as sorceress or magician. 'Witch' came much later and referred to anyone thought to have allied with the devil in order to make black magic. Finally, 'Mother Goose' represents the triumph in western European consciousness of the harmless old woman; the malicious ugly witch has been tamed and relegated to the world of fairy tales. In short, one prominent motif regarding ordinary females in Europe had them first as somewhat problematic, then a huge threat (in certain areas at certain times) and finally a charming old grandmotherly figure. Western Europe traversed this distance in the relatively short time of three centuries.

Part of the problem with the old title was that it was out of order chronologically. I could not write 'Wicce, Witch, Mother Goose', or 'From Wicce to Mother Goose', because then the book would have seemed pitched largely at modern wiccans. Not that I have anything against them! But the intended audience was much wider – all those interested in Europe, the fate of women, mass violence, why a great fear would rise and fall in a society, and much more.

I hope that the new title is a better invitation to consider one of the most controversial and chaotic episodes of European and North American history.

INTRODUCTION

Strasbourg, France, lies along the Rhine, for centuries one of the world's busiest waterways. Here the valley of the Rhine is broad and fertile; corn and cows line both the French and German sides before giving way to vineyards as the land climbs gradually in both countries, rising to the low mountains of the Vosges to the west and the Black Forest to the east. The density of the trees in this part of Germany darkens the ground, giving the forest its name and helping to spawn a vast array of legends and stories. Across the valley in France the woods are still thick, and disturbing tales circulate here, too.

In Strasbourg's old quarter the cathedral, half-timbered houses and narrow streets decked with flowers at every window bespeak the wealth enjoyed by the city for more than half a millennium. This cross-roads of western Europe is now the seat of the European Parliament and European Court. However, business and politics can produce severe congestion in Strasbourg, and the heat of the flat Rhineland can be exhausting. Going from the city into the Vosges hardly means going back in time, but it is possible to find places where the same families have lived for centuries, where tourists are not thick on the ground, and where witches were once executed.

The Bruche River is little more than a stream as it flows east through the mountains to join the Rhine. Close to the headwaters of the Bruche are a number of steep side valleys, on the slopes of which are perched the nine villages of an area called Ban de la Roche in French, Steinthal in German, signifying the ancient bilingual character of the region. The names may be translated respectively as 'district of the rock' and 'rock valley'. For centuries the Ban has been ruled as one administrative unit, and today it forms a French 'commune'. It was here that, in the early part of the seventeenth century, a series of vicious and deadly witch hunts took place. Let us begin with an incident from one wave of Steinthal's witch trials, and look at what questions this one case might conjure up about the witch hunts in general, which occurred roughly from 1400 to 1700.

On 11 July 1629, a grandmother and widow, Catharina Ringelspach, was arrested in Ban de la Roche on charges of 'child murder and witchcraft'. She was accused of causing the death of her grandson, Colla, by poisoning him. The day before, several people testified, the boy had been healthy. He had gone out to pick berries and had returned home at about two in the afternoon. His grandmother had made soup for him in the evening, which he had eaten 'without indication of difficulty or sickness'. Colla had then gone out again 'completely cheerfully', but when he returned he sat by the fire and complained about pain in his thigh. Catharina put him to bed. After lying there a little while, he got up to defecate, which out of dire need he did in the room itself. At that moment his grandmother, wanting 'to get in the cat so that it could catch mice and rats', entered the room. Seeing what the boy had done, she hit him and made him go back to bed. She cleaned up the mess, then sat in the main room by the fire and began to spin wool. Colla's sister, also in the house, heard him complain again from the room where he was lying that he felt bad. Catharina, she said, picked up a stick and went into the bedroom; whether she hit the boy at that time or not the granddaughter could not say. She heard no scream. The widow told Colla that he could not stay in the bed but had to lie on a straw pallet on the floor.

The granddaughter went to milk the cow; hearing the boy complain once more, she suggested that her grandmother should go to him, but was told that the boy was making noise because he was bad, and that there was nothing wrong with him. Catharina would not permit her granddaughter to go in to the boy and instructed her to go to bed. Half an hour later the widow went to bed; after another half an hour had passed, she came out of the room and said that the boy was dead. The granddaughter entered the bedroom and found her brother dead on the straw.

Six days later, a court, authorized by Count Georg Gustav Veldenz, who owned all of the land and fixed assets in the Ban, assembled to hear Ringelspach's case. The tribunal consisted of local men, among whom was the Lutheran pastor Nicolas Marmett. Johann Wolders, Veldenz's bailiff, headed the group. At first the court questioned the widow Ringelspach with 'good words'. But the men had already made up their minds about her guilt, as they asked by what means the widow had brought the boy to an 'unnatural death'. They knew that her grandson had been 'fresh and healthy' when he had eaten his last soup. Ringelspach must have done something besides hit him to make him die so suddenly.

The members of the tribunal examined Colla's body closely. According to the interrogation record, they found red and blue spots under the boy's arms, while the area around his heart was completely white. On his back they found an open wound the width of a penny. The neck was broken in two at the nape, one man announced. Although Colla had been dead for days, his joints were all still flexible.

Wolders then ordered that if Ringelspach did not tell the truth, 'with the help of torture the truth be brought out from her'. When she persisted in her denial of witchcraft or any wrongdoing, Wolders directed his assistants, who probably included a man who was both a specialist in torture and an executioner, to bind her and 'hoist' her off the ground. The procedure in all likelihood used a form of the strappado, in which the victim's hands were tied behind the back. Another rope then passed from the hands to a pulley or beam set near the ceiling of the chamber. The torturer would pull on the second rope until the accused's hands were wrenched up and back behind the shoulders. Then the whole body was lifted from the floor. The agony caused by having one's full weight on the arms and shoulders, especially twisted as they were into such an unnatural position, was intense; on occasion torturers would attach heavy weights to the feet to increase the pain. The handlers might jerk the victim up or drop her suddenly to the floor. In many cases dislocation of the shoulders resulted.

We do not know exactly how Ringelspach was tortured; the record only states that she was questioned again as she hung in the air. But she was a tough woman who refused to change her previous testimony.

The investigation alternated between sessions of torture and questioning of other witnesses. Villager Jean Daillon told the court that Ringelspach had wanted to teach his wife a 'suspicious art' for dealing with illness. The prisoner denied having done so. Next a woman came forward to say that Ringelspach had offered to teach her how to cure an illness by using several candles and wax formed into the shape of a heart. The sick woman should say a prayer in the name of the Father, of the Son and of the Virgin Mary, but should deliberately exclude the Holy Spirit. To the judges, this was a sign that Ringelspach had diverged from the 'true' religion. The other villager had refused to accept Ringelspach's advice.

After being subjected to further torture, the accused began to change her story. She now said that three days before her grandson's death, she saw him in her garden, but when she approached him, the 'thing' disappeared. It must have been an angel or a devil, she told the judges. The tribunal responded by having her hoisted yet again off the floor, this time with some sort of screw mechanism tightened on her legs. Despite what must have been great pain, Ringelspach altered her previous statements only by adding that during the day of the boy's death, she had given him herbs to eat several times.[1]

Here ends the paper trail on her case. We do not know Ringelspach's fate, but given the testimony against her and the nature of her grandson's death, so suspicious to the court, it is highly likely that she was executed as a witch. The same set of documents shows that in Steinthal at least 50 other women and 30 men were burned for witchcraft between 1620 and 1630. Available evidence indicates that during that decade, 174 of some 1200 residents in the nine villages, or close to 15 per cent of the local population, were accused of witchcraft.

From the farmhouse where I stayed for a few days one July, I walked along a trail that led to the spot where witches and other convicted criminals of the Ban had been executed. I followed the path along the edge of a thick forest and came to open ground where a few tall trees stood around the remains of a recent campfire. The site has a name: Perheux. Although I could see several villages above and below me on the hills, I was alone, with little sound of human activity able to reach me. It was a bright day; the sky was postcard blue.

I tried to strip away several hundred years and visualize a crowd of people jostling for a better view of one of their neighbours as she received a final blessing by the pastor, who days before had served as one of her judges. Were the other peasants frightened, and if so, of what? Of the presence of a witch or of the thought that one of them, especially a woman, might be the next victim? Or did they feel relief because they believed that a real criminal was going to her death? Continental witches were often strangled before their bodies were burned; however, no record told me if that had been the practice here. Was Catharina Ringelspach burned alive?

I failed to imagine a vivid scene. Maybe the place was too quiet and pretty. All I could get was a fleeting picture of a crowd (silent?

screaming?), low flames, maybe the odour of something foul. It was easier to visualize the scene in a quiet library or study, with a document from the period in my hand. Nevertheless, in the 1620s the crowd was there, many times. Both the spectators and the participants must have been more or less normal people, or the term 'normal' has no meaning. Why did they deliver each other to the pyres?

Nothing was simple here. Before a large group of cases from 1620 to 1622, only one accusation of witchcraft is recorded for Ban de la Roche, from the year 1607. After the wave of trials from 1629 to 1630 that included Ringelspach's ordeal, no more are mentioned. The witch hunt in these relatively isolated mountain hamlets thus fits well into the general chronology of the persecutions across Europe; the first recorded trial of a witch took place in 1324, in Ireland, while the last recorded legal execution for witchcraft occurred in 1782, in Switzerland. But the number of trials climbed slowly and erratically after 1324, and the peak of the witch burnings was roughly from 1580 to 1630. In the early 1620s, a particularly large and vicious wave of persecutions struck several parts of Germany. Altogether, the greatest number of cases by far were in German-speaking lands; one could draw a circle with a 300-mile radius around Strasbourg that would encompass well over 50 per cent of all known witch trials.[2] Such a circle would take in most of Germany, the Netherlands and Switzerland, as well as much of France; however, it would also leave out a great deal of Europe, and within its sweep many areas did not register any witch trials at all.

Immediately several problems demand consideration: why did the witch persecutions occur only during a certain period of European history, and why only in certain parts of Europe? And what was a witch? On one level the latter question is much easier to tackle than the other issues. In various European languages, a witch was different from a sorcerer. French is not one of them, as it never produced a word more precise than the inclusive *sorcier*, female *sorcière*. But German and Spanish provide good examples: the *Zauberer/Zauberin* (magician or sorcerer) began to yield around 1420–30 to *Hex/Hexe*. In Spanish the transition was from *hechicero/hechicera* to *brujo/bruja*, although an especially clear distinction between the two terms never developed. The Anglo-Saxon *wicca/wicce* originally referred simply to someone who used magic, whether for good or ill; the word eventually evolved into *witch*, a term that had a vastly darker set of associations. The European witches allegedly made a solemn agreement, a pact, with the devil. They voluntarily and of their own free will – this point will be terribly important – agreed to be his servants and to have sexual intercourse with him in any manner or position he chose. However, sometimes, the judges and witch finders maintained, Satan would assign a lesser demon as sexual partner for a witch, or would detail a female spirit to accommodate a male follower.

The witches were said to fly to great gatherings, the sabbats, a word taken from Jewish services. When the witches congregated, they ate coarse food, danced to mournful tunes, celebrated a kind of anti-mass with their master and engaged in repulsive sexual acts with each other and the demons. Coupling with the devil was far from pleasurable, the witches of Steinthal and many others reported; the male and female demons both felt cold, 'like ice', and for female witches the experience was sometimes as painful as giving birth.

The old magicians and sorcerers had not, in the popular and the elite mind, held sabbats. The witches did supposedly mimic the bad magicians, or more precisely their bad side, by carrying out evil acts, *maleficia*, to use the Latin word that appears so often in the documents for both categories of supernatural power users. However, the witches were charged with particularly horrendous deeds, especially against human and agricultural fertility, committed at the command of their master. They were fond of destroying crops, animals and humans. Their favourite prey was babies, a motif that appears steadily in the trial records. According to the witch hunters, these renegade humans would obey the devil's command to kill and eat infants.

For centuries, the European imagination could create such creatures – for there is no credible evidence that they really existed, or that anyone performed nocturnal rites that remotely resembled the witches' sabbat – but these anti-humans were central figures in everyday outlook only during a certain period. What had happened? What cultural and perhaps political currents came together to produce the stereotype of the witch and to make people act upon it? The witches had a long prehistory, as it were; they sprang, as did the big Western Christian devil, from a tangled set of sources and fears. To find the origins of the witches, it is necessary to look well back in time, especially to the Bible and the early church fathers, and then to take a more detailed look at key themes in Western culture starting around 1000 CE.

The word 'belief' often figures prominently in discussions of how the Europeans and their branch in Massachusetts regarded the witches, but a book that treats the history of attitudes would actually be better off avoiding the term, if only that were possible. We often have little enough confidence that we know what *we* really believe, let alone what people believed five centuries ago. If religion in particular is 'a cultural resource' that different people understand quite differently,[3] it will be more useful to consider the matrix of ideas and symbols within which we operate as providing the usual boundaries and the ground for our imaginations. From such a matrix, people pick and choose images, or combinations of them, to emphasize and to use as explanatory devices for the experiences they encounter. Behaviour rarely runs flagrantly counter to the dominant cultural menu.

Few people have imaginations that range outside the set of words and symbols they absorb from their culture. Those who do go further are usually called insane or geniuses. Ordinary, uneducated Europeans produced folk dances, wonderful melodies and a great array of art, but left to themselves they probably did not picture a large devil doing battle on virtually equal terms with Christ. Rather, the common folk pictured devils or petty, rather stupid demons in their tales whom they could overcome by wit or luck.[4]

Over the course of about a thousand years, the great Satan of our period was created by some Europeans through new symbols, words and images. The elite of the Continent also probably did not produce such a figure on their own; there was a long interaction between those things named by the educated and those named by the common folk. Together they developed an outlook that included an active, energetic devil and his attentive converts, the witches. Yet the belief system was one of possibilities, perhaps more accurately of probabilities; we cannot know to what extent those alive in the years 1000–1700 took any part of the existing matrix to heart and became convinced that it correctly described reality.

This study will argue that, given the prevailing belief system in western Europe in the period 1400–1700, witchcraft was considered a real crime, one taken with deadly seriousness. 'Western Europe' in this book refers approximately to the territory of the 'capitalist' countries during the Cold War. A line could be drawn from the Baltic Sea a little east of Berlin down to Vienna and on to the Adriatic, at the border between Italy and the former Yugoslavia, to divide western from eastern Europe; this would put much German-speaking territory, especially in the early modern period, in the eastern section, but would provide a reasonably accurate division of Europe for the purposes of discussing the witch hunts.

In the western part of the Continent, the new image of the witch spread widely. Yet in many areas the governing elite did not necessarily accept the stereotype as an indication of clear and present danger to society. Published guides to the unmasking and trial of witches circulated in Venice and Spain, for example, but never engaged the elite's attention enough to provoke a large hunt.

In eastern Europe, Russia provides a good example of the new witch stereotype's failure to become an established part of the cultural setting. The Russian language uses *koldun/koldun'ia*, *ved'ma* (a feminine form) and a long list of other words to refer to people who practise good or evil magic. Even in recent years, *kolduny* have been invited to Russian weddings, obviously in the hope of a good outcome. Suspected witches were not invited to Western nuptials, but the *wicce* or the 'cunning folk', the more traditional healers and practitioners of magic in the villages, surely did attend. They were too important, and possibly too dangerous in their own way, to be excluded.

Before there could be witch hunts, a new concept of the magicians, that they drew their powers from Satan, had to be in place within a culture. In short, the witch had to make her appearance as a new kind of creature. Sorcerers and old-fashioned magicians were often known to their communities because their business depended on reputation. However, few admitted to witchcraft in Europe after about 1440, as execution often followed.

Although some older studies, and in recent years new research, have uncovered witch hunts where the majority of victims were men, it is still probably safe to say that 75 per cent or more of all executed witches were female. Why? This is one of the thorniest issues of all. Gender – roles and ideas assigned to the realm of one sex – must be considered within the context of what women did in Europe, what marriage meant for them, and how their image in art and thought worsened as the Middle Ages waned. Why were women so often identified in the first place as the sex more likely to consort with the devil?

One part of the answer to this question is that, as both cause and effect of a change in women's image that began in the high Middle Ages, a new conception of male and female purity arose.

Dyan Elliott has described a figurative 'splitting' by the eleventh century of men from women, women from holiness, and even breasts from female genitalia.[5] Purity was now ascribed to more men but fewer women than ever before. The cultural origins and significance of this division directly relate to the coming of the witch hunts. Much later, during the seventeenth century, the image of women improved, if only relative to what had gone before. It is no accident that the curve of the witch burnings moved roughly in the opposite direction from that of the general image of women.

Yet focusing on the victimization of women in the hunts can obscure more than it illuminates. This book also pays great attention to where the persecutions occurred. Locale varied widely, so that often one jurisdiction suffered through trials while neighbouring districts, even of the same religion and more or less the same social make-up, did not. At the same time, persecutions in villages typically differed from those in towns or cities. The social and political geography of the witch persecutions deserves as much study as does the issue of gender, partly because precise location bore significantly on the implications of gender. Women's activities in towns were often distinct from those in villages, and diverse surroundings gave rise to sets of ideas on the proper roles for each sex that varied significantly. Even more important, standards of evidence applied in any witchcraft trial were often different in towns than in the countryside.

Women were indeed accused of witchcraft much more often than men. However, once an accusation arose the European and New England courts came to the business of looking at the available evidence. On the whole, the European judicial system, especially outside of England, changed fundamentally in the high Middle Ages. Courts operated on the basis of reason and evidence more than ever before. Ironically, the new jurisprudence helped lead to a vast increase in charges of witchcraft. The new courts made the witch hunts in many places.

But, almost together with the new demonology of the fourteenth and fifteenth centuries, voices in Europe and Massachusetts raised objections to the standards of evidence being used against witches, and to the use of torture to gather that evidence. However erratically objections and scepticism appeared, they were always present. It is crucial to understand that the European elite neither spoke nor acted uniformly at any time regarding witch persecutions.

The critical voices were overwhelmingly those of men. If men began and conducted the witch hunts, they also brought them to an end. Focusing on the issue of what was considered good evidence of witchcraft, and on why attitudes toward evidence changed dramatically by the end of the seventeenth century, will bring us closer to understanding what the witch persecutions were all about.

The large body of literature on the hunts has grown substantially in recent years. A significant part of these studies, especially ones that appeared after the late 1960s, suggests that the witch hunts were an attack on women by the men who held virtually every position of importance at the time. Men wished to murder uppity women, to teach acceptable female behaviour by way of fiery example, and sometimes, it has been argued, to indulge their sadistic lust by probing and harming women's bodies.[6] While investigations along these lines have revealed a wealth of information about the witch hunts, these claims do not stand up to a careful look at how the trials unfolded in Europe and North America.

Sociologists and historians influenced by these and similar ideas have argued that the hunts were a way of getting rid of marginal residents who had disturbed the community and hence might be erased for the common good. The thesis that witch persecutions served as a means of eliminating or curbing deviant residents of both sexes has been around for decades.[7] Once again, available case studies do not usually support such conclusions. Often the argument is circular: people who were deviants were executed; we know they were deviants because they were executed. It is possible to go well beyond this tautology.

Witch trials frequently occurred in political or religious border regions; Ban de la Roche was a Protestant district ruled separately from the Catholic areas that surrounded it. Did tensions or competition in such borderlands, including fear of strangers, contribute significantly to witch burnings? The pursuit of witches often happened where central political authority was weak, and some scholars maintain that deploying the charge of witchcraft was part of the process of strengthening higher levels of political power.[8] In other words, witch hunts were a part of state-building. Another variation describes the accusation as an attempt by urban officials to assert their authority in the countryside.[9]

Many studies have discussed a rise in social and economic tensions or in the ambitions of civil and church authorities during the late medieval–early modern period. The new anxiety and aspirations have sometimes been identified as the key factors, if not the causes of the witch hunts. Religious strife after the beginning of the Reformation is also sometimes given a central role,[10] and indeed most of the trials occurred after the division of the Western Church.

Explanations that follow these broad lines frequently hinge on 'function': in the witch trials the elite supposedly pursued a political, social or ideological goal, or a combination of the three. The best example is probably the notion that the patriarchal society attempted to discipline or terrorize women, using a thin legal cloak to hide its true intentions. Writers who see such functions in the hunts usually imply that the men who directed them rarely if ever did what they said they were doing, hunting people they perceived to be dangerous criminals.[11]

For many years, sociological and anthropological literature on witches and their persecution has mentioned another kind of function. Especially in this usage, 'function' does not mean the same thing as 'purpose'. Even if the initiators of an action do not have a specific outcome or intention in mind, their deeds may serve or fulfil a function, so the argument goes. One social science description of a function in witch accusations is that members of many communities, from English villagers in the sixteenth century to the herding Navajos of the American Southwest in the twentieth century, have relieved social tensions and displaced their own aggression by charging others with witchcraft. Anthropologists sometimes deem the accusation an expression of hostility toward someone who cannot be directly attacked under existing social rules. Such transferral has also been called scapegoating,[12] as it supposedly allows a society to shift the burden of its hostilities on to a few members. Ironically, the writer best known for taking this approach to European witch hunts, Alan Macfarlane in *Witchcraft in Tudor and Stuart England*, then rejected his own thesis in a later book.[13] His change of heart has not prevented more than a few academics from citing and praising the first study as a model of how social science can provide functional explanations.[14]

Beyond the difficulty of finding precise evidence that supports such discussions of the hunts, the sociologists themselves have all but abandoned the term 'function' in describing communal behaviour. Robert Merton, the great proponent of the idea from the 1940s until his recent death, indicated that the term function was adapted from the biological sciences, where it refers to 'the vital or organic processes' that 'contribute to the maintenance of the organism'.[15] 'Vital' and 'organic' obviously suggest that a living creature, or a society, cannot exist without certain processes. If that is correct, why did so many parts of Europe cope reasonably well without witch hunts? Why did officials in areas where hunts raged for a time often bring them abruptly to a halt?

Nothing is clarified – on the contrary, the waters are muddied further – by bringing into the discussion the adjectives 'manifest' or 'latent', which Merton attached to 'function' in 1949. He now borrowed from Freud as well as from biology. 'Manifest' functions are 'consequences . . . intended and recognized by participants in the system'. So far, so good; 'manifest' means something that any intelligent person can see. But latent functions are by definition not visible; they are 'neither intended nor recognized' by those who carry out an action.[16] Then how does anyone know that such functions are there? Scholars have deduced latent functions from actions, in effect maintaining that they can see deeper into the witch hunts than the people involved did.

If a given society sought relief from tension or wanted to indicate the boundaries of acceptable behaviour, why should such functions have taken the specific form of executing accused witches? In other respects, European authorities were hardly reticent about directly indicating the boundaries of acceptable behaviour through law and punishment; attempting to conceal a pregnancy was a capital crime in France in the early modern era, for instance.[17] The lower classes, especially peasants, were typically considered quite stupid by their social superiors; there was little point in giving the brutes indirect lessons in conduct, especially when, as we shall see, witch trials were as a rule quite expensive.

Sociologists still approvingly quote Merton's ideas on manifest and latent functions in introductory texts, but rarely are the 'concepts themselves employed in the research context'. They have not 'found a home in sociological theory'.[18] They are vague and unprovable; they do not work. Merton himself had strong words for those who would apply his ideas too broadly: 'functional social scientists' might be too quick to find the ideas they were already looking for in societies that are not their own, which Merton called 'strange' or 'primitive'. For people alive today, Europe from 1400 to 1700 can indeed be a strange place, for its symbols and belief system do not have the same significance to us. What does 'Jew' or 'heretic' mean today in Western Europe compared to their emotive power for Christians in 1400?

It is now abundantly clear that, while most European witches were executed after some sort of judicial procedure, however filled with pressure and torture it may have been, many other suspected witches were killed by crowds acting outside the law. That is, these victims were lynched. In recent studies of mob action, 'lynching' is usually defined as any illegal killing by a group, usually of three or more persons, acting 'under the pretext of service to justice, race, or tradition'.[19] The mob carries out what it sees as an act to serve the public, not private vengeance or punishment. Sociologists who examine lynching argue that it had the function of releasing tension within the dominant group or of intimidating a target population and keeping it 'in its place'.[20]

Assuming for the moment that the functions of witch accusations were to relieve tension, channel aggression, or keep a group properly frightened and manageable, it seems strange that more societies do not have witch trials. Hunts should affect a relatively small number of people at any one time but should be more or less periodic events if the persecutions are a means of venting aggression or enacting social control. Yet if any generalization about the European witch hunts is on solid ground, it is that they were highly erratic. In looking at a phenomenon as complex as the hunts, sociology and anthropology can make a great contribution, but only if we bear in mind that societies and their cultures do not remain static. Some level of social tensions may be found in every era of European history, and several periods before and after the early modern period witnessed greater dislocation but no witch killings.

Many groups that possessed power or superior force over others, for example Nazis, ordinary German soldiers, Soviet officials, and mobs of white American southerners, have abused and murdered people without scruple. Yet in the grim history of mass persecutions, the European witch hunts stand out as episodes where specific charges of criminal acts were lodged against suspects. The accused then usually underwent established judicial processes, however skewed the trials might have been as a result of the use of torture. Physical pressure was not common in England but was legal in Scotland and on the Continent of Europe. Judicial torture was carried out behind closed doors, though it was not an altogether secret procedure; its use was regulated and even required in the law codes in certain circumstances, the names of those condemned by the courts were made public, and their executions were spectacles open to all.

Catharina Ringelspach passed through a legal process and was in effect judged an enemy of the Christian community. We know little else about her. The documents do not mention her grandson's mother and father, so perhaps Ringelspach had assumed care of the boy after his parents' deaths. She lived in what seems to have been a substantial household; the dwelling had various rooms, already placing it above the housing of the poorest people crammed into one undivided space. There were pigs and milk cows on the farm. No evidence indicates that Ringelspach was marginal or a deviant in the sense of having violated established social norms. Was she a scapegoat for others' aggressions? There is no way to judge, just as there is not for the great bulk of available evidence on witch trials; however, we must doubt that she was simply or even largely a victim of others' guilt transference. After all, a substantial legal apparatus, voracious in its consumption of time and money, was brought to bear on one woman. At the least it is necessary to explain why anyone's hostility towards a member of the same community would be focused and directed through a legal trial, endorsed and led by the local elite, to produce her execution.

Without denying for a moment that males have been vicious brutes all too often in societies around the world, it is worth touching briefly on the implications that follow from functional explanations of the witch hunts. These interpretations suggest that men coldly and cynically chose their (largely female) victims, charged them with crimes that had not and could not have happened, and tortured and burned them. The sparse evidence on lynchings of witches, of course less well documented because of the nature of the homicide, suggests that the victims were socially and economically like those convicted and put to death under the law. All this supposedly occurred in order to punish some people for breaking the prescribed rules of conduct and to deter others from doing the same. Were men that callous? Perhaps they were, although then the problems re-emerge of why some men in some places behaved so badly, while in neighbouring villages or towns they did not, as well as of why the pyres burned only for a certain period of time.

The idea that scapegoating and transfer of aggression were involved raises another gender issue. One of the first sophisticated studies to advance the scapegoat argument was Clyde Kluckhohn's study of the Navajo, published in 1944.[21] Kluckhohn found that Navajo males were overwhelmingly the target of witchcraft accusations. But why should everyday hostilities in some poor, agrarian societies be taken out on men, while in other such settings the targets were women?[22] More history and a closer look at the nature of relationships among western European peasants are clearly needed.

Several recent studies of witchcraft as a whole have moved beyond the European and North American episodes to emphasize the universality of witch beliefs and hunts. Extensive and terrifying outbreaks of witch hunting have been reported in recent decades, on a relatively small scale in Latin America but sometimes involving dozens of deaths in Africa.[23] Yet emphasizing the African story in particular has the drawback of making the European hunts seem merely one part of a long human tendency, a misleading impression, and one which moreover brings us again to the idea of witchcraft accusations as fulfilling some basic human need. There is also the implication in such accounts that witch persecutions have to do with a certain level of development in a society, a more 'superstitious' or 'backward' level that used to exist in Europe but is now found more in Africa.

The point must be stressed again that the witch hunts in Europe and North America were unique. Nowhere else has the pact with the devil been so emphasized, or has appeared at all. Attacks on village cunning folk occurred in Europe before and well after the organized hunts, and it is those persecutions of common people by their peers that resemble African witch killings much more than the 'judicial murders' of the period 1400–1700 did. The European hunts emerged from the Christian world, but only as that milieu changed and became a much more fearful setting than earlier. If all societies talk about harmful magic and are concerned with throttling it, only in the western part of Europe and its colonies in America, and only for a discernible period of time, did those attitudes bring together elite and popular views to produce officially sanctioned capital punishment of witches. Neither the African killings nor the deaths of cunning folk in Europe before and after the major persecutions are usefully illuminated by describing them as universal human behaviour.

To begin to do justice to these issues and to a terrible aspect of Western history, it is necessary to start well before the first witch hunt recorded in Europe. The early chapters of this book look at three strands that helped bring about the witch persecutions. These themes, which came together between about 1000 and 1400, were the formation of a new, more coherent Christian cosmology and design for daily life; a decline in the status of women and hence in their worth, in various senses; and a growing sense that Western Christendom was under attack by enemies from without and from within.

NOTES

1. 'Originale Hexen-Protokolle aus dem Steinthal', Rare and Manuscript Collections, Carl A. Kroch Library, Cornell University, 197–207v. Hereafter cited as Steinthal ms. A typescript of the manuscript,

prepared in 1926 by Bertha Sutermeister Merritt, is available at Kroch Library.

2. William Monter, in a book whose findings have held up well, guessed that 'probably more witches were killed in the confines of present-day Germany than in the rest of Europe put together'. E. William Monter (1976) *Witchcraft in France and Switzerland: the Borderlands during the Reformation* (Ithaca, NY: Cornell University Press), p. 191. More recently, Wolfgang Behringer has argued that 'by far the majority of persecutions occurred within the boundaries of the Holy Roman Empire', an area covered by our hypothetical circle. 'Witchcraft Studies in Austria, Germany, and Switzerland', in Jonathan Barry, Marianne Hester and Gareth Roberts (eds) (1996) *Witchcraft in Early Modern Europe: Studies in Culture and Belief* (New York: Cambridge University Press), p. 66.

3. Charles Zika (2003) *Exorcising our Demons. Magic, Witchcraft and Visual Culture in Early Modern Europe* (Leiden: Brill), p. 9.

4. Robert Darnton (1984) *The Great Cat Massacre and Other Episodes in French Cultural History* (New York: Basic Books), p. 30, gives one of many European examples of folk tales in which peasants or other ordinary people outwit the devil. In a Flemish comedy of the fifteenth century, *The Entertainment of the Apple Tree*, a simple farmer outwits both the devil and death; cited in Gary K. Waite (2003) *Heresy, Magic, and Witchcraft in Early Modern Europe* (New York: Palgrave Macmillan), p. 18. A broad treatment of this theme, among others, is Robert Muchembled (2003) *A History of the Devil: From the Middle Ages to the Present*, trans. Jean Birrell (Cambridge: Polity Press). Peasants across Europe 'dominated' the devil in their tales, brought him 'closer to the people' and 'limited the fear he could inspire', pp. 25–6.

5. Dyan Elliott (1999) *Fallen Bodies: Pollution, Sexuality, and Demonology in the Middle Ages* (Philadelphia: University of Pennsylvania Press), pp. 82, 111 and 126.

6. Carol F. Karlsen (1987) *The Devil in the Shape of a Woman* (New York: W. W. Norton), esp. pp. 164–8 and 180–3. For an argument that men used witchcraft accusations to deal with women 'thought of as threatening or opposing' male authority in Europe, see Bonnie S. Anderson and Judith P. Zinsser (1999–2000) *A History of their Own: Women in*

Europe from Prehistory to the Present, 2 vols, rev. edn (New York: Oxford University Press), p. 161. On a male desire to torment women's bodies, see Anne Barstow (1994) *Witchcraze: A New History of the European Witch Hunts* (San Francisco: Harper), esp. pp. xiii and 1–5.

7. For example, Nachman Ben-Yehuda (1980) 'The European Witch Craze of the 14th to 17th Centuries: A Sociologist's Perspective', *American Journal of Sociology* 86 (1): 14; Kai T. Erikson (1966) *Wayward Puritans: A Study in the Sociology of Deviance* (New York: John Wiley and Sons).

8. Brian P. Levack (2006) *The Witch-Hunt in Early Modern Europe*, 3rd edn (Harlow: Pearson Education).

9. For example, Brian P. Levack (1992) 'Introduction', in Brian P. Levack (ed.) *Witch-Hunting in Continental Europe: Local and Regional Studies* (New York: Garland Press), p. x. Robert Muchembled (1979) *La sorcière au village* (Paris: Plon), p. 23, suggests that the hunts were an effort to impose urban cultural and political control in villages.

10. Joseph Klaits (1985) *Servants of Satan: the Age of the Witch Hunts* (Bloomington: Indiana University Press), p. 4.

11. For a recent critique of functional analyses, see Robin Briggs (1996) *Witches and Neighbors: the Social and Cultural Context of European Witchcraft* (New York: Viking), pp. 6–8, 399 and 404.

12. René Girard (1986) *The Scapegoat*, trans. Yvonne Freccero (Baltimore: Johns Hopkins University Press), pp. 13–14.

13. Alan Macfarlane (1970) *Witchcraft in Tudor and Stuart England: a Regional and Comparative Study* (London: Routledge and Kegan Paul), esp. p. 168; Alan Macfarlane (1978) *Origins of English Individualism: the Family, Property and Social Transition* (Oxford: Oxford University Press), pp. 12, 59, 130 and 163. A new edition of the first work is *Witchcraft in Tudor and Stuart England: a Regional and Comparative Study* (1999) 2nd edn, Introduction by James Sharpe (London: Routledge). However, the argument of 1970 is unchanged. Keith Thomas, Macfarlane's doctoral advisor, broke new ground by analysing English witchcraft accusations in the same terms as his student did; Keith Thomas (1971) *Religion and the Decline of Magic: Studies in Popular Beliefs in Sixteenth and Seventeenth Century England* (London: Weidenfeld and Nicolson), pp. 553–67.

14. Recent examples of studies that laud Macfarlane's first book but ignore his *Origins of English Individualism* are James Sharpe (1996) *Instruments of Darkness: Witchcraft in Early Modern England* (Philadelphia: University of Pennsylvania Press), p. 11; and Waite, *Heresy, Magic, and Witchcraft*, p. 173.

15. Robert K. Merton (1957) *Social Theory and Social Structure*, rev. and enlarged edn (Glencoe, Ill.: The Free Press), p. 21.

16. Ibid., pp. 21, 51.

17. Following an edict issued by King Henry II of France in 1557, women in the extensive part of the country under the jurisdiction of the Parlement (an appeals court above all) of Paris were fifteen times more likely to be executed for this crime than for witchcraft; Robert Muchembled (2006) 'Introduction', in Richard Golden (ed.) *Encyclopedia of Witchcraft: The Western Tradition* (Santa Barbara, Calif.: ABC-CLIO), xxviii.

18. Colin Campbell (1982), 'A Dubious Distinction: An Inquiry into the Value and Use of Merton's Concepts of Manifest and Latent Function', *American Sociological Review*, 47(1) (February): 29, 30, 37; Charles J. Erasmus (1967) 'Obviating the Functions of Functionalism', *Social Forces*, 45(3) (March): 319; Jon Elster (1998), 'Merton's Functionalism and the Unintended Consequences of Action', in *Robert K. Merton and Contemporary Sociology*, ed. Carlo Mongardini and Simonetta Tabboni (New Brunswick, NJ: Transaction Publishers), p. 129. In Merton's chance to reply to critiques of his work, he spoke of '"latent" as distinct from "manifest" *consequences*', ibid., p. 304; my italics.

19. Christopher Waldrep (2002), *The Many Faces of Judge Lynch: Extralegal Violence and Punishment in America* (New York: Palgrave Macmillan), p. 2. And see his (2000) 'War of Words: The Controversy over the Definition of Lynching, 1899–1940', *The Journal of Southern History* 66(1) (February).

20. Stewart E. Tolnay and E. M. Beck (1995) *A Festival of Violence: An Analysis of Southern Lynchings, 1882–1930* (Urbana: University of Illinois Press), pp. 18–19.

21. Clyde Kluckhohn (1944) *Navaho Witchcraft*. Papers of the Peabody Museum, XXII, no. 2 (Cambridge, Mass.).

22. E. E. Evans-Pritchard (1937) *Witchcraft, Oracles and Magic among the Azande* (Oxford: Oxford University Press), p. 31, found that among this African people men and women were deemed witches in equal proportions.
23. See, for example, Justus Mozart H'Achachi Ogembo (1997), 'The rise and decline of communal violence: an analysis of the 1992–94 witch-hunts in Gusii, southwestern Kenya'. PhD dissertation, Anthropology, Harvard University. Ogembo refers to these hunts throughout as lynchings.

CHAPTER ONE

NEW FEARS IN EUROPE: 700–1500

In the film *The Return of Martin Guerre* (directed by Daniel Vigne, 1983), set in early sixteenth-century France, a young peasant cannot consummate his marriage. Everyone around him knows that he is unable to perform sexually, and he is the object of a cruel mockery, called a *charivari*, in which most of the other village males humiliate him. Nonetheless, all of his neighbours want him to carry out his conjugal duties.

At one point an old woman with cloudy eyes comes to chant over Martin. Peasants commonly saw impotence as caused by an evil person or spirit who had 'tied' a man. So the old woman intones, 'I unbind thee, blessed flesh, I unbind thee!' She gestures ponderously over Martin as she sprinkles a powder onto his trousers. As this mumbo-jumbo ends, the film cuts instantly to the next scene, in which the village priest makes his own attempt to help. The priest circles around the couple, who have been bound loosely to a pole inside a dark room, and flicks holy water on to their naked backs. 'Accursed demon, leave this body. Holy Spirit, I ask Thee to help Martin', he prays. 'It worked, that same day', the young peasant's wife later tells a visitor.

What worked, we suppose now, was the power of suggestion, not the old woman's counter-spell or the priest's holy water. But the problem posed by these two scenes is in trying to figure out what the villagers believed. The film, based closely on surviving documents, implies that the peasants wanted to leave nothing to chance with regard to a 'cure' for Martin. If a doctor had been available and they could have afforded to consult him, the family would probably have done that as well. Had they lived close to a shrine or the relics of some saint reputed to help in such matters, they would have journeyed there.[1] What they did do in this case was to appeal to traditional sources for aid: the old woman might have some special knowledge or connections to supernatural forces, and so might the priest.[2] In this respect *The Return of Martin Guerre* puts the traditional 'healer', as we shall call her for the moment, and the representative of organized, official religion on the same plane.

BELIEF SYSTEMS AND 'SUPERSTITIONS'

Martin Guerre's story illustrates the difficulty of trying to decipher what people really believed in the early modern period – or, for that matter, in any time and place. Did the peasants of south-western France in the 1540s themselves know what they believed in? Did they sometimes change their minds about what to think? Did they perhaps not believe in much at all, but merely opted for a kind of insurance policy by trying different methods and sources when problems arose? After all, neither the Church, the doctors, nor the healers were of much help in most illnesses. People died young, crops sometimes failed, and invaders spread devastation no matter what.

Early modern Europeans at all social and educational levels tried many means to solve misfortunes,[3] which suggests that they did not have great confidence in any one kind of remedy or appeal. They probably turned to various putative aids, ranging from herbs to magic, to religion, not so much from a firm belief that they would help as out of desperation or a sense that it was unwise to leave any possibility unexplored. Even today, people can 'accommodate different and even contradictory beliefs, one coming to the fore at one time, another at another'.[4] For the purposes of trying to understand why the people of Europe behaved in any way or changed their behaviour in a given period, it is best to note first the symbols and words they used to describe their world.

Relatively few sources provide direct glimpses into the ideas of the lower classes in the early modern era; when their words were recorded, it was by educated people, who imposed their own frames of reference on what they heard. Nevertheless, scholars have found scattered remarks that appear to come directly from the peasants; some of these indicate popular doubt in the existence of hell or even of the soul.[5] Certainly the common folk often felt resentment toward the clergy, especially those in its higher ranks who came from the elite and reflected its outlook.[6] Yet lower-class critics of a society may also be among its staunchest patriots, as the experience of American and British workers shows. In all likelihood, their lower-class European counterparts until quite recently picked and chose among the symbols available to them, fashioning their own interpretations of the universe around them in the process.

Religion can be seen as a 'cultural resource' from which people drew, producing different understandings according to 'social, professional, age and gender groups';[7] of course, individuals within any group fashioned their own outlook. One of the most persistent features of European world views, as we shall see, was the presence of humans who used magic to help or hurt their neighbours.

It is not especially useful to call such a notion a 'superstition'. Gustav Jahoda wrote that 'there is no objective means of distinguishing "superstition" from other types of belief and action'. Superstitions are relative to time and place, and they refer merely to ideas and practices which reasonable people do not accept at the moment as valid. Any use of the word has an 'emotional element' that people notice, even if they do not act on it. Jahoda added that in the Middle Ages, 'the world as people saw it included witches, devils, fairies and all kinds of strange beasts . . . magic and miracles were commonplace'. Certainly this picture can be extended to cover most people in the early modern period. 'Sceptics were in an important sense maladjusted, deviants who risked their lives if their doubts were too openly voiced.'[8]

Virtually all the phenomena Jahoda mentioned as part of the medieval belief system, as well as his deviants, require more discussion, which will follow later in this book; in the meantime, he was correct to point out that during the era of the witch trials, strong pressure to accept certain views of the universe existed in many places. However, neither coercion nor the frequent repetition of certain images could guarantee that people would believe in them. In any event, the words, concepts and pictures that provided a matrix for beliefs in western Europe changed rapidly between 1000 and 1400.

THE PERSECUTING SOCIETY

At the start of the new millennium, western Europe was hardly a tranquil setting. However, society was relatively open and tolerant. Jews and Christians lived near each other, heresy within the Church was not a pressing problem, sexual behaviour was a personal (or at least a local) affair, and authorities did not try to prescribe daily conduct for their subjects. There was a lot of talk and many laws, judging by extant codes, against people who practised evil magic. But as yet the *sorciers*, wicca, and so on were persecuted only sporadically. From time to time these 'cunning folk' or 'wise' people were arrested and put to death, legally or otherwise, for supposedly using black magic. But into the late medieval period, these judgments did not amount to a regular pattern of persecutions; such magic did not yet appear to be a major danger, at least in the eyes of the elite.

By 1400, western Europe had changed dramatically in these respects and more. Jews, now forced to live in ghettos across the

Continent, had been attacked, tortured and murdered by Christians on many occasions. Heretical movements had appeared, spread, and been the targets of gruesome campaigns of extermination in France and elsewhere. In earlier centuries, lepers had been fastidiously avoided by almost everyone but had not been the object of special persecution; by the fourteenth century local and royal authorities were rounding up lepers, confining them, stripping them of all civil rights and often murdering them. Homosexuality had been outlawed and made a capital crime in every land. Finally, Christian church and lay authorities had become deeply concerned with how people lived on a day-to-day basis and adopted legislation designed to regulate their behaviour.

In the words of R. I. Moore, by the late Middle Ages a 'persecuting society' had arisen in western Europe. Governments, courts and other institutions practised 'deliberate and socially sanctioned violence . . . against groups of people defined by general characteristics such as race, religion or way of life; . . . membership of such groups in itself came to be regarded as justifying these attacks'.[9] Jews, heretics and lepers were the first three major categories to fall victim to the persecuting society. In fact, many of the images and accusations that mainstream Christians attached to one of these three groups were also ascribed to the others: that they were sexually hyperactive and dedicated to luring innocent people into their ranks through their sexual prowess; that they engaged in disgusting anti-human practices, sexual and otherwise; and that they were determined to infiltrate and bring down the larger society around them. In short, the idea became popular that one or more vast conspiracies were trying to destroy Christianity from within. The plotters were reputedly financed and abetted by an outside, evil force, often the Muslims.

All societies, it seems, create images of the 'Other'. Humans appear to need ways to distinguish themselves from members of different societies. It is common in preliterate cultures to refer to one's own group as 'people' and to members of other groups as monkeys, crocodiles or any other handy animal. The 'we' and 'they' mentality appears in the earliest written records of civilization, from Sumer. Literate societies often expend considerable effort to develop images of the Other; Edward Said has documented the myriad ways in which western Europeans constructed images of 'Orientals' (Middle Easterners) as devious, imitative but uncreative, romantic, emotional instead of rational, childlike, undisciplined, lazy and sexually perverse.[10] From at least the 1500s onwards, Western accounts of Russians retailed many of these same features. Within the West, Germans and English held each other in polite contempt but reserved their most careful denigration for peoples on the periphery of the Continent, especially the Irish and Spanish.

However much the Other appears as a socially necessary figure – in other words, an anthropologically functional device – around the world, it is certain that western Europeans became especially adept at manufacturing and using the construct. Any major collection of art from late medieval and early modern Europe, virtually the time frame of the witch hunts, contains paintings of twisted men in turbans or Jews' conical hats tormenting Jesus, to cite one common motif. There is an almost constant emphasis, especially in the 'northern' European art of France, Germany and the Low Countries, on repulsive figures who differ from the decent stock around them. Although these Others are usually shown as stupid and bestial, it is clear that they can cause serious trouble if they so choose.

Along with these images and labels came the rise of the devil. His meteoric career after 1000 is a story unique to western Europe. Rarely has a culture produced one powerful and widely publicized devil determined, so a great many words and pictures indicated, to destroy the world of goodness and faith in the true God. Demons and petty, evil spirits apparently exist in every society; people seem to need them to explain misfortune. But one big devil, almost as powerful as God, or equally powerful in some variants, is largely a Western creation, although it possibly derives from Persian traditions that there is a realm of good and a realm of evil in the universe. The bright and benign part is that of the spirit and the heavens, while the dark and evil side is that of the flesh and the earth. The two are equal, or nearly so, in this outlook, called dualism. Chinese, Indian, African, even Russian or Byzantine Christian art, representing societies in which dualism is not prevalent or has been suppressed, does not depict one great devil. Naturally, 'no other religion ever raised hell to such importance as Christianity, under which it became a fantastic underground kingdom of cruelty, surrounded by dense strata of legend, myth, religious creed, and . . . dubious psychology'.[11]

By the late Middle Ages, the chief of this realm became the most widely cited outside force striving to annihilate the good society. Like the heretics, lepers and so on, the devil was supposedly busily recruiting agents – the witches – among the Christians. Petty demons do not seem to need human help; why should they, if there are many of them? The big devil, on the other hand, supposedly had many human assistants; at least that was the argument of leading witch hunters. But why would a big devil need any help at all? Critics of the witch hunts posed this question almost from the time they began; for the moment, we may note that the zealots answered that the devil supposedly profited from tempting souls into his service – the more witches, the more guaranteed residents of hell.

Here, then, is the persecuting society in about 1400, full of dreadful words, images and fears that decent life was close to disappearing. Armageddon, the final battle between the forces of God and those of the devil's son, the Antichrist, often said to have a Jewish mother, was discussed in many works as an imminent event. Good would triumph, but the victory would not be easy, and many souls would enter hell. This is hardly a picture of confident

Christian faith. To reiterate a point, there is no way to tell how many people believed that a multifarious crisis was upon them, but it is possible to discuss the actions, including the witch hunts, that appear to reflect a sense of such impending disaster. Why did such broad anxieties and fears, undoubtedly related in their origins and effects, notably the torture and execution of thousands of people, arise in western Europe?

EUROPE UNDER SIEGE: 700–1500

New enemies of Western Christendom, and some old ones in new form, began to appear by the eighth and ninth centuries. They continued to arrive, to harass the edges of the western subcontinent, and even to strike deep into it, until the late 1600s. The most devastating of these attacks came from the Vikings across an arc from Russia through England, Ireland, France and even Sicily; from Muslims in the Middle East and Spain; from Magyars (Hungarians) in central Europe; from the Mongols (or Tatars) in eastern Europe; and from the Ottoman Turks in the south-eastern and central parts of the Continent.

In 711, an ethnically mixed Islamic army entered Spain. The 'Moors' were defeated in southern France in 732, but remained in control of much of Spain through the Middle Ages and were not completely driven out until 1492. For more than 700 years, with strong effects that linger to this day, Spanish society, values and culture centred on the *Reconquista*, the effort to retake the country from the Moors.

Viking assaults on Ireland, England, France, Russia and elsewhere are recorded from 787 onwards. The destruction was so extensive in Ireland, for example, that the great monastic sites, among them Glendalough and Kells, with their treasures of gold, silver and books, were left in ruins. For a long period, the only real protection against Viking attacks was storms that prevented them from crossing the sea to reach Ireland. Thomas Cahill refers to the 'constant fear of the monks', as illustrated in an old gloss:

> *Bitter is the wind this night*
> *Which tosses up the ocean's hair so white*
> *Merciless men I need not fear*
> *Who cross from Lothland on an ocean clear.*[12]

If the Vikings seemed to be of the same race as their victims in western Europe, this was of little consequence; they were still non-Christian barbarians from an unknown part of the globe. For centuries, no one in the West could stand against them. The Norsemen finally tamed themselves by staying in places they conquered, from Ireland to Sicily, to Russia, and adopting the ways of the local people. But the terror they had long provoked remained within the European psyche, partly because the Vikings were hardly the only successful invaders.

During the ninth and tenth centuries the Magyars, who appeared from Asia, raided frequently from the base they secured in today's Hungary into Polish, German, French and other territories. As far away as Bavaria and Alsace, settled life became nearly impossible.

In 1240, the Mongols, who had devised a special kind of cleated horseshoe for their wiry ponies, used the frozen rivers of Russia as ice highways to clatter into the country and capture all but a corner of it. The highly disciplined Mongol cavalry, numbering between 150 000 and 200 000 troops, smashed any army foolish enough to try to block its advance. Besides the Russians, forces of Poles, Germans and Hungarians failed in the attempt. To this day in Krakow, in southern Poland, trumpeters play a call every hour. The notes are suddenly cut off, marking the legend that the watchman who tried to sound an alert as the Mongols approached was silenced by an arrow in the throat.

However, the new Asian invaders turned around almost as suddenly as they had arrived; the Great Khan had died in Mongolia, and the lesser princes had to return to select another leader. Having reached Liegnitz in Silesia (then German territory but today in Poland) in 1240, and the coast of the Adriatic Sea opposite Italy the next year, the Mongols could probably have gone anywhere in Europe they wanted to.

Although they withdrew from the central part of the Continent, the devastation the Mongols caused further east was widely known. Archbishop Plano Carpini travelled from Rome through southern Russia in 1245–46. He reported that the invaders:

went against Russia and enacted a great massacre in the Russian land, they destroyed towns and fortresses and killed people . . . when we passed through that land, we found lying in the field countless heads and bones of dead people; for this city [Kiev] had been extremely large and very populous, whereas now it has been reduced to nothing: barely two hundred houses stand there, and those people are held in the harshest slavery.[13]

When the Mongols first conquered Russian soil, their religion was a form of Asian animism. But in the early fourteenth century the newcomers adopted Islam. This faith now inspired, or designated as fundamentally different, most of the major enemies of Western Christendom. Muslim forces, entrenched in Spain as well as in eastern Europe, held a wide swathe of territory on two of the Continent's flanks.

The violence of the Tatars, as the Russians call the Mongols to this day, sank deep into popular consciousness across Europe. In 1590, Christopher Marlowe described another Mongol conqueror in *Tamburlaine the Great: who, from a Scythian shephearde, by his rare and woonderfull conquests, became a most puissant and mightye monarque, and for his tyranny, and terrour in warre, was tearmed, The scourge of God.* Shakespeare's witches in *Macbeth*, first performed in 1606 for King James I, put 'Tartar's lips' into one of their foul brews. Yet the greatest Islamic threat to Europe was still to come.

For many centuries the most glorious and powerful Christian country was one that today is all but forgotten, except for an adjective meaning convoluted and devious. The Byzantine Empire remains, to those outside of Greece who have even heard of it, a mysterious and negative phenomenon. Yet from the fourth century until 1453, the Byzantines, who spoke Greek but styled their realm the Eastern Roman Empire, carried on the legacy of the ancient world, produced fabulous churches and mosaics that rank among the world's greatest artistic achievements, and governed a large territory centred on the capital, Constantinople. Certainly the Byzantines lost many battles, and the area they ruled shrank at times to very little. Still, they managed to survive attacks by Mongols, Vikings, various Bulgarian and Serbian rulers, and even the occupation of the capital by errant Western crusaders from 1204 to 61. However, the next wave of invaders from Asia proved to be too much for the Byzantines, and for many another Christian forces as well.

The Ottoman Turks started small. This branch of the Asian peoples loosely linked by their Turkic languages, which today include tongues such as Uzbek, Kazakh and modern Turkish, achieved their first real success by seizing a zone just east of Constantinople in 1326. Perhaps the Ottomans would have amounted to only a minor danger if the Byzantines had not been so badly weakened by outside attacks and internal divisions; likewise, the Mongols began to divide and fight among themselves by 1359. In any case, the problems of the Ottoman Turks' nearby enemies provided breathing space and time for the new power. With the help of an Italian artillery expert, an Ottoman army overran Constantinople itself in 1453. The Turks quickly changed the city's name to Istanbul and converted the great cathedral of Hagia Sophia into a mosque.

Western Europeans had hardly displayed brotherly love for their fellow Christians in the Byzantine Empire, and now they shed few tears at the fall of an old antagonist. They should have wept bitterly. A character in Johannes Nider's *Formicarius* (The Ant Hill), written 1435–37, wonders at how Europeans suffer at the hands of Turks and Saracens.[14] For more than 200 years, Ottoman forces probed deep into central Europe. Having overrun the Balkan peninsula decades before they conquered Constantinople, the Turks pushed on into Hungary, by now a settled and Catholic country, where they won a great victory at Mohács in 1526. Christian forces rallied enough to defend Vienna in 1529 and to crush a Turkish fleet in 1571. However, it was not until 1683 that a Christian allied army led by King Jan Sobieski of Poland managed to halt the Turks' last major attempt to expand into the heart of Europe, defeating them outside Vienna. It took many more years of fighting, particularly by Austrians and Russians, before the Turks turned finally into the 'Sick Man of Europe' and no longer presented a threat to the West.

Looking back, then, at the attacks over a period of nearly a thousand years around the edges of western Europe, and the thrusts into its heartland by outside forces, especially those riding under Muslim banners, we can imagine a massive impact on the way the people of the West felt about their world. When would the next group of invaders from the East appear? Given the prejudices of the day, it was disturbing to think about living under the rule of darker-skinned people speaking unfamiliar languages and worshipping in strange ways. There were in any event many thousands of European dead, many a destroyed village or city. We do not know what peasants in northern Italy, for example, felt about such threats. But the familiar puppet theatres that featured Western knights fighting dark Turks with drooping moustaches and scimitars suggest that ordinary people perceived an evil force nearby. In many plays and stories the latest Muslim invaders were identified as the devil's agents; just before the witches of *Macbeth* add Tartar's lips to their concoction, they drop in 'nose of Turk'.

If it is sometimes puzzling that in the late Middle Ages and early modern period the European nobility, in most areas about 1 per cent of the population, ruled over the other 99 per cent, the perennial need for a common defence provides part of the explanation. Peasants armed with sticks or axes stood no chance against invaders; only a highly trained force of professional fighting men on horseback had any real possibility of stopping an outside attack. The 'gunpowder revolution' of the fifteenth and sixteenth centuries marked the final end of the mounted knight as an effective fighter but also meant that the men who designed, built and directed the fire of the new weapons required even more training and financial support than knights had received. Any area's military had to be led by professionals, whose skills gave them an edge that, when applied at home, enabled them for the most part to keep the lower classes in line. Yet the trained fighters also drew upon some popular support, if they did not push their privileges and demands beyond traditional limits, because of the protection they provided against invaders.

When the military caste dominated European society, it followed that the children, friends and allies of this group would supply the rest of the elite. Superfluous sons of the upper nobility tended to occupy high positions in the clergy; excess daughters went into convents. Delivering ideological support for the warrior societies, the Western religious hierarchy relied on affinities of upbringing; shared values; a common written language, Latin; and a mutual dedication to combating enemies from other faiths. This cohesion would assume vast importance for the witch hunts, which would not have occurred without intense cultural direction from the elite.

Religious unity under one Church, broken at times by heresies that will be discussed below, characterized the western part of the Continent until the Reformation. But a fundamental division between Eastern and Western Christendom occurred almost 500 years before Luther began his public protests. The earlier schism usually merits only a brief mention in histories of Europe, but it had a profound effect on both parts of the Continent. The churches of eastern and western Europe split in 1054, nominally over issues of theology but in reality over territorial and political matters. What is now called the Catholic Church, which extended into Poland and the Baltic lands, was of course based in Rome; the bishop of that city had increasingly asserted claims to head all Christianity, but those pretensions were always rejected in Byzantium, Russia and south-eastern Europe. There the influence of the Byzantines held sway after the ruling strata converted to Eastern Orthodoxy in the ninth and tenth centuries. This attraction stemmed from proximity to Constantinople, which was relatively easy to reach by travelling along the Adriatic coast to the Mediterranean Sea, or down the Russian/Ukrainian rivers to the Black Sea. Besides, while Rome was a small town with impressive ruins, Constantinople boasted brilliant art, architecture and a number of successful military campaigns. Most important, the Byzantine Empire remained a major independent state. Its clerics and their followers hardly felt like taking orders from a pretentious bishop in Rome, a third-rate town into the high Middle Ages.

As the West regrouped and enjoyed a hiatus from outside attack, roughly from the eleventh to thirteenth centuries, the Orthodox (sometimes called Greek Orthodox, although the Greek branch is only one of a number in the faith) Church became feared as yet another outside power dedicated to the destruction of the good Christian society. A perceived threat from the East now became personified in one of the first major heretical groups of the period, the Bogomils. By 1143, Bogomil infiltrators supposedly in league with Satan had arrived in Germany from Byzantium.[15]

It was not enough simply to label these outsiders as evil; they had to be smeared as extremely unpleasant people. Thus English and other languages have the term 'bugger', the derivation of which followed in this manner: Middle English *bougre*, from Old French *bolgre*, from Middle Latin *Bulgarus*, literally a Bulgarian, originally used in the eleventh century to mean Bulgarian heretic. The word 'bugger', someone who commits sodomy or is otherwise generally contemptible,[16] thus has its roots in the church schism of 1054.

Perhaps some Orthodox believers did attempt to convert Catholics in the West, but the main point is that the Eastern Church became identified as a source of depravity that would somehow seduce true Christians – a well-established theme in European culture suggests that respectable folk will be turned immediately to the dark side by homosexual experience, as if it were the ultimate addiction – and in the process make them into the devil's henchmen. To say the least, this picture will reappear.

The advent of the persecuting society in western Europe should now be clearer. Cruel acts unthinkable in the year 1000 attracted no particular notice several centuries later. The chronicle of the French monastery of St Stephen of Condom reports that in the year 1321, 'a great deal of snow fell in the month of February. The lepers were exterminated. There was another great snowfall before the middle of Lent; then came a great rain.' In various parts of France, similar accounts continue, lepers were burned at roughly the same time. They were accused of having gathered secretly and poisoned the good people by spreading deadly powders in fountains, wells and rivers. Within a few years, other chroniclers added the charge that the Jews had been the lepers' partners in these acts, the object of which was to take over the kingdom of France. A durable rumour insisted that both groups had been sponsored and financed in their evil by the Muslim king of Grenada, in present-day Spain.[17]

But the murderers of the lepers cannot be dismissed as superstitious and ignorant. First, such terrible persecution had not happened earlier and hence was not somehow a fundamental part of European practice. Second, the twentieth century, and now the young twenty-first century in its turn, have witnessed far too much methodical killing to label early modern authorities as completely different from those of our own age. Nor were the earlier judges and priests irrational in terms of the belief system in which they lived. Rather, it makes more sense to see the lepers' executioners as people who had become deeply frightened of plots led by others designated as basically unlike the good Christians. The fear of such conspiracies, especially ones thought to be organized and funded by outside powers, begins to make sense in the long context of attack and destruction that western Europe experienced.

When caught in the midst of a crisis, people often have little time and energy to spare for reflection on their general situation. But when the immediate danger subsides, 'greater opportunity for speculation' exists, as Bernard Hamilton noted for the period around 1000. Communication became easier, and a revival of scholarship began.[18] The barbarian invasions were over, for the moment, and the new waves of invaders from Asia were yet to appear. If the West had constantly been under attack, it seems doubtful that Christian institutions, cosmology and exclusion of groups now labelled hateful would have been created with nearly as much effectiveness. It was the combination of grave threat followed by respite that impelled westerners to rethink their unity and identity; in the relative calm of the eleventh century, the Latin Church 'began to devise its grand program of sanctifying the world'.[19]

MASS DEATH THROUGHOUT EUROPE

The lepers of St Stephen's met their deaths in 1321. The year is important for the purposes of this book as it came late in the formation of the persecuting society but before the outbreak of the greatest disaster ever to hit Europe, in terms of the spread and percentage of deaths among the populace. This was the plague, or Black Death. Before referring briefly to its impact, let us consider a simple proposition: despite all that has already been said about the rise of fear in Europe and its connection to persecution, if there had been no plague there would have been no witch hunts.

That witch trials would have taken place seems beyond doubt, and indeed the first case with all or almost all the ingredients of the standard witch accusations was held in 1324. But it seems equally unlikely that without the profound dislocation and mortality produced by the plague, not once but repeatedly across Europe, witch trials would have remained relatively isolated affairs. It is not possible to draw a clear and direct line between the plague and the rise of the witch hunts, but the disease provided the essential background for their growth. Only the sheer, massive terror induced by the plague grounded the notion that absolutely anyone, not just those identified by religion or disease, could be an agent of the kingdom of evil. After all, only something like the plague could appear at any time, take a toll of victims from all social strata, and then disappear – for a while.

One-third or more of Europe's population died in the first wave of the plague, which began in Constantinople, jumped to Italy and spread quickly from there. In some areas mortality was 80 per cent. Although pestilence was known from the Bible and other accounts of the ancient world, and contagious disease had devastated the Roman Empire in the sixth and seventh centuries, no pandemic had occurred in Europe since the eighth century. The plague, a periodic scourge until well into the eighteenth century, therefore appeared as an onslaught on humanity that seemed unprecedented.

Needless to say, the impact on human behaviour was immense. Affluent residents fled the large towns for the relative safety of the countryside, only to die there in many cases. One immediate effect of the disease was often fundamental disruption of ordinary activity and the economy. In England, a contemporary observer recorded this picture:

That most grievous pestilence penetrated the coastal regions by way of Southampton and came to Bristol, and people died as if the whole strength of the city were seized by sudden death. For there were few who lay in their beds more than three days or two and a half days; then that savage death snatched them about the second day. In Leicester, in the little parish of St. Leonard, more than three hundred and eighty died; in the parish of the Holy Cross, more than four hundred, and in the parish of St. Margaret, more than seven hundred . . .

And the price of everything was cheap, because of the fear of death, there were very few who took any care for their wealth, or for anything else. For a man could buy a horse for half a mark [about 7 shillings] which before was worth forty shillings . . . There is no memory of a mortality so severe and so savage.[20]

Given the inclination that Western Christians already displayed to blame their problems on plots to destroy humanity, it is not surprising that they now rushed to adopt such explanations of the plague. Although some voices described the disease as God's punishment for general sin and iniquity, it was common to hold the Other responsible. Particularly in Germany, Jews were accused of poisoning the wells, and they suffered mass executions at the hands of the local Christians. In some instances the authorities at first tried to prevent such killings but had to yield to enraged mobs. This was the case in Strasbourg, where a thousand or more Jews were burned alive in 1349.

No matter how the plague was explained, it terrified people. If they chose to believe that evil-doers among them had spread the disease on the orders of an opposing faith, or perhaps of the devil, they would have become even more concerned than before about attacks on the good society. As the pestilence swept across the Continent, it made people more anxious about the future as well as about who might be working for the destruction of Christians in particular and perhaps of humankind in general.

Yet the Black Death provided a sort of movable feast of accusations: at first the Jews and lepers, with the aid of the Muslims; then, as we shall see, witches in some instances; and finally, in Hungary during the eighteenth century, vampires.[21] Clearly witches were not necessary to explain the plague; it seems that whatever group was already in the sights of the elite and common folk would serve. On the other hand, a recurring phenomenon as baffling and terrifying as the plague begged for an explanation through human agency, or by humans with satanic help.

In the wake of the Black Death came peasant rebellions, notably in France in 1358 and in England in 1381. These incidents were protests against traditional exploitation but also against the ruling nobles' attempts to hold down wages and re-establish control over the rural folk, who had gained some freedom and opportunity as the demand for labour soared following the pandemic. The French, English and other lower-class rebellions were put down ferociously, but they reinforced the upper-class view of rustics as dangerous brutes who required firm guidance by their betters.

Nevertheless, rebellion by the poor, which had happened before and would happen repeatedly in later years, did not directly prompt the European elite to think that witchcraft was a grave danger. If rebellion was 'as the sin of witchcraft' to some witch hunters,[22] it was not the *same* as witchcraft. Rebels were punished, usually with great severity, as such; there is no evidence that leaders of lower-class uprisings were charged with satanic activity. They did not need to be. It is also true that, for the most part, peasant revolts were not directly followed in the same area by witch trials. Finally, the chief rebels were not women, the stereotypical witch in European prosecutions.

Although the witch hunts gained some momentum a few years after the peasant uprisings of the late fourteenth century, the mentality which facilitated the rise of the trials related to a much broader set of factors. The most basic of these were the fears provoked by invasions and the plague. But the new anxiety was only part of the background to the witch persecutions; the following sections explore another essential aspect of the story, changes in Christian outlook, practice and conceptions of the devil.

THE DEVIL'S CLIMB TO PROMINENCE

Satan was originally a minor and innocuous biblical character. The derivation of the name is unclear, but it probably came from the Semitic root *stn*, the early meaning of which is debated. Currently the most popular guesses are that the root meant 'to be remote', or 'to obstruct'. In any case, in the Old Testament, more properly called the Hebrew Bible, the name 'could refer to any human being who played the role of an accuser or enemy (1 Samuel 29.4; 2 Samuel 19.22; 1 Kings 5.4; 1 Kings 11.14). In Numbers 22.32 the satan refers to a divine messenger who was sent to obstruct Balaam's rash journey. . . . In Job 1–2, the satan seems to be a legitimate member of God's council.'[23] In all these passages except the last, the New Revised Standard Version of the Bible translates satan as adversary; in Job this Bible simply leaves the word satan in its original form.

It is only in the New Testament and contemporaneous Jewish writings that Satan becomes identified as the arch-enemy of God and mankind. Also called the tempter, prince of demons and so forth, Satan gains a capital letter in many versions of the Bible. The term is often translated as the devil, a word taken from the Greek *diabolos* (the Latin is the same). Persian dualism, which argued that the powers of good and evil were of separate origin but of equal strength, may well have influenced the early career of the devil. In the New Testament he can do many things, apparently on his own: enter and possess the bodies of people, cause illness, imitate an 'angel of light' (2 Corinthians 11: 14),[24] and tempt Jesus in various ways. 'In an instant', he shows Jesus 'all the kingdoms of the world' and says he will give them to Jesus for the small price of worshipping him. The devil takes Jesus to the top of the temple in Jerusalem, through the air and therefore by flying (Luke 4: 1–12), a point later stressed by the major witch hunters and writers, with lethal results. Petty demons are found throughout the Gospels, possessing various people.

Jesus drives them out, once into the bodies of a herd of swine, which then drown themselves, apparently out of self-loathing.

Elaine Pagels has argued that the four Gospel writers tell Jesus' story as a struggle between supernatural forces. It is an escalating tale of confrontations between Jesus and the devil; Jesus wins each time, until, as Matthew and Mark imply and Luke states explicitly, the devil returns in the form of Judas Iscariot to betray the Saviour. The crucifixion establishes Jesus' continuing importance because for the devil it is 'not a final defeat but only a preliminary skirmish in a vast cosmic conflict now enveloping the universe'.[25] Jeffrey Burton Russell adds that the 'basic premise' of the New Testament is that 'the world is at issue between Christ and Satan'.[26]

Jesus says he will return and establish the Kingdom of Heaven on earth. The book of Revelation further announces that after a thousand years Satan 'will be released from his prison'. He will be defeated in a final battle, taking the sinners with him to a lake of fire, while the saved will remain with God. After all this, what assurance did ordinary people have that they would be able to resist the devil's powers? A creature who could challenge Jesus repeatedly and carry him to the top of a temple might overwhelm the vast majority of humanity with no difficulty.

The New Testament emphasizes the devil's connection with the Jews as it sets up the possibility of virulent Christian anti-Semitism. While the Gospels of Matthew and Mark fix some responsibility for the Crucifixion on the Roman governor Pontius Pilate, Luke's version essentially absolves him by shifting the blame on to 'the chief priests, the leaders, and the [Jewish] people', who repeatedly urge him to allow Jesus' execution (Luke 23: 13–25).

The book of John makes continual negative references to Jews in general. In this Gospel, Pilate finally bows to great pressure from Jesus' 'own nation' to kill him. Pilate 'went out to the Jews' gathered before his residence to ask one last time whether they will not agree that Jesus should be spared. But they answer that 'we have a law' according to which Jesus must die for his blasphemy (John 18: 35–40, 19: 4–7 and 19: 12–16). For Luke and John, Pilate and the Romans do not desire Jesus' death and are merely the instruments of it, while the Jews as a whole are its instigators.

According to John, Jesus had earlier said that the Jews 'who had believed in him' were the devil's children: 'You are from your father, the devil; and you choose to do your father's desires. He was a murderer from the beginning . . . [he is] the father of lies' (8: 31–44). It was easy enough to move from Jesus' imprecise statement to the idea that all Jews were the devil's spawn.

As Pagels makes clear, the broader point is that the New Testament identifies the devil and his evil deeds with people on earth who act as his agents. But the problem is not only that some or, in certain passages, all Jews are such agents; as John quotes Jesus, these evil people *choose* to follow their father's wishes. The notion of a conscious choice to join the loathsome, anti-human forces was at the heart of the European witch trials. Nothing in the Bible or Western culture as a whole suggested, moreover, that only Jews could be the devil's agents; members of other groups, including the Christians, could also make the fatal choice.

Satan's progress in the West remained chequered for the next few centuries. In Jewish writings dating back to around 150 BCE, Satan becomes not merely a great enemy of the good people but the 'intimate enemy – one's trusted colleague, close associate, brother'. He has turned 'unexpectedly jealous and hostile'.[27] These works, close as they are to much that is in the Bible, undoubtedly influenced early Christians. Two church fathers, Tertullian (c.155–220) and Origen (c.185–254), established the idea that before Satan's fall he was the greatest of the angels; thus his power was so great. Christian life was by this point explained as 'a constant struggle with the powers of darkness'.[28] This problem helps explain why Christianity has been so insistent on having its followers avoid sin, or at least in finding ways to forgive them for sinning.

St Augustine (354–430) renewed the biblical theme of human choice to do evil when he dwelled on 'agreements made with devils', which were 'untrustworthy . . . treacherous . . . disastrous'. Christians 'must fear and avoid this alliance with demons, whose whole aim, in concert with their leader, the devil, is to cut off and obstruct our return to God'.[29] For well over a thousand years, Western religious writers were heavily influenced by Augustine, the pivotal figure in the development of early Christianity.

A Greek story about an actual pact with the devil appeared in the West by the sixth century. Theophilus, a church steward, is dismissed from his office on the basis of slander by his enemies. In despair he turns to a Jewish sorcerer, who puts him in touch with Satan. Theophilus signs a document renouncing Christ and pledging himself to the devil, who restores him to office. Theophilus then feels bitter remorse and performs penance for years, moving the Virgin Mary to intercede for him and to snatch the document from Satan. The story, translated into Latin by the eighth century and into vernacular verse by the tenth, became the basis for many popular variants and plays in the high Middle Ages.[30] Although Theophilus was male, the elements of the witch stereotype were moving slowly into place, with a Jewish minion of the devil thrown in for good measure.

Yet this story, early church writings and the merging of Jewish tradition with the new faith did not quickly produce a devil who personified clear and present danger to society. In 563, the Church Council of Braga defined the official Christian view that Satan did not have an independent origin and that he did not create the material universe, as another dualist movement – the Manichean heresy – had recently claimed. The devil could act only with God's permission, an idea, one might think, that should have greatly calmed Christian fears of diabolical activity.

However, the notion of humans doing Satan's bidding was a time bomb planted in the heart of Western culture, or better yet a

47

landmine buried in it which would not explode until enough protective layers of habit and practice had been removed. Even though some early clerics identified heretics with Satan in the next centuries, for example the bishop Irenaeus at Lyons in about 180 CE, persecution of Jews and heretics was not a major pursuit in Europe until after 1000. To bring on large-scale attacks on heretics, which in turn provided images and attitudes all too easily applied to suspected witches, a more fearsome devil was required. Western artists and writers produced him over time, surely in connection with the rise of the new fears.

The first known Western depiction of the devil is a sixth-century mosaic in the Church of San Apollinare Nuovo, in Ravenna, Italy. This Byzantine work shows Christ with an angel on his right and what appears to be a virtually identical angel, complete with wings, on his left. The three are in the process of literally separating sheep from goats; figuratively, they are determining which souls will enter heaven and which will go to hell. The figure on Christ's left, Satan, appears to be helping in the work just as efficiently and calmly as the good angel on the right. Certainly the devil is not an evil figure out snaring souls for his domain.

A more human form is given to Satan in an illustrated manuscript of the ninth century, the *Utrecht Psalter*. Here he is still not especially gruesome, but rather obese and slothful. Never shown stirring from hell in the *Psalter*, the devil commands some helper demons equipped with hooks and pitchforks to pull in or torment souls. Jesus has no trouble with these figures; in one scene he calmly tramples a skinny one.[31]

The devil's time had not quite arrived. It would require increasing fear in Europe to act upon him as a growth hormone, and the advent of the millennium to boost his status and visibility. Around 1000, Christians referred widely to the coming of the final days and the prophecies that the Evil One would be released from his prison. For example, Ralph Glaber, a monk of the great Cluny monastery, finished his *Five Histories* in about 1048. His stated goal was to produce a universal history since the reign of Charlemagne, but he tossed in many anecdotes, theological speculations and reports of miracles and disasters. Glaber, or people he had heard of, saw demons on earth from time to time; putting all this together, the monk declared that: 'These signs accord with the prophesy of John, according to which Satan will be unchained after 1000 years have passed.'[32] Glaber did not seem especially worried about this event, noting that all ages had their problems, and he did not make any prediction about when the final days would be; nonetheless, his rambling book reflected a new uneasiness about the devil's presence on earth.

More depictions of Satan began to appear, and he gained his familiar horns, hooves, tail and grotesque features, although sometimes he was depicted as purely animal. The goat was especially useful, for it came equipped with horns, cloven feet and a reputation for sexual energy. Satan was no longer a lazy, passive creature waiting in hell for souls to fall into his clutches; he was out wandering the earth and collecting them personally.[33] By the time of the Anglo-Norman Holkham Bible (*c.*1330) the devil is shown as large as Christ, and appears to be no pushover should they fight. Satan has several souls in a basket on his back, and Jesus does not try to take them from him.

Meanwhile, warnings arose from various sides that the devil or his demons might have sexual intercourse with humans. A tenth-century Anglo-Saxon book warned specifically against women who engaged in this practice, while St Thomas Aquinas (d. 1274) was more evenhanded. He discussed a theme already widely accepted in Europe that demons could appear in male form (*incubi*) or female form (*succubi*) for the purposes of having intercourse with either sex. But Aquinas stopped well short of the later witch stereotype: he did not connect such activity with *maleficia* (evil deeds), or suggest that humans became witches through sexual contact with demons.

Still, Aquinas did help to spread and make respectable the idea that demons were active, aggressive creatures who might interact with humans in secret.

Soon the devil was everywhere that illustrations might appear; besides in books, he could be found on many church walls, tapestries, and as a character in popular plays. In some of these spectacles whole towns participated, and the devil would be played by a man dressed in a suit of hair or feathers. To enliven the show, this figure would hold a firecracker in each hand, protected by a thick layer of mud, and would have another attached to his buttocks.[34] Truly it was dangerous to play around with Satan. These productions were occasions for humour and excitement, but they brought home the concept that hell awaited all sinners.

By about 1200, it would have been difficult to be a Christian and not frequently hear of the devil. It is not so clear that ordinary people, especially in the countryside, would yet have seen depictions of him; the great wave of church building was still to come, and the mystery plays were held in towns. However, by 1500 scenes of the devil were commonplace in the new cathedrals and small parish churches that had sprung up in many regions.

To combat the big devil required a strong and well-organized set of institutions. There were many reasons for the growth of the medieval Western Church; among the most important was the need to develop the means to counter the good Christians' enemies.

THE CONSOLIDATION OF WESTERN CHRISTIANITY

For all that the medieval Church spread and intruded on Europeans' lives and purses, it did not at first make far-reaching demands on ordinary people's daily behaviour. Nor did it claim to explain the whole universe; until about 1100, 'Christian cosmology was not considered a literal blueprint of God's creation'.[35] The Church, 'full of optimism, still sure of its faith and of the triumph of that faith',[36] did not execute heretics, as we have seen. Into the early Middle Ages the Church 'had not yet developed the means, or . . . the inclination, to demand uniformity of worship and practice throughout western Christendom'.[37] Marriage, especially among peasants, was not necessarily something to which clerics paid much attention or solemnized in a ceremony. Indeed, priests often took concubines or even wives in the same way that other villagers did; in fifteenth-century Bavaria, for example, only an estimated 3 or 4 per cent of village priests did not have concubines.

But as Europe came under increasing attack from the outside, and the persecuting society developed, the Western Church became a different creature. By the time of the Fourth Lateran Council, 1215, the Catholic hierarchy demanded certain types of behaviour and at least external fidelity to its teachings from every Christian under its sway. Starting about the same time, the Church began to shift its emphasis on rules for everyday conduct from the seven deadly sins to the Ten Commandments. Easily memorized, the commandments were 'much easier to use for an annual moral check up' by the priesthood. Heresy or witchcraft now became a specific crime against the first commandment and hence against God himself.[38] While this change did little by itself to spur attacks on heretics or witches, it did give theorists writing on their supposed activities more ammunition to fire at their targets.

Within a few more years, church and secular authorities proved willing to undertake not just isolated violence to enforce their religious will but wholesale campaigns of bloodshed, some of them on a scale (relative to population size) that approached recent standards of mass murder.

It may be easier to imagine the processes that urged greater conformity in western Europe by looking again at the micro level. Communities under attack or living close to the margin of existence – which would include most peasant villages from the beginning of human organization until close to the present – require a high degree of conformity from their members. Why did Martin Guerre's neighbours think it appropriate to humiliate him for a problem that modern people consider completely private? The simplest answer is that 'private' is an unfamiliar or relatively recent concept for most people around the globe. Peasants' lives were not private matters when the village had to stick together in order to survive. For the most part, fellow peasants remained the only source of aid if a fire struck a family's house, if a draught animal or a bread-winner died, or if orphans had to be taken in. Standards of behaviour required strict enforcement because peasants had to act in a co-ordinated, disciplined manner if they hoped to stave off hunger or endure the constant demands of the outside world for food, money and recruits for the army. Sharp differences among peasants in any respect would undermine their ability to act in concert. A military metaphor works fairly well for peasant societies: just as members of army units are expected to look, dress and behave alike as far as possible, so peasants demanded similar uniformity of each other. In both situations the need for defence and coordinated action dic-tates solidarity. Of course conflicts and competition existed in the villages, yet until quite recently European peasants lived by a highly developed set of rules that dictated certain common behaviours.

Hence the charivari for Martin Guerre. The issue was not his will or even necessarily his actions with his wife, which everyone in the village evidently thought were beyond his control. Rather, the point was simply that he was not living in the manner expected of him. Why or whose fault were not the most important problems in this instance; to the community, results counted for virtually every-thing, and by not producing children Martin was not meeting the social norms of the village. Once he fathered a child, all was forgotten. The Jews of eastern Europe pre-1939, hippie communes in America, or the British gentry in the late nineteenth century, to take just a few examples, all felt the need to require a high degree of conformity in order to perpetuate themselves.

At this point it is necessary to raise the issue of the connection between social solidarity and the witch hunts. Deviants of any kind were not at all coterminous with witches, and deviant behaviour was not equated with witchcraft. However, on the other hand, the cohesion of European villages was an essential component in the appearance of witch accusations, a matter to be discussed in more detail later on.

The plague and the many invasions of western Europe prompted a replication of local solidarity on a much broader scale. Repeatedly attacked, the Christian community came to view internal coherence as necessary to survival. Perhaps the first step in creating the requisite bonds was self-definition. As this issue became more acute, and as the elite had the time between assaults to ponder it, the Church's role in articulating what Christians were and were not expanded.

The eleventh century was a vicious turning point in various respects. The first execution of heretics since the fourth century took place at Orléans, France, in 1022. A group of highly-placed churchmen and women were put to death on charges of holding orgies, which included sex with near relatives, killing infants and using their blood to make a potion that all participants drank, and worshipping the devil, who appeared among them as a large black cat or other animal. Such accusations had ironically been made centuries earlier by the Romans against Christians, and again around 720 by an Armenian bishop regarding followers of a rival group. Now the same set of charges was applied within western Europe to people said to have deviated horribly from the true path to salvation.

We cannot know whether the persecutors believed in any sense in their accusations or cynically used them to eliminate people they disliked. In either case, the timing of this heresy trial fits well with the trends just discussed. Stereotyped images of the repulsive Other had long been available; now they were trotted out to show what the enemy within was capable of. 'Let this [the Orléans affair] be enough to warn Christians to be on their guard against this evil work', wrote a monk of Chartres around 1090.[39] The trial thus helped define good Christians by indicating both what they were not to do and what they should fear. The Western community was delimiting itself more carefully and creating the concept of the enemy within as it closed ranks to meet new dangers.

Led by the Roman Church, the persecuting society developed rapidly, further impelled by the schism with the Eastern Church in 1054 and the resulting suspicions that its agents were hard at work among the good people. In 1063 the first known slaughter of Jews occurred, the work of French troops travelling through Spain to help fight the common Christian foe, the Moors. By 1084 the first ghetto for Jews had been created, this time in Germany. Finally, in 1095 the heightened religious zeal combined with a sense of being under siege to produce the First Crusade, which Christian soldiers on their way to the Holy Land punctuated by murdering Jews. Western Christianity had become a militant, aggressive faith.

As these events unfolded in a span of less than 50 years, the problem, from the point of view of the good society's leaders, was not just that visible or identifiable enemies might be striving to defeat Christendom. Jews and Moors might convert on the surface to the true faith yet still remain dedicated anti-Christians; lepers might not always be noticeable, since the disease could produce only slight traces; or agents of the Orthodox Church might conceal their real intentions. Any of these opponents might be able to seduce Catholics, especially through their purported sexual prowess and appeal. Then presumably the power of the lust unleashed in the recruits would draw them after their sexual masters into nefarious anti-Christian, anti-human conspiracies.

Partly as a result of these perceived problems, which the Roman Church had done so much to create, the Western clergy reorganized and strengthened its bureaucracy, its claims to power and ideological guidance, and its view of the cosmos. Society, especially the elite, needed a stronger Church to provide the coherent ideas that the times and their dangers called for. Sharp political fights between secular rulers and the Church, and others within the Catholic hierarchy, characterized the drive to build a more solid Christian world view and the institutions to support and enforce it. Such struggles lasted into the nineteenth century, yet the emergence of an ideologically powerful Church equipped to meet the challenges of the new fears was not in doubt. Again, the timing cannot be accidental: the eleventh century was the pivotal period for this and other key developments in the history of the church; beginning in 1049 the papacy finally began to become simultaneously more than an office controlled by local nobles and to expand its claims to spiritual and even political leadership in the West.

Only a few years later, following the schism with the Orthodox Church, Roman popes had even more reason to assert their authority. By the reign of Pope Gregory VII (1073–85), the pontiff claimed that the Roman Church had never erred and could never do so, that the holder of the office was the supreme judge of Christendom, and that all princes owed him homage. Conflicts with secular rulers continued, and in 1302, during a struggle with the king of France, Boniface VIII reiterated the Church's right to lead: 'There is one holy, catholic [universal], and apostolic church we are bound to believe and hold, our faith urging us, and this we do firmly believe and simply confess; and that outside this church there is no salvation or remission of sins.'[40]

But what were this Church's tenets? Simple statements like the Apostles' and Nicene Creeds had been available for centuries, but even the Bible was not an agreed-upon text in the Catholic Church until the mid-thirteenth century (of course, different Christian faiths use different Bibles to this day). Complete Bibles remained rare, and it is unlikely that many people in the Middle Ages ever saw one, let alone read one. Bibles had been available in vernacular languages in many areas, but that fact had not caused concern in the Church until about 1000. Most Bibles had been in Latin for centuries; after 1000 the Church strengthened its control over the text by insisting it be used in that language, denying it a wide audience, and ruling that only priests were qualified to interpret its meaning. The seven sacraments were a medieval development, and the concept of purgatory did not appear until the thirteenth century; it was accepted as a definite article of faith only in 1437. Purgatory quickly became an essential part of Catholicism, however, as people were now instructed that their final judgement would occur only after their deaths. The delay made the concept of intervention by Jesus or a saint for a soul, as mediated by the clerics, more understandable. Purgatory also enhanced the idea that ordinary people could be saved; until about 1200, the Church had maintained that by and large only men of the cloth would go to heaven. This must have been discouraging for lay folk and probably prompted many to ask why they should follow the Church's rules on earth if they would not help in the long run.

A pivotal moment in the expansion of the Church's claims to the direction of human consciousness and behaviour came at the Fourth Lateran Council (1215) under Pope Innocent III. This gathering, attended by more than 1200 churchmen, opened its decrees with a declaration of faith, itself a departure from tradition, which clearly aimed to refute the Cathar heresy. The Cathars, who preached simplicity, reincarnation, rejection of the official church hierarchy and a form of dualism, had become well established in recent generations in southern France. The Church reaffirmed its commitment to maintaining a proper level of wealth and organization and declared anathema on all heretics, who were to be seized, stripped of their property and turned over to secular authorities for punishment. Even those suspected of heresy would be barred from church ceremonies for a year, during which they could try to clear themselves. Lay authorities were exhorted to 'exterminate' on their territory 'all heretics pointed out by the Church'. Soldiers fighting in such a cause would be given the rights and privileges of crusaders.

Beyond these threats and injunctions, all Christians were now required to take communion and to confess their sins at least once a year, preferably at Easter. Anyone failing to do so would be excommunicated and thus condemned to hell after death. Bishops were to make visitations throughout their jurisdictions once each year to make sure that no heretical activity was going on.[41]

The Fourth Lateran Council therefore marked two major departures for the Church. Although, as we have seen, actions to counter heresy had been under way in western Europe since 1022, attacks on religious deviance now took on new legitimacy and importance. Ferocity against heretics was encouraged. Second, to ensure that the Church had its way, ordinary people's lives would now be subject to scrutiny. The Roman Church had begun to shift from forbidding certain kinds of behaviour, as in the Ten Commandments, to prescribing what Christians should do on a daily basis. Acting at a moment of strength following the Western conquest of Constantinople in 1204 and the hope it produced for reconciliation of the Orthodox and Catholic faiths – on Western terms and through the support of considerable loot brought from the East – Lateran IV nonetheless illustrates the West's reaction to the recent fears. The Church had to be strengthened; to do that, it needed to define more precisely than before what constituted a good Christian.

Did the Roman Church create heresies when it found them useful? After all, not every protest movement against the church hierarchy, not every group that spoke about the need to return to poverty and simplicity within the Church, was declared heretical. The movement back to simplicity begun in the early thirteenth century by Francis of Assisi resembled in various ways the ideas of the Cathars, who at virtually the same time, starting in 1209, became the objects of a bloody assault in the name of orthodox

Christianity. Largely because Francis himself had much respect for the majesty and authority of the Roman Church, his order was co-opted by it. The Franciscan order grew rapidly, the Cathars were destroyed.

As the Catholic Church expanded both its territorial coverage and its claims to order Christian life, it found a purpose in labelling some dissent as heresy. Not all groups that attacked clerical splendour, wealth and power could be tolerated, especially as the religious hierarchy claimed the right to determine what constituted good Christianity. The Franciscans could be useful as a way of appealing to humble social strata, but too broad a movement with too many poor people was dangerous. However, ecclesiastical authorities could point to such a group to delineate unacceptable beliefs and behaviour. The Cathars, based in southern France, could be physically conquered and the region brought into an expanded French kingdom that swore fealty to the pope. When vicious tales spread about the Cathars' sexual behaviour and homage to the devil, the whole affair was even more functional. Contemporary French writers drove home the point and made familiar connections by occasionally referring to the Cathars as *bougres*. In any event, the situation and pretensions of the Church by the high Middle Ages meant that large divergent movements could not be ignored; they needed to be co-opted or crushed.

The Inquisition, which developed as a formal institution dedicated to the pursuit and extirpation of heretics after 1227, should be seen as a logical result of the Church's growing concern about splinter groups. As late as 1148, treatment of confessed heretics had been lenient, but the campaign against the Cathars became both cause and effect of a changed attitude. A papal bull issued in 1184 instructed to seek out heretics and turn them over to secular authorities for punishment, although the sanctions to be applied were not specified. As noted, the Fourth Lateran Council (1215) demanded death for heretics who remained stubbornly attached to their ideas. But as yet any developed mechanism for finding heretics, or declaring people to be such, was lacking.

To enlist heretic hunters, the energetic Pope Gregory IX had only to look to the new mendicant (literally begging, as in theory they were supposed to exist on alms) orders, the Dominicans and the Franciscans. In 1231, Gregory issued the fundamental constitution of the Inquisition, the bull *Excommunicamus*. This stipulated life in prison for repentant heretics and death for obstinate ones who refused to acknowledge the error of their ways and return to the true faith. The pope at first limited the Inquisition to Germany, but in 1232 ordered its spread to Aragon, a part of Spain, and the next year to all Catholic territories.

Needless to say, the Inquisition has a terrible reputation as a machine for torture and punishment. Acquiring the right to torture in 1252, as long as its practices did not mutilate, draw blood or maim, the Inquisition inflicted terrible pain and suffering upon many people. However, ultimately its procedures became regularized, careful and thorough. It was a highly centralized institution that may have been responsible for far fewer deaths than its popular image would suggest; in Languedoc, France, when the campaign against heresy there was at its peak in the thirteenth century, on average three people were burned per year. The regularization of investigations and the requirement of due process of law, however biased against the accused, brought 'the pyromania which had characterized lay attempts to suppress heresy . . . to an end'.[42] In other words, the Inquisition became a means to stop lynching.

As we shall see, these features meant that where the Inquisition was most powerful, notably in Spain and Italy, it played a significant role in keeping the witch hunts from becoming particularly large affairs. Chapter 5 will return to this issue in discussing torture and the issue of evidence during the witch persecutions.

On the other hand, the Inquisition capped and epitomized the development of the persecuting society. In 1000, a relentless and pitiless quest to unveil heretics would have made sense to few minds in western Europe; 250 years later this task was a perfectly acceptable idea across the subcontinent, even in the cases when secular officials resisted the inquisitors' activities as a challenge to their political authority. The Inquisition and all that had helped produce it provided fuel for the fires that would soon consume the witches.

[*]

Taken together, a number of new trends in the mid- to late Middle Ages constituted much of the background to the witch hunts. These developments were the almost concurrent rise of the Bible, heresy, prescriptions for daily life, purgatory, the devil, and the claim of the Church to decide who would be damned and who saved. An enemy within had been identified, perhaps even created, and linked to the forces of evil. The Western elite had entered a campaign mode and frame of mind.

It is unnecessary to repeat details here of the attacks on heretics such as the Cathars and the Waldensians, a movement that arose in southern France in the twelfth century. The Waldensians, while placing less emphasis on personal purity than did the Cathars, also advocated poverty and direct access to the Bible in the vernacular, points that posed a direct challenge to the Church's authority. As campaigns against the heretics gained momentum, the persecuting society tightened its grip on lepers, homosexuals and Jews as well. The latter were expelled from various countries, including England in 1290, France in 1306 and Spain in 1492. The stories of disgusting behaviour retailed about the Orléans group in 1022 spread along with the wars against heretics, and such tales were applied to Jews as well. None of this soothed Christian sensibilities, it seems, partly because the appearance of new threats and setbacks continued.

These debits included the arrival of the Mongols, the loss of the westerners' grip on the Byzantine capital in 1261, and the capitulation of their last stronghold in the Middle East by 1291. The crusades to reconquer land from the infidels had become merely an attempt to keep them out of Europe. The fall of Constantinople to the Turks in 1453 represented another major advance for Islam. Westerners remained deeply uneasy: 'missionary efforts in Asia had largely petered out; heresy had struck hard in central Europe; converts from the non-Christian minorities within Europe were feared as a fifth column undermining the purity of the faith; Antichrist was at the gates and Satan's minions within them'.[43]

As these events proceeded, major facets of the witch stereotype, especially descriptions of perverted sex, devil worship and infanticide became commonplace throughout Europe. But before turning to the witches themselves, two themes must be added to the picture of culture and attitudes drawn thus far: the situation of women in Europe and popular notions of the spirit world, including the activities and capabilities of the dead.

NOTES

1. Brigitte Rochelandet (1997) *Sorcières, diables et bûchers en Franch-Comté aux XVIe et XVIIe siècles* (Besançon: Éditions du Cètre), p. 140, details the pilgrimages and appeals to saints that the peasants of Franche Comté made in the fifteenth and sixteenth centuries when they were ill or beset by any misfortune.

2. The cinematic treatment is supported by the historian Natalie Zemon Davis (1983) in *The Return of Martin Guerre* (Cambridge, Mass.: Harvard University Press), pp. 19–21. Davis, who acted as a consultant for the film, reports that the family did bring in a 'cunning woman' to help and had four masses said for the young couple.

3. Katharine Park, 'Medicine and Magic: The Healing Arts' (1998), in Judith C. Brown and Robert C. Davis (eds) *Gender and Society in Renaissance Italy* (London: Longman), pp. 129–32.

4. P. G. Maxwell-Stuart (2001) *Witchcraft in Europe and the New World, 1400–1800.* New York: Palgrave), p. 15.

5. See, for example, Alice K. Turner (1993) *The History of Hell* (San Diego: Harcourt Brace & Co.), pp. 111–12; Peter Biller (1990) 'The Common Woman in the Western Church in the Thirteenth and Early Fourteenth Centuries', *Studies in Church History*, 27. *Women in the Church* (Oxford: Basil Blackwell), p. 146; Emmanuel Le Roy Ladurie (1978) *Montaillou: Cathars and Catholics in a French Village, 1294–1324*, trans. Barbara Bray (London: Scolar Press), pp. 134 and 320; Carlo Ginzburg (1980) *The Cheese and the Worms: the Cosmos of a Sixteenth-Century Miller*, trans. John and Anne Tedeschi (Baltimore: Johns Hopkins University Press), esp. pp. 4 and 11.

6. One of many works touching on this point is Richard Wunderli (1992) *Peasant Fires: The Drummer of Niklashausen* (Bloomington: Indiana University Press).

7. Charles Zika (2003) *Exorcising our Demons. Magic, Witchcraft and Visual Culture in Early Modern Europe* (Leiden: Brill), p. 9.

8. Gustav Jahoda (1969) *The Psychology of Superstition* (London: Allen Lane/ Penguin), pp. 9–10, 3 and 6.

9. R. I. Moore (1987) *The Formation of a Persecuting Society: Power and Deviance in Western Europe, 950–1250* (Oxford: Basil Blackwell), p. 5.

10. Edward S. Said (1979) *Orientalism* (New York: Vintage Books).

11. Turner, *History of Hell*, p. 3.

12. Thomas Cahill (1995) *How the Irish Saved Civilization: the Untold Story of Ireland's Heroic Role from the Fall of Rome to the Rise of Medieval Europe* (New York: Anchor Books), p. 210.

13. Quoted in Nicholas V. Riasanovsky (2000) *A History of Russia*, 6th edn (New York: Oxford University Press), p. 72.

14. Michael Bailey (2003) *Battling Demons: Witchcraft, Heresy, and Reform in the Late Middle Ages* (University Park: Pennsylvania State University Press), p. 102.

15. Moore, *Formation of a Persecuting Society*, p. 22.

16. *Webster's New World Dictionary of the American Language* (1982) 2nd College edn (New York: Simon and Schuster), p. 185.

17. Carlo Ginzburg (1992) *Ecstasies: Deciphering the Witches' Sabbath*, trans. Raymond Rosenthal (New York: Penguin), pp. 33–5.

18. Bernard Hamilton (1981) *The Medieval Inquisition* (New York: Holmes and Meier), p. 21.

19. Edward Peters (1988) *Inquisition* (New York: The Free Press), p. 40.

20. Henry Knighton (1949) 'Chronicle', in J. B. Ross and M. M. McLaughlin (eds) *The Portable Medieval Reader* (New York: Viking), pp. 218–19.

21. Gary K. Waite, *Heresy, Magic, and Witchcraft in Early Modern Europe* (New York: Palgrave Macmillan), p. 227.

22. Brian P. Levack (2006) *The Witch-hunt in Early Modern Europe*, 3rd edn (New York: Pearson/Longman), p. 66. A more recent translation of the biblical verse in question is 'rebellion is no less a sin than divination': I Samuel 15: 23.

23. Hector Ignacio Avalos (1993) 'Satan', in Bruce M. Metzger and Michael D. Coogan (eds) *The Oxford Companion to the Bible* (New York: Oxford University Press), pp. 678–79.

24. All references to and quotations from the Bible are to the *Holy Bible: The New Standard Revised Version* (Nashville: Thomas Nelson, 1989).

25. Elaine Pagels (1995) *The Origin of Satan* (New York: Vintage Books), pp. 11–12.

26. Jeffrey Burton Russell (1981) *Satan: the Early Christian Tradition* (Ithaca, NY: Cornell University Press), p. 37.

27. Pagels, *Origin of Satan*, p. 49.

28. Ibid., p. 143.

29. St Augustine (1997) *On Christian Teaching*, trans. with an introduction by R. P. H. Green (Oxford: Oxford University Press), pp. 51–2.

30. Norman Cohn (1975) *Europe's Inner Demons: an Enquiry Inspired by the Great Witch-Hunt* (New York: New American Library), p. 233.

31. E. T. De Wald (n.d.) *The Illustrations of the Utrecht Psalter* (Princeton: Princeton University Press).

32. *L'An Mille* (1947) trans. and ed. Edmond Pognon (Paris: Gallimard), p. 80. Included in this book is Glaber's *Five Histories*, translated into modern French.

33. In Dante's *Divine Comedy*, written 1302–21, the devil is almost perfectly immobile, frozen as he is up to his chest in the middle of hell. Dante and his guide Virgil climb unmolested down the body of Satan. Yet the immense size of this version of the devil and the great number of his demons, who are extremely mobile, should be a frightening image. He is 'emperor of the world of pain' and 'the source of every

evil in the world'. Dante Alighieri (1998) *Inferno*, trans. and ed. Elio Zappulla (New York: Pantheon Books), p. 302.

34. Turner, *History of Hell*, pp. 90 and 117–20.

35. Alan Charles Kors and Edward Peters (eds); revised by Edward Peters (2001) *Witchcraft in Europe, 400–1700: A Documentary History*, 2nd edn (Philadelphia: University of Pennsylvania Press), p. 5.

36. Cohn, *Europe's Inner Demons*, p. 67.

37. Moore, *Formation of a Persecuting Society*, p. 69.

38. John Bossy (1988) 'Seven Sins into Ten Commandments', in Edmund Leites (ed.) *Conscience and Casuistry in Early Modern Europe* (Cambridge: Cambridge University Press) pp. 217, 230.

39. Quoted in Cohn, *Europe's Inner Demons*, pp. 20–21.

40. Quoted in R. N. Swanson (1995) *Religion and Devotion in Europe, c.1215–c.1515* (Cambridge: Cambridge University Press), p. 1.

41. Moore, *Formation of a Persecuting Society*, pp. 6–7.

42. Hamilton, *Medieval Inquisition*, p. 57.

43. Swanson, *Religion and Devotion in Europe*, p. 260.

CHAPTER TWO

TOWARDS THE WITCH PYRES: IMAGES AND REALITIES OF EUROPEAN WOMEN TO 1500

MISOGYNY AND CULTURE

Women comprised perhaps 75–80 per cent of known victims of the European and North American witch persecutions. But to call the witch hunts an attack on women or to point to misogyny as the pre-eminent factor in producing the trials leaves several problems unexplained. First, as always, there is the question of chronology. Misogyny has long, deep roots in ancient, Jewish, Christian, Muslim and many other cultures. The Bible wastes no time in getting to Eve's story, in which the flightiness and lack of faith of the first woman are portrayed as the source of human suffering.

In the year 197 CE, Tertullian addressed all women:

And do you know that you are (each) an Eve? The sentence of God on this sex of yours lives in this age: the guilt must of necessity live too. You are the Devil's gateway. You are the unsealer of that (forbidden) tree . . . you are she who persuaded him whom the Devil was not valiant enough to attack . . . On account of your desert – that is death – even the Son of God had to die.[1]

Similar statements can be found throughout the writings of the early church fathers. The warrior cultures of Europe from ancient Greece through early modern Spain and Russia devalued women.

Misogyny, or at least a profound distrust of women's abilities and morals by men, reflected in many laws and customs, has certainly survived into our times. And that is precisely the problem in trying to decipher the relationship between male fear or hatred of women and the witch hunts: such feelings existed long before and long after the persecutions themselves.

Another difficulty in identifying misogyny as the fundamental impetus of the witch trials is that images of women have varied a great deal in Western culture. While many highly negative depictions have been produced, other, much more positive representations have also appeared. Indeed, in the centuries just before the witch hunts began, women often enjoyed benign images as more pious, closer to God, more inclined to read and better child-rearers than men. What must therefore be explained is why, for a period that more or less coincided with the witch persecutions, females were often shown in Western culture as dangerous creatures more likely than males to league with the devil. Yet even to say this is somewhat misleading, as some prominent witch hunters did not emphasize women's perfidy, while some anti-persecution figures demeaned them.

In any event, the overwhelming predominance of females among victims demands that careful attention be paid to the issue of gender. Several questions in particular require discussion: first, how were images of women constructed, and what was the philosophical or ideological message behind the creation of gender? (I do not agree with those who argue that *sexual* differences are created by language and culture; biology, to say the least, is important.)

As material cited already demonstrates, some men wrote vicious attacks on women because of their purported nature. However, Stuart Clark argues for a reappraisal of women's position in medieval and early modern thought. From ancient times, commentators emphasized the oppositeness of 'elements' like fire and water, earth and air, as well as of culture and nature. Philosophers separated the sacred from the profane, good from evil, Christ from Antichrist. In such schemes, all phenomena were divided into binary opposites that placed women, the devil, disorder and untamed nature, for example, on one side, and males, Christian faith and so forth on the other. There could be nothing between these antithetical qualities. Clark uses the image, one sometimes depicted in the writings he discusses, of two columns of opposites. Women were placed in the same column as the devil and other problematic or dangerous phenomena. This division was not necessarily a malicious devaluing of women, since in the world view of the period they had to be construed as one of a pair of opposites.

It was not until the period of the twelfth to the fourteenth centuries, partly for reasons discussed earlier, that portrayals of women as the opposite of men began to harden into negative and dismissive ideas. But, Clark continues, the broad acceptance of such notions by the fourteenth century meant that in practice most people, male and female, simply felt that women were more susceptible than men to the devil's blandishments. The majority of writers on witchcraft were entirely representative of their age and culture, and they 'showed little interest in exploring a gender basis of witchcraft or in using it to denigrate women'. The positioning of females in the same column as the devil and disorder did not necessarily produce misogynist attacks on women; such hatred characterized only some witch hunters' writings. In Clark's view, there was much less of a vicious assault on women in the witch hunts than has frequently been argued.[2]

Gender is a matter of what people do as well as how they are perceived. It is of course difficult to separate the two aspects of gender, and the roles women filled in Europe were both cause and effect of concepts of the feminine. But the tasks and responsibilities of women, rather than ideas regarding their inherent nature, need to be addressed as specific contributors to the broad perception that females were more likely to be witches.

67

A discussion of these questions will be woven into the rest of this book, especially the next two chapters. It is appropriate to start almost from the ground up, with what women did, made and earned in the West.

WORK, MARRIAGE AND WOMEN'S STATUS IN EUROPE

As the persecuting society arose in Europe, the status of women declined. Their worth, in the various senses of that word, diminished from the ninth or tenth century onwards. Women became limited to certain roles as they were ousted from a number of occupations or from the more lucrative and independent positions within other trades. Strengthening the institution of marriage protected women in certain ways and helped to make sure that wealthy and powerful men would not monopolize available females; on the other hand, in some respects marriage proved to be a new trap for many women. All this may demonstrate preconditions – not causes – for the witch hunts.

The vast majority of women around the world have always worked. In European peasant households of the early modern period, their labour was vital; an adult trying to live on his or her own was doomed to failure by both community and economic pressure. Where the nuclear family came to predominate, especially in Europe north of the Mediterranean regions, villagers understood the situation and moved to marry when an economic niche opened upon the death of a parent;[3] if a spouse died and the remaining partner was still relatively young, the survivor quickly remarried.

Although peasants did not necessarily object to profound affection within marriage, they did not marry for love but to form an economic unit. In Sennely, France, a typical north-west European village, marriage was 'a partnership established for the purpose of continuing the timeless battle against hunger and solitude'.[4] In this context, the dowry that a bride of even modest means brought to the marriage had a dual meaning: first, it represented a transfer of wealth from her father's household to her new husband's family. Second, girls often began in childhood to work on the sheets, towels, embroidery and other products they would bring to their marriages; these things were necessary household items but also physical manifestations of the skills, thrift and discipline a wife needed to make a peasant union successful.

Even the celebration of a bride's virginity found in many cultures or, on the other hand, the difficulty of making a good match for a girl known to have had sex before marriage with someone other than her intended groom, may not have related at bottom to moral standards. Instead, the fact (or reputation) of virginity at marriage probably symbolized the likelihood that a woman would be a hardworking member of an economic team. As Olwen Hufton has pointed out, for rich and poor alike, preparation for marriage involved careful planning beginning in early adolescence or even childhood.[5] A female who had not been able to discipline herself or protect herself from sex until marriage was probably too flighty, especially in the eyes of peasants, to make a good wife. What if she was promiscuous after the wedding? Although affection was not the main issue, peasants realized that jealousies could erupt and threaten not only the marriage but the solidarity so needed by an entire village. Meanwhile, the economic unit of husband and wife could become unworkable, damaging not only their own household but the community itself.

Needless to say, in almost all cultures men have not been held to the same standards of sexual behaviour as women. This difference is not solely the product of gender constructs. Men are larger and stronger on average and have, because their bodies produce 10–20 times more testosterone, more natural aggression than women.[6] But physical dissimilarity opened the way to elaborate appraisals of gender and to groundless ideas about biology. Aristotle, whose writings were popularized in the Renaissance, argued that women were imperfect men. Early modern doctors also often maintained that women were unrealized or defective men, and that their smaller craniums indicated smaller mental capacity. Popular wisdom had it that males were conceived when things went right, but that female offspring were fathered by old men or young ones temporarily enfeebled by sickness, fatigue or other problems. The birth of a female child produced widespread disappointment, and twice as many girl babies as boys were abandoned in Renaissance Italy. Infant girls were put out to wet nurses more often and for longer periods than were boys.[7]

Whatever men thought of women, marriage became the most acceptable state of being for adult non-clerics in most societies. Yet there is intriguing evidence, directly related to the issue of women's worth, that the nature of marriage in the West changed dramatically beginning in the eighth or ninth century. Developments in the wedding ceremony were markers of what happened to marriage as an institution. Into the ninth century, most weddings appear to have occurred without any participation by the Church whatsoever. By the mid-1200s priests did celebrate weddings, but typically outside of a church building. The ceremony then moved inside the churches. Marriage is mentioned as a sacrament at the Fourth Lateran Council (1215), but for Catholics the wedding ceremony required the blessing of a priest to become official in the eyes of the Church only in the 1560s. This long shift in the way weddings were performed denotes a heightened desire of the Church at least to participate in, if not control, the formation of recognized couples. The authorities' efforts to insert themselves into the lives of ordinary people, to demarcate, define and regulate, as well as the timing of such a quest in Europe, should be familiar by now. These efforts became much more successful as the Church's institutions and power expanded.

The terms of Western marriage also shifted in the direction of undermining women's financial worth. The historian David Herlihy showed that until well into the Middle Ages, western European marriages tended to favour females: the dowry, or more precisely bridewealth,[8] so called because it represented a transfer of wealth to the bride's family, tended to move to females. That is, the husband would contribute goods to the marriage, although in many cases these were items intended for only his use, such as spears, war horses and so forth. Nevertheless, bridewealth brought items of value to the woman's family, which presided over their handing down to subsequent generations. Finding a good match for a daughter, or better yet for several, could make a family rich. Herlihy argues that this transfer of resources enabled numerous women to become wealthy and powerful – up to a point – and to found convents and other institutions.

Lineage was always important, but in early medieval Europe it could be traced most reliably through the women of a family, for the simple reason that it was beyond doubt who the mother of a child was. 'Women, and relationships to women, were the surest indicators of close kin' into the eleventh century, and families with status tended to trace their descent equally through the female and the male lines.[9] In this situation, it was logical to designate women as the bearers of family wealth. Females had value and were valued.

But gradually the terms of marriage shifted against women, and the dowry, with its transfer of wealth from the wife's family to her husband's, replaced bridewealth. By the 1400s well-to-do families in Florence put a third or more of their entire wealth into a single marriage, which meant that marriageable sons were a blessing and marriageable daughters a curse. The size of the gift was a sign of a family's position in society, and a ruinous competition developed to display social rank. The problem became so severe that Florentine officials moved to place legal limits on dowries. Before 1650, wealthy Milanese families solved the problem, in a certain sense, by sending three-quarters of their daughters to convents. When females no longer had financial value, and instead caused huge drains on their families' resources when they married, their figurative value inevitably decreased as well. Trying to marry off more than one or two daughters could ruin a wealthy family.

Other aspects of marriage in the early modern period also contributed to a decline in the position of women. When members of the Italian upper classes married, often a man in his 30s took a bride 10–15 years younger. An experienced male thus formed a couple with someone who was barely more than a girl, and who had in all likelihood been carefully protected, especially against having intercourse, as she grew up. In the upper reaches of society, the tendency of men to think that they were superior to their wives was therefore strengthened, and youthful wives were marginalized among their husband's relatives. To be sure, young brides sometimes gained revenge of a sort by outliving their spouses.

However, such widows posed a problem for society. They had tasted the pleasures of the flesh, as popular attitudes had it, and were considered likely to continue sexual activity. Particularly among male guardians of honour, widows' libido was seen as a threat: a sexually experienced woman living outside marriage was deemed an undisciplined creature who might seduce any man and bring shame to her family. Moreover, complications could develop as widows attempted simultaneously to hold on to the dowry, maintain connections with their natal families, please society and remarry. The results of this juggling act produced a negative picture of widows in Italy, where they were accused of being grossly avaricious, flighty and disloyal to their husbands' families. 'There is no doubt that the growing misogyny and mistrust of women at the dawn of the Renaissance were reinforced by structural contradictions' that made it difficult to combine the issues connected with the dowry with the demands of the dead husband's lineage.[10] This situation was not limited to the upper classes, as the custom of giving dowries spread to the lower strata at least of Tuscan society, if not to other areas as well. The great humanist Marsilio Ficino summed up a common male attitude of the day with the remark that, 'Women should be used like chamber pots: hidden away once a man has pissed in them.'[11]

Such problems help explain the passage of laws in many German cities during the sixteenth century that pronounced women living on their own as dangerous. Unmarried women were not allowed to move into these towns, and single domestic servants had to leave the municipalities if they gave up their jobs and did not immediately take others.

In the ways marriage changed into the early modern period are major clues to why Western culture came increasingly to portray women as troublesome figures, helping to pave the way for the witch hunts. Such attitudes changed from the top of society down, and elite views proved crucial in creating the preconditions for the witch hunts and then in facilitating the persecutions themselves.

Why did the reversal in the terms of marriage occur? Herlihy cites two factors: first, that Western society had literally settled down and changed from a warrior economy, in which the capture of booty and slaves was the major source of wealth, to landownership. When land and not loot became the basic source of wealth, the issue of bequeathing that wealth became much more important. Each new generation of males could not seize its own booty. Land was a limited resource, and the way to maintain it in financially significant parcels was through the family, by giving most or all of it to one descendant. Especially in warrior societies or in ones evolving away from the warrior ethos, men were going to protect their status somehow as changes in the nature of wealth took place. The eldest son thus became the focus of inheritance, whether by law as in England or by custom as in most of the rest of Europe. To this picture the anthropologist Jack Goody adds that the Western Church accumulated vast amounts of land through bequests and gifts as early as the sixth century, making the issue of who controlled the remaining territory even more critical.[12]

The second basic cause of the decline in women's position, according to Herlihy, was the growth of towns from the twelfth century onwards, first in Italy and then elsewhere. Several factors were intertwined in this story. Increasing competition in some trades meant that men drove women out of them or restricted them to low-paying, low status positions. Specialization and the need for increasing amounts of capital to make a business successful put women at a disadvantage, as they had on average fewer resources to draw from. Whatever the reasons, no doubt exists about what happened in town after town. Women made up 15 per cent of independent taxpayers in Paris in 1292; among them were skilled workers and doctors. By 1313 the percentage of such taxpayers had dropped to 10, while only 8 per cent of all taxpayers showing an occupation were women. By the early fifteenth century, the second figure had fallen to 2.5 per cent. Women helped establish the wool trade in Barcelona and worked as masters in its early stages, around 1300. Two centuries later, women held only lower-paying jobs in the wool industry.[13] According to another study, the growth of guilds led to the exclusion of women from many trades as established men sought to limit competition; 'women were an easy group to single out' for exclusion from work.[14]

As their financial worth and opportunities declined, how could women's figurative worth not also have fallen? Having some money and a job that requires skill and judgement means having a degree of independence; by 1500, women had lost considerable ground in their efforts to be self-reliant. Perhaps the wonder here is that women's status did not fall even further than it did.

WOMEN AND THE MEDIEVAL WESTERN CHURCH

The problem of women's deteriorating image was exacerbated by the Church. Once again, the higher Roman clergy contributed substantially to new or newly heightened images of a nefarious group within the larger society, in this case women. As the Church tried to define itself and proper Christian behaviour more precisely, the old idea that sex was a bad thing gained ground. The Synod of Rome (1047) had demanded celibacy of all priests; that the injunction had to be repeated several times demonstrated both how frequently clerics cohabited with women and how determined the higher church authorities were to end the practice. By the high Middle Ages sexual intercourse became in the eyes of the Church a necessary evil usually tolerated only within marriage and only for the purposes of procreation or to keep men away from illicit activity.

It is true that before the Reformation the church was 'ambivalent in practice about fornication'.[15] St Augustine had set the example of a male who might indulge in sex outside marriage but then be saved by a change of heart and penance. The Dominican Order promoted brothels or areas of towns where prostitution was allowed into the late fifteenth century, on the manifold theory that the women involved had already fallen; that a small number of them could serve a large number of men; that prostitutes had a useful function as a ready symbol of sin; and that by providing an outlet for certain men, some families might actually be preserved by the sex trade.[16] But these ideas imply that for the general good of society a limited amount of evil should be tolerated, and clearly the emphasis was on preserving as many men as possible from its touch. The women involved were 'fallen', the term applied to miscreant angels who became the devil's helpers, as if their status was determined once and for all.

Although men of the cloth endorsed and sometimes ran sexual establishments, they had no business using the services themselves. Priests and monks were most definitely not supposed to reproduce; they had to avoid sex in order to keep themselves pure and dedicated to a higher purpose, as well as to keep any property they accumulated within the church. Thus the line between animal grossness and purity was drawn between those who engaged in sexual activity and those who did not.

A bad thing must have a bad cause or agent; given Eve's original mistake, with its sexual overtones, and men's constant efforts to see their status maintained, females were the only choice for the wicked role. From the eleventh century forward, church reforms 'all emphasized the importance of controlling female sexuality and the inappropriateness of female religious [nuns and other categories of women dedicated to the religious life] being in contact with lay society'.[17] Except for the Dominicans' role in the exchange of sex for money, the Roman Catholic hierarchy increasingly assigned women to a corner marked in effect 'do not touch except when needed for procreation or to avoid a still greater evil'. Only men could aspire to the highest category of being, those who remained above earthly desires. Women were not worthy, since they were considered by nature to be temptresses with burning desires for sex. Or, to put it another way, women had been pushed into a category opposite to men. Even females who lived in convents and refrained from intercourse had second-class status in the Church. A mere handful of female saints could hope to find the ultimate in grace. Yet for all that the image and reputation of women was constructed by men, it is also worth keeping in mind that it was easier in one sense to point to women's sexual activity, for females alone produced unmistakable proof of sexual intercourse by becoming pregnant.

Dyan Elliott underscores the point that as celibacy became more strongly emphasized in the Church, the image of women and of their bodies declined. The first liturgies surrounding 'purification' of a new mother appeared in the late eleventh century. Women were seen as polluting the male ministers of the altar, and ecclesiastical authorities now waged 'institutional war' against adult females. Although women were supposedly passive during intercourse, churchmen now argued, they were also said to be much more lustful and to have a vast 'imaginative power' regarding sex.[18] Meanwhile, a popular view in the Italian Renaissance and long after held was that in order to conceive a woman had to reach orgasm during intercourse. It seems that various bits of imaginative thinking about women's sexuality were available, to be woven as authors chose into narratives about female evil or goodness. The flexibility of female images will appear repeatedly in the witch hunters' manuals.

By the late fifteenth century, elite rhetoric about the dangers women presented was useful in making the binary oppositions of the day clearer than before: male/female, priest/lay people, celibate/married were now supposed to be antithetical categories of being. The depiction of women themselves was also split, between the pure Mary, who had never had intercourse, and women who had, or indeed all other women. Following this logic, the picture of the female body also bifurcated: breasts and their milk were good, the vagina was the source of great evil. As this happened, church rites became more male dominated; transubstantiation, in which an 'involved male cleric [was] handling the body of a male God', became the central mystery of the faith. From all this, Elliott remarks, it was easy to envision the witch as the embodiment of everything that was wrong with women. The new emphasis on clerical celibacy and its obverse, the condemnation of women and their bodies, made 'materialization of the witch virtually irresistible'.[19]

This is a powerful argument, and there is no doubt that Elliott has identified central trends in the thought of the high Middle Ages. These developments were deeply harmful to women. But, as we shall see, the line from such words and rituals to the killing of women for witchcraft by no means took the direct and 'virtually irresistible' path that Elliott suggests. Nor did male theorists and officials share any single view of women.

Given the social, economic and cultural trends discussed above, which were layered over existing denigration of women, their image in late medieval Europe was largely negative. Nevertheless, other aspects of Christianity, in which much religious tradition centred on women, tempered this picture. Mary, Mary Magdalene and Mary and Martha of Bethany represented some of the most important figures in Jesus' story. At the Crucifixion it was women who gathered to wait and weep. Male disciples wavered in their faith and even betrayed Christ, while the women trusted in his resurrection. In many depictions of the Holy Family, Mary and sometimes her mother St Anne appear as strong, confident, truly religious figures; Joseph, who everyone knew was cuckolded by an angel, is often shown as old, feeble, of no particular importance and confined to the background.

Women 'increasingly appear as the prime readers of the devotional and instructional works' of the late Middle Ages.[20] Images of St Anne teaching her daughter to read became widespread. Mothers, not fathers, had the duty of passing on religious knowledge within the family. Fathers could impart practical knowledge to children, but in the medieval hierarchy of activities, matters of the spirit were accorded greater value than anything that involved earth, blood or money.

Alongside the anti-women tracts and sermons were positive statements. The Franciscan monk Berthold of Regensburg was 'the greatest mid-thirteenth-century German preacher',[21] or simply the 'greatest preacher' of the day.[22] Among positive remarks he made about women in his sermons were:

You women, there are many serious sins that you do not commit as men do . . . you do not commit murder.

You women, I know you follow my thoughts better than men do.

You women, you go more readily to church than men do; speak your prayers more readily than men; go to sermons more readily than men.[23]

The case of Joan of Arc also tempers any impression of unmitigated misogyny in the late Middle Ages. She was executed in 1431 by the English – as a heretic, not a witch, although some were quick to call her one – but for months before her capture by the enemy she had amazed and inspired the French with her sanctity. Joan personifies the argument that at the time, 'the privileged conduit for divine revelation was young, poor, and female'.[24] Caught as she was in a war, and too much an inspiring symbol for the English to tolerate, Joan's execution does not diminish the point that her bravery and evident devotion to God won the admiration of many thousands of Frenchmen. In any event, Joan's second trial, held in 1456 and supported by both the pope and the king of France, resulted in her rehabilitation. While the second verdict came 25 years too late to help Joan herself, it certainly indicated that her memory was to be respected in all of Catholic Europe.

If no more wealthy convents were founded by women in the late Middle Ages, many of the ones begun earlier remained viable. Into the sixteenth century the Abbess of Quedlinburg (Germany) governed a large territory; under her jurisdiction were nine churches and two male monasteries. Women retained their economic importance in the peasant milieu and continued to enjoy a positive image in many texts and paintings.

At the same time, misogyny's ugly face remained prominent. Women experienced a decline in their fortunes, opportunities and status in various towns after about 1200. The difficult position of widows in affluent families contributed to a growing negative reputation for all females in western Europe.

Around 1400, these contending aspects of women's situations tended to produce an equilibrium, albeit one definitely on the negative side. Voices like Tertullian's had identified all women as bad and as allied with the devil. But, just as with biblical passages that suggested all Jews were the devil's offspring, words alone did not spur men to attack the smeared group. The really determined witch-haters turned to another, older tradition in Europe for images that suggested all women might be capable of disgusting, anti-human behaviour.

WILD AND FURIOUS WOMEN

Across Europe stories were long told of processions of the dead, usually led by women, who moved about the land at night. The spirits, who walked or rode animals, were called by various names: the Wild or Furious Horde, the Wild Hunt and so forth. In what must be a blend of Norse, Celtic and Roman traditions, the leader of the processions was often said to be the goddess Diana. The wandering dead were not necessarily malicious, although villagers often put out food and drink for them at certain times of the year; failure to do so might result in unpleasant mischief, for example that the spirits might urinate in the beer kegs. Such tales are recorded by 906, although they surely circulated long before that, and were repeated, at least in some areas of Germany, into the sixteenth century.

Ordinary people in Italy spoke of the 'women of the good game' or the 'game of the good society' in the fifteenth and sixteenth centuries; in Scotland somewhat later peasants described gatherings of the 'good people' or 'good neighbours', fairies who did no harm. Carlo Ginzburg calls these legends an 'ancient stratum of beliefs' in Europe. Between the middle of the fifteenth and the beginning of the sixteenth centuries, the elite mounted a 'frontal attack' on these old stories and twisted them into malicious reports.[25] Once again, this new campaign must be set into the context of a felt need to close Christian ranks.

Ginzburg's view might be challenged only in that the diabolization of the old beliefs began in some cases well before the period he identifies, although there is little question that the main transformation occurred when he said it did. The spirits might have been called the Good Ladies in German-speaking regions, but that did not prevent St Germanus from recounting an unpleasant incident about nocturnal marchers in 1264. He lodged one night in a poor man's house, where the owner mentioned that he put out food for the Ladies. Germanus determined to stay up and watch; what he saw was male devils who came and sat at the table.[26]

The key document of Western Christianity on the processions of the dead, one that both discusses the belief and illustrates the disturbing effect it was beginning to have on clerical consciousness, is the *Canon Episcopi*. Its name derives from the first word of the text, the Latin for bishops. Throughout the Middle Ages, the document was thought to be a church canon dating from 314. In fact it was not a statement of faith at all, but an order to churches issued under Charlemagne, and it dates only from the turn of the eighth to the ninth centuries. No matter; it was taken to be an authentic and venerable prescription to bishops, noting that:

some wicked women perverted by the devil, seduced by illusions and phantasms of demons, believe and profess themselves, in the hours of night to ride upon certain beasts with Diana, the goddess of the pagans, and an innumerable multitude of women, and in the silence of the dead of night to traverse great spaces of earth, and to obey her commands as of their mistress, and to be summoned to her service on certain nights ... such phantasms are imposed upon the minds of infidels and not by the divine but by the malignant spirit. Thus Satan himself, who transfigures himself into an angel of light, when he has captured the mind of a miserable woman and has subjugated her to himself by infidelity and incredulity, immediately transforms himself into the species and similitudes of different personages ... the faithless mind thinks these things happen not in the spirit but in the body.

Whoever believes that any force except the creator can change the form of a being is an infidel, the text continues.[27]

The *Canon Episcopi* established in the Roman Church the view that women, widely deluded by the devil, often believed that they went out at night to march with Diana. For the purpose of examining the witch hunts, several points are important here: first, that women were identified as having minds that Satan could easily influence; second, that talk of the night processions must have been common; and third, the Church maintained that the nocturnal marches did not actually happen; they were a product of dreams and illusions produced by the devil. What must then be explained is why, when a supposedly venerable canon said there were no such processions – or that there were no nocturnal gatherings of people for the purpose of committing evil, since the procession of the dead is clearly the cultural forerunner of the witches' sabbat – many witch hunters, clerics and officials later maintained that the night meetings did occur. And why did the change in elite attitudes occur in a certain period, in the fifteenth and sixteenth centuries?

FROM SORCERER TO WITCH: THE CREATION OF THE WITCH STEREOTYPE

The idea exists in many societies that some people have supernatural powers or supernatural acquaintances that will lend them such powers. But traditionally the people equipped in this way are not necessarily seen as subordinates of the devil, who did not exist in any event in Greek or Roman theology and who assumed a leading role in Western Christendom only in the late Middle Ages. Among the Azande people of Africa, what has been translated as 'witchcraft' was considered to be a substance people were born with; it could be identified in an autopsied corpse by the elders.[28] The Navajo deem some people 'witches' but explain their powers as deriving from contact with mysterious materials or forces, not including the devil.

In this study, 'witch' has a particular meaning: the word refers to a highly developed image of malicious persons that arose in Europe in the fourteenth and fifteenth centuries, drawing on legends and images that already dated back thousands of years.[29] The new witches were accused of making a pact with the devil in which he granted them the use of evil powers. He might also provide some money, food, other material aid and sexual activity, although these, at least

82

in available testimony from witch trials, often turned out to be worthless or painful. Witches had the ability to fly, but that seemed to work only to get them to gatherings of their sisters. In what already sounds like a really bad bargain, the humans had to shun Christianity, attend sabbats presided over by the devil and lesser demons, become the sexual partners of any demon or other witch who wanted to use their bodies (especially at the sabbat), and harm people, animals or crops at the devil's command. The witches of course forfeited their souls to the devil after death and spent eternity in hell. People who fell into the devil's clutches in these ways did so with full knowledge of who their tempter was, in the outlook of the day. The new recruits then became Satan's servants, as opposed to the sorcerers who might try to invoke and control demons.

In the European context, the Azande and Navajo wielders of supernatural powers would not be called witches, although that term is hardly likely to be dislodged from writings about them. It would be better to use a word such as sorcerer to designate such people.

European popular cultures considered extraordinary, magical abilities to be either innate or learned. Innate power was often associated in Europe with certain signs at birth. Italians of the Friuli, for instance, considered that anyone born with a caul (part of the amniotic sac) over the head had specific, limited connections to supernatural powers as well as a duty to use them for the good of the community. People of this group, called the *Benandanti*, 'the good walkers', were certainly not the devil's spawn or servitors.[30] But in many parts of Europe there did not need to be any particular marks announcing a person's ability to see or act beyond the natural world. A reputation for such talent was all that mattered.

The word 'magician' into the early modern period usually implied a learned ability, obtained either from books or from experienced common folk, to alter the course of events, identify a criminal, heal the sick, prepare love potions and so on. 'High' magic referred to knowledge gleaned through careful study, especially from books. 'Low' magic was the garden variety practised by the lower classes; it often involved the use of charms, looking glasses, cards, dropping raw eggs into water to watch the patterns they made and a host of other simple devices.

The 'wise' or 'cunning' people of Europe engaged in low magic. They were usually lower-class folk sought out by others because they were considered good at finding lost or stolen objects, making love potions, seeing the future and/or healing. Probably the reputation of such people did not have to be especially great to draw clients, who were typically poor, desperate or lacking in alternate means of relief. The Catholic Church and secular authorities into the early modern period tended not to attack the cunning folk, partly because the elite also sometimes sought them out, unless they became too notorious or were charged with committing tangible evil acts. The development of the persecuting society, including the fourteenth-century attacks on Jews and lepers, and the periodic arrivals of the plague, did increase officialdom's desire to act against the traditional magicians in some areas. For example, burnings took place in Lorraine in 1327, 1358 and 1372. In the last year, three women and a man were executed in Metz.[31] Yet superstition, magic and even witchcraft did not become major concerns to European authorities into the fifteenth century. Laws and theoretical discussions of these topics 'remained a very small part of the immense literature on the social and spiritual life of Christian Europeans'.[32] As we shall see, no sustained, effective campaign against the cunning folk ever developed. They continued to appear in numerous sources in England, across the Continent and in North America into the nineteenth century.

Ordinary Europeans usually avoided the issue of where supernatural insight or power came from and simply went to consult those reported to have it. But people might visit a wise person one

day and on the next go to great lengths to avoid him, since mani-
pulators of the world could probably perform harmful as well as
good magic. A love potion might be wonderful for the one who
purchased it but miserable for anyone who lost in romance because
of it. The cunning peasants or artisans who could heal might be
able to cause sickness as well. Thus the neighbours of these local
conjurors and finders treated them with a mixture of awe, respect
and fear, and sometimes even assaulted them.

At the risk of greatly oversimplifying a complex subject, religion
is usually distinguished from magic: the first involves requests for
aid from the supernatural, help that may or may not be granted but
that is never under the control of the supplicant.[33] Magic, on the
other hand, purports to give the one using it command of supernatural forces. Thus witchcraft was frequently called a heresy in
our period, a depraved form of religion or an anti-religion, since it
was described as a cult of the devil; its practitioners asked him for
assistance but by no means controlled him. On the contrary, they
became his dupes.

How did the transition occur from sorcerer or village magician
to witch, and from occasional trials of people for conducting evil
magic to frequent proceedings against witches for using the devil's
power? The mixture of ingredients that produced the image of the
witch took a long time indeed to come together, to simmer in the
minds of European writers and artists, and finally to boil over into
accusations and trials themselves.

Antecedents for the European witch came from many sources.
Besides the figure of Diana, available in much of Europe for transformation into a potentially harmful figure, the ancient world provided other dubious female characters who lived on in popular
and especially elite culture. The *Odyssey* furnished several of these,
notably Circe, who uses her evil magic to transform Odysseus'
crew into pigs, for no apparent reason other than it pleases her to
do so. Calypso, although not inherently evil, uses magic drugs to

keep Odysseus on her island as her sexual partner for seven years. In these two cases, men are saved from the evil of women or their sexual power only by the intervention of the gods. There is, of course, Penelope, Odysseus' faithful wife, who waits long years for him, but the story shows how easily even a good man may be drawn from the right path by powerful women.

Hebrew legends of Lilith, said to be Adam's first wife, depict a woman recalcitrant and evil almost from the moment of her creation. In these stories, Lilith is fashioned by God, not from Adam's rib but from the earth, the way Adam himself was made. The couple immediately begin to fight, as Adam claims the right to lie on top during intercourse. But Lilith vehemently objects, saying that because they were both made from earth they are equal. Neither will yield, and Lilith then 'pronounced the Ineffable Name' (of God), a great sin in the Bible, and flew away into the air. Three angels who race after her cannot persuade her to return. From that moment on Lilith has dominion over newborn children and can kill them until a boy is eight days and a girl twenty days old, unless they are protected by special signs or amulets. In return, a hundred of Lilith's children, the products of sex with demons, must die each day.[34] If ever a model of an uppity woman with a voracious sexual appetite, malicious and evil to boot, was needed, here it was. Lilith may well have derived from the Babylonian-Assyrian word *lilitu*, a female demon. An extant statue of this figure from Sumer, dating back to 2500 or 3000 BCE, features a woman's face, large wings and powerful claw feet.

Lilith is found in the Bible, though not explained, in Isaiah 34: 14; she must dwell in a desert with snakes, jackals and goat-demons for company. The King James Bible, among others, translates the Hebrew word 'lilith' as screech owl; this bird, as we shall see, became important in the construction of the witch. Besides this conduit to western European lore, she also arrived via Jewish writings beginning in the eighth century CE. In late medieval Europe, Lilith became Satan's concubine in stories and legends. Masaccio decorated the walls of the Brancacci Chapel in Florence with a fresco of the temptation of Adam in 1424–27; a snake with a woman's head has already given the apple to Eve. In 1467–68, the Flemish artist Hugo van der Goes produced the painting *Original Sin*, now in the Kunsthistorisches Museum, Vienna. Van der Goes places a rather plain-looking Adam and Eve in the Garden of Eden; instead of a snake tempting Eve with the apple, a sort of furry ferret with a woman's face holds out the fruit. Michelangelo's *Temptation and Fall*, painted on the ceiling of the Sistine Chapel in 1508–1512, portrays the serpent with the upper body and face of a woman. A sixteenth-century Italian translation of an older work by a converted Jew depicts Lilith 'with the face of a woman and the body of a snake lurking behind the trees in the garden and spying on Adam and Eve'.[35] A sexually insatiable woman linked to original sin, who in some guise flies and kills children: in a few years this will be a familiar figure indeed.

Yet it took centuries for the Western Christian world to draw widely upon such images and to associate them in general with female potential to do harm. As the Introduction noted, in various European languages the words for someone who could wield supernatural power did not necessarily have evil connotations at first. This is most easily seen in the French terms *sorcier* (male) and *sorcière* (female), which can be translated into English as both witch and sorcerer. Merlin the sorcerer, for example, may be good at heart and use his magic for beneficent purposes. The English *witch* derives from the Anglo-Saxon words *wicce* (female) and *wicca* (male), used to indicate one who practised sorcery or magic. On the other side of the Continent, Russian dictionaries consider *ved'ma* and *koldun* to be synonyms; both referred originally to the use of magic or supernatural powers, and not necessarily for evil purposes.

Until the late sixteenth century, and in many cases for another hundred years, Latin dominated in educated European discourse.

Treatises on witchcraft appeared solely in that language until the 1580s; therefore the Latin words for witch are of grave significance. One of the relevant terms is *saga*, which more properly refers to a seer or fortune-teller. Another word, *venefica*, which originally meant poisoner, was commonly used in medieval and early modern texts. Human societies do not allow known poisoners to go unpunished. Perhaps the most widely used Latin word for witch in the early modern period was *maleficus/malefica* (malefactor). This term had been employed in the ancient world without reference to the devil, unknown at the time, to designate anyone who carried out evil magic. Law codes carried the same concept forward as late as the sixteenth century.

The King James Bible (1611) boldly uses the word *witch* where the original Hebrew terms are not entirely clear. In particular, Exodus 22: 18, part of the laws of behaviour brought to the Jews by Moses and following in order closely after the Ten Commandments, reads: 'Thou shalt not suffer a witch to live.' Bibles in other languages are more cautious; in Russian scripture, for example, the word used is *magesnitsa*, an archaic term derived from *magiia*; it was not used in known accounts of Russians accused of using black magic. French Bibles use *la sorcière* for this passage, while the German is *Zauberin* (also feminine) or, in Luther's translation, *die Zeuberinnen*, an old plural feminine form. Neither French, German nor Russian injunctions in Exodus 22: 18 meant much in practice, since the broader and more vague 'sorcerer' lacks the implication of immediate threat that 'witch' conveys. Ironically, as later chapters will show, James I did not promote witch hunts once he assumed the throne of England.

The Bible known by his name translates various Hebrew words as witch that can also be rendered in English as sorcerer, sorceress, medium or necromancer (one who calls forth the dead to carry out commands). In general, the references to witches in the Hebrew Bible 'reflect a category of ritual specialist whose status and function are now virtually unknown'. The original text refers to women in several of these passages, for instance in the Exodus law, where the word *kasaph* (more properly seer, not witch) is used; this may be because women were forbidden to conduct official religious rites. The repeated mention and condemnation of sorcerers in the Old Testament perhaps indicate that ancient Hebrew clerics tried to distinguish their official religion from popular practice,[36] just as many Catholic documents did in the period after about 1000 CE. In both cases the exclusion of women from the performance of church rites was a powerful symbol of females' lower status. This relegation in turn made them more suspect of seeking aid from other, unholy supernatural forces.

Whether we are talking about the ancient Hebrews or the English in the seventeenth century, governments in the Judaeo-Roman-Christian tradition disliked magicians or sorcerers. But this attitude related more to punishing their alleged acts than to any drive to impose state-approved forms of religion on the people. Roman law largely ignored magic unless it was thought to cause harm. In early written Visigothic, German and Carolingian law, magicians could be punished for their evil acts or for engaging in ceremonies which were clearly residual pagan rituals. But there does not seem to have been much prosecution on the latter grounds.

Teutonic laws of the sixth and seventh centuries condemn the old wandering nocturnal spirits, *strigae* and *lamiae*, who were said to fly out at night to suck people's blood or otherwise injure them. *Strigae*, from the Latin *strix*, plural *striges*, taken from Greek, originally meant screech owl. *Strega*, from the same derivation, remains the modern Italian word for both witch and sorceress. *Lamia* is a much older word; it first appears in a passage written by Heraclitus in about 500 BCE. The Lamia was a snake woman who bore a child by Zeus. She was 'named Sibyl by the Libyans', Heraclitus continues.[37] In other versions Lamia was the name of a beautiful queen of Libya who became Zeus's lover. His wife Hera then took vengeance on the couple by destroying their children. Lamia, distraught and alone, reacted by slaying other people's children. Here again a conflation took place over time of the seer, the child-slaying mother and women in general, for the Sibyls were brought intact into early Christian writings as useful prophetesses. Nonetheless, their evil side remained available for other cultural uses.

Laws against *strigae* and *lamiae* suggest that rulers entertained the notion that such creatures were human; why else talk about punishing them? Isidore of Seville, writing in the seventh century, added the idea that these figures could be females who had sexual intercourse with demons. The transformation was already under way from considering the night-flying evil-doers only as spirits, and sometimes only as delusions produced in people's minds by the devil, to thinking of them as maleficent humans at work among the good people.

Germanic rulers, as they began to absorb more Christian influences in the Middle Ages, did not cease condemning the old evil spirits and creatures, called *zoubere, vergiftnisse* (poisoners), and 'those who swear (by the devil)'. But a number of Germanic laws also prohibited mob action against alleged sorcerers and specified fines for false accusations of evil magic; whatever happened to the evil-doers had to occur in a regulated manner. By the early ninth century, magic or sorcery (*zouberey* or *zauberey*) meant sacrificing to, praying to, or invoking either the old pagan gods or the devil, as well as carrying out evil acts with the help of such supernatural forces. The law codes did not yet mention the pact with the devil or night flying, nor did they indicate that women were the most likely perpetrators of witchcraft. Trials of magicians did take place and resulted in death sentences, but in this early period officials still emphasized that the guilty parties had fallen victim to illusions created by demons.

Since various pagan rituals were still celebrated by the common people, including one at New Year in which they donned the skins of animals, a traditional way of asking the spirit world for help in hunting, the Church and its secular allies had much to criticize in popular behaviour. But the elite did not consider such practices to be especially threatening to society, at least in part because 'high' and 'popular' culture had hardly begun to diverge. Well-born Europeans told the same stories and sang the same songs that the ordinary people did. Even into the 1400s, the sources do not suggest that, through folk magic or practices of any kind, the devil was directing a vast conspiracy against humanity; Satan was still only growing into his starring role in Western culture.

The persecutions of the fourteenth to eighteenth centuries treated here, with all their apparatus of trial, torture and execution, involved a different kind of miscreant; at least, the charges against the accused did not centre on magic or sorcery as they have been discussed above. The chief persecutors hunted people they called witches. In some places, particularly English- and German-speaking territories, new terminology makes the transition clear; *witch* was not *wicce*. Even if the label applied to people suspected of diabolical acts did not change, as in France, the description of their deeds shifted dramatically, and the concept of the witch in trials held from the 1320s on differed from that of the old magician or sorcerer. One of that ilk might have invoked and controlled petty demons; the new witches were voluntary servants of a mighty master.

Officially supported attacks on witches were not assaults on the English cunning folk, even after their practices became somewhat less acceptable to the Church with the coming of the Reformation. The magistrates were not much concerned with villagers who simply claimed to be able to find lost cows or lockets.[38] In Germany the people in demand for their healing skills, potions and the like were left alone as the witch hunts progressed – except when they were accused of inflicting perceptible, physical harm through their supernatural connections. Scottish folk magicians were sometimes charged with witchcraft, but this happened only when large-scale witch hunts were in progress.[39] There was a link between magic and charges of diabolical activity, which will be explored in its turn, but it was not as simple as attempts by the authorities, whether Catholic or Protestant, to crush popular practices. If the authorities had wished to attack folk magic, they could certainly have done so head-on. Yet even the Protestant elite, which ostensibly had more reason than its Catholic counterpart to distrust magic, never undertook a 'major prosecution of cunning folk'.[40] When Swedish authorities attempted in the 1680s to 'educate the populace in desired directions' by punishing the wise people, the campaign was an embarrassing failure. Some village magicians were brought to court, but there were long trials and counter-suits, witnesses turned up drunk or skipped the proceedings altogether, and various cases ended in acquittals.[41] Witchcraft was another matter that, when prosecuted, was taken extremely seriously by the courts.

While the *Canon Episcopi* had pointed the way 600 years earlier to the idea that the devil could control people's – or at least women's – minds, the Catholic Church long remained relatively indifferent to the idea that females were somehow naturally inclined to become the devil's helpers. Then with the book *Formicarius*, written 1435–37, the German Dominican monk Johannes Nider made a substantial contribution to implanting exactly that likelihood in elite culture. Nider reported that he had spoken at length with two men, one a lay judge and the other a Dominican inquisitor, who had presided over numerous witch trials, involving male and female defendants. Nider mentions that they were charged with using spells to produce disease or to make someone fall in love; so far this is a traditional picture. But he also introduces the idea that there were sects of people who not only used the old charms, but also ate infants and conjured up a demon in the shape of a man. Abjuring the Christian faith in every way possible, these witches boiled the flesh of children they had killed, making of it both a powerful magic ointment and a drink given to new initiates in the sect. There is nothing in Nider about flying, orgies or night gatherings, yet the outlines of a deadly anti-human conspiracy, able to spread rapidly by recruiting new members, are in place.

Although Nider wrote of male and female witches, he also made clear his belief that women might be more drawn to the repulsive sect than were men. He referred to Joan of Arc, burned only a few years earlier (as a heretic and not a witch, we remember), and now claimed that she 'had a familiar angel of God . . . judged to be an evil spirit; so that this spirit rendered her a sorceress'. Two other women then came forward, Nider continues, to claim that they had been sent by God to help Joan. 'Doctors of Theology' determined that they had been 'deceived by the ravings of the evil spirit'. One repented, but the other refused to and was burned. Nider refers to Joan and her purported helpers as 'magicians or sorceresses [*mage vel malefice*]'.[42]

Formicarius is written in the form of a dialogue between a naive pupil and a learned master. The pupil remarks about Joan's story that 'I cannot sufficiently marvel how the frail sex can rush into such presumptuous things'. That is, he represents popular attitudes, not yet convinced of the inherent inclination of women to ally with Satan.

The master replies that:

These things are marvelous to simple folk like you, but they are not rare in the eyes of wise men. For there are three things in nature, which, if they transgress the limits of their own condition, whether by diminution or by excess, attain to the highest pinnacle whether of goodness or of evil. These are the tongue, the ecclesiastic, and the woman; all of these are commonly best of all, so long as they are guided by a good spirit, but worst of all if guided by an evil spirit.[43]

Since women had long been identified as far worse chatterers and gossips than men, Nider in effect dealt their image a double blow, even as he indicated that they might sometimes be among the best people. But Nider has come in for some revisionism regarding his views on women and the devil. First, Nider wrote more about good people than about bad. He described witchcraft as a 'terrible threat' to humankind, but he emphasized 'false visions' of demons and their ability to deceive people. Witches could do real harm, but they could be combated through piety. It also appears from what is known of Nider's life and other work that his main concern was heresy, especially the growth of the Hussite movement in Bohemia. Nider may well have propounded a negative image of women more to make another point than to denounce them: he 'clearly realized he could use the basic fear of *maleficium* to his own spiritual needs', which were above all to promote the fight against heresy.[44]

Perhaps this smearing of women because they were handy vessels for other campaigns made no difference; their image suffered just as much as if they had been the primary targets. But if the point of *Formicarius* and other works on demonology was to raise fear of a conspiracy against Christians, women might still be seen on the whole in a more neutral way, above all in the courts.

Virtually simultaneously with the creation of Nider's main book, and in the same setting, the Council of Basel (1431–49), Martin Le Franc wrote a long poem that featured pro and con arguments about the nature of women and their possible links to the devil. Entitled *Le champion des dames* (The defender of women), this work of almost 25 000 lines includes a debate between 'Defender' and 'Adversary' of women. Defender recites achievements of women from antiquity to the present moment, while Adversary insists that they practise sorcery, fly to sabbats, eat babies, cause impotence in men, and indulge in orgies with demons. Defender says all that is illusion; Adversary draws from recent trial records to make his points.[45] Since the title of the book may also be translated as The champion of women, it can be said that a positive view of women prevails in the debate. Nonetheless, here was another set of charges against women that served in the course of the next 250 years to bolster those inclined for whatever reason to prosecute females as the devil's agents on earth. Material linking women's sexual activity with the presence of a grave threat to the good society was mounting up in Europe.

But the images of women debated in *Le champion* must be seen in the context of a long debate, the *querelle des femmes* – the dispute about women. Lasting for some four centuries, it was launched by the Frenchwoman Christine de Pisan in 1399. Born in Venice about 1365, she moved with her father to the French court when she was three years old. Happily married to a court notary around 1380, she was left a widow with three children upon his death in 1390. She received offers to live at French and Italian courts but decided to try to make her own living as a writer. Besides producing love poetry and other non-political works, she attempted to deflect men's attacks on women's minds and bodies, rejecting the argument that women were basically vile. In particular, she tried to counter the coarse images of women and their desires in the highly popular *Roman de la Rose*. This illustrated tale, begun by Guillaume de Lorris in about 1237 but left unfinished by him, was picked up and completed by Jean de Meun around 1277.

Although de Pisan's efforts to counter the attitudes reflected in the *Roman* evoked a storm of criticism and further slander against women, she also won considerable renown and financial rewards for her work.[46] One of her characters, Lady Reason, defends women's sexuality as moderate and normal. Her most famous defence of women was *The Book of the City of Ladies*, 1405, in which she creates a metropolis populated by famous and virtuous women of the past.

By the time that Nider and Le Franc wrote in the 1430s, presentations of the *querelle* often took the form of a debate between a defender and a critic of women. This tradition is repeated, for instance, in Baldesar Castiglione's *The Book of the Courtier*, written in the early sixteenth century. Castiglione also presents a champion and a critic of women, but neither hints that the female sex has anything to do with the devil. Women may be particularly lustful, deceitful and emasculating, according to the critic in *The Courtier*, but even he admits that they may also be wise and self-disciplined.[47]

Compared to commentaries on women that preceded it, Castiglione's book was mild indeed. In any event, from Nider forward such works presented two contrasting opinions about women. Stuart Clark's discussion of medieval and early modern thought as relying on opposites, often grouped together in columns, is important to remember when considering views of women into the sixteenth century. Defenders and Adversaries are another reflection of the tendency to invoke such opposites, which did not necessarily suggest that one side was clearly superior to the other. Was air better than earth?

Of course men had created a general framework of thought that was derogatory towards women, but many specific voices were raised in their defence and their virtues continued to draw praise from male speakers, even when figures such as Castiglione's Signor Gasparo also complained about their fickleness and lust. The witch hunts did not grow out of woman-hating per se because there was still a great deal of room in the western European tradition for according virtue and self-control to females.

Similar ambivalence also appears in comments on the nature of women by a famed itinerant preacher, St Bernardino of Siena, a contemporary of Nider and Le Franc. Bernardino wandered about Tuscany speaking in the open air and in churches for some 30 years. On the one hand, his sermons touched on the need for mutual love in marriage. He seemed to respect women greatly when he said, 'Mark me, women, that I hold with you so far as to say that you love your husbands better than they love you.' Women are sometimes represented as flighty in his remarks, but they also make thoughtful statements with which he agrees.[48]

Bernardino was one of the most popular Italian preachers of his day, drawing large crowds in Rome, his home town of Siena, Florence and other cities. Part of his success lay in his skill in using the language of the common people, part in the vivid images and stories he produced, and part in extolling devotion to the name of Jesus. The last appeal skirted heresy, as Bernardino invoked Christ's name almost as a charm. In the late 1420s Pope Martin V, who had learned of Bernardino's immense success in preaching devotion to the name of Jesus, summoned him to Rome for an examination. Perhaps Bernardino used his charm on the pope, for a papal tribunal cleared him of all charges. Bernardino then returned to open-air preaching.

This was fortunate for Bernardino but not for the witches. As early as 1424 he had referred to night gatherings of what he called in Latin *strigones* and *dyabolicas strigatrices*; in his vernacular sermons he must have used variants of the old *stregi*. Without much initial success, he urged crowds in Rome and Padua to denounce witches, who should be burned. He had long maintained that there was an evil sect whose rites included taking an infant and tossing it from one person to another until it was dead. The members of the cult then ground the body to dust, put the result into a liquid and drank it. He appears to have been largely responsible for a witch trial in Rome in about 1426. Although he had spoken of males and females involved in witchcraft, the defendants were solely women; of these, however, only two were executed. Bernardino later claimed much greater success in persuading listeners to name witches, such that after a sermon in Rome, a hundred accusations were filed with the city's inquisitor. There could be no mercy for these monsters, Bernardino exclaimed at one point; 'Make sure that they are exterminated in such a way that their seed will be lost.'[49] The zeal and popularity of this itinerant preacher had done much, if his own accounts of his success in evoking accusations of diabolical magic can be trusted, to implant the new image of the witch in the public mind. Yet other clerics resisted his lead in Italy, and he did not create a major witch hunt.

The story of the infamous *Malleus Maleficarum* (The Hammer of Witches) and its author, the Dominican monk Heinrich Kramer (sometimes called by the Latin form of his name, Institoris), further illustrates the twists and turns of the route to the witch pyres. First published in 1486 in the German city of Speyer, the *Malleus* demonstrates both the newly emerging horrid image of women and the difficulty of generalizing too much from it. Institoris had gained favour with the pope and was named inquisitor for southern Germany in 1474. He became involved in witch trials as early as 1476.

The *Malleus* is the best-known witch finders' treatise. It is the one book of this type mentioned in every study of the witch hunts, partly because the formidable Protestant scholars of the persecutions who wrote in the late nineteenth and early twentieth centuries made it famous. It became the centrepiece of their view that superstition, ignorance and fanaticism had produced the hunts and that the Enlightenment's breakthrough to reason had ended them. In 1878 the president of Cornell University, Andrew Dickson White, showed a newly acquired early edition of the *Malleus* to 'his shuddering class', saying that it had 'caused more suffering than any other [work] written by human pen'.[50]

The book offered almost nothing new in its depiction of witches and their evil acts; in particular, Kramer cited *Formicarius* at least seventy times. But the *Malleus* presented the witch stereotype in a complete and reasonably clear fashion. At the time of its publication and in subsequent reprintings, the *Malleus* appeared to some educated Europeans to present the weight of earlier authorities as well as a considerable body of evidence about witches' recent misdeeds. The book also served as a how-to manual for magistrates who tried witches; it gave detailed advice on how to treat the accused during interrogation and trial, including how to torture them, and on ways judges could protect themselves against witches in court, for example by wearing 'Consecrated Salt' around the neck.

The semblance of usefulness, gravity and profound knowledge in the *Malleus* was heightened by the fact that the author used a bull issued by Pope Innocent VIII in 1484 as the preface to the book. In this way the tome seemed to have the pontiff's direct blessing. But Innocent had merely written a standard kind of directive for the period reaffirming the authority of his inquisitor. The bull repeats conventional wisdom of the day on the sexual depravity of heretics, not witches. It does not mention nocturnal flight and refers to the sabbat only indirectly. Women are not singled out as Satan's whores.[51]

The *Malleus* itself remains disturbing reading to this day for its thorough condemnation of women. A small sample of its views follows:

All wickedness is but little to the wickedness of a woman . . . What else is woman but a foe to friendship, an unescapable punishment, a necessary evil, a natural temptation, a desirable calamity, a domestic danger, a delectable detriment, an evil of nature, painted with fair colours! . . . the root of all woman's vices is avarice . . . Women are easily provoked to hatred . . . They are more credulous; and since the chief aim of the devil is to corrupt faith, therefore he rather attacks them. . . . Women are naturally more impressionable, and more ready to receive the influence of a disembodied spirit . . . They have slippery tongues . . . and since they are weak, they find an easy and secret manner of vindicating themselves by witchcraft . . . Since they are feebler both in mind and body, it is not surprising that they should come more under the spell of witchcraft. . . . Women are intellectually like children. . . . [A woman] always deceives.

But all this is prelude to the most important reason Kramer gives for women's attraction to the devil. A woman is 'more carnal than a man, as is clear from her many carnal abominations'. The author reiterates this point obsessively, finally concluding that 'the mouth of the womb' is never satisfied and that 'all witchcraft comes from carnal lust, which is in women insatiable'.[52]

Kramer did mention 'chaste and honest women' and at a few other points in the book indicated that females might not be entirely repugnant, but such remarks pale beside his general misogyny. Clearly he deeply feared women, as shown by the many references to impotence caused by witchcraft and even to the removal of penises by witches.

Although the *Malleus* represents an important strain in contemporary male attitudes toward women, it does not point to misogyny as the pre-eminent factor behind the witch hunts. To begin with, the extent of the book's influence is far from clear. While later works on witches drew heavily on the *Malleus* for material and theses, its publication history was erratic. It appeared in two waves, 1486–1520 and 1574–1621; that is, the book was not reprinted during a 50-year span that witnessed a significant upsurge in the number of trials. Nor did it appear during another great round of hunts, from the early 1620s to roughly 1650.

The reception that Kramer received at the time his book appeared shows vividly that agreement on witchcraft did not then exist among the European elite. On the contrary, the early response to his efforts was largely negative. This was partly due to his own conduct. Kramer had been arrested in 1482 for allegedly stealing silverware and money in the course of his duties as an inquisitor; he was pardoned in October 1483 by Pope Sixtus IV only, it appears, for political reasons. Kramer was a staunch supporter of papal authority and an opponent of conciliarism, the movement which argued that church councils possessed higher authority than the pope did. When leading clerical figures proposed a new council, Sixtus felt that Kramer's pen could be a strong weapon on the side of the Holy See.

Free to pursue his role as inquisitor once more and armed with the bull issued in 1485 by the newly enthroned Innocent VIII,

Kramer proceeded to arrest some fifty women in the prince-bishopric of Brixen, near Innsbruck. In such an administrative arrangement, which played a great role in the German witch hunts of the next two centuries, a bishop was also the reigning prince of a region. Nominally at least, such prince-bishops were in turn under the legal and administrative control of the Holy Roman Emperor. In practice, as we shall see, these bishoprics often had wide autonomy.

Kramer had his accused women tortured immediately, a gross violation of inquisitorial rules. The ways he had exceeded his authority evoked strong opposition from other officials on the scene. They agreed to a trial of the women, but it led to Kramer's downfall in Austria. When he questioned one of the accused about her sexual practices and moral standing in her community, other members of the tribunal objected to his query as irrelevant and overruled him.[53] Soon the whole trial came to an end, as episcopal members of the court – those appointed by the local bishop, not by the pope – objected that Kramer had exceeded his authority. All the arrested women were released.

Georg Golser, bishop of Brixen, now wrote that Kramer was 'completely childish' because of his advanced age (he was about 55 at the time!) and advised him to return to and stay in his monastery. Kramer 'still wants perhaps to mix in women's affairs', the bishop continued, but 'I am not letting him do that, as formerly he erred almost completely in his trial'.[54] In the autumn of 1485, Golser sent a message to Kramer that his presence in Innsbruck had become unwelcome, and warned that a popular uprising against his witchcraft proceedings might develop. The local population indeed seemed incensed by Kramer's behaviour. But it took a second threatening letter from Golser in early 1486 before Kramer finally departed for Salzburg.

It was at this point that, humiliated publicly and by the local church authorities, Kramer set to work on the *Malleus*. 'His failure at Innsbruck and his apocalyptic fears drove Kramer to develop his ideas further.'[55] The book was 'revenge' for his 'bitter defeats'.[56] Hastily written and with odd lapses in organization and presentation of the argument, the volume was in print by late in the year. Kramer then followed his criminal inclinations once more; he had a forgery endorsing his book inserted into letters from the theology faculty at the University of Cologne, which offered only limited support for his ideas. The real and fake letters were gathered into a notary instrument, a public, legal document, about the *Malleus*. When this latest inquity became known, Kramer's reputation took a further dive, and his former inquisitorial partner Jakob Sprenger opened prosecution against him for the forgery. Kramer moved further north, to the Mosel region, where he again fell foul of his superiors by approving a local community's effort to create counter-magic by erecting a large crucifix. The Church, of course, could not openly approve such quasi-pagan measures.

No further witch trials ever took place in Brixen; Kramer's own evil conduct served to discredit the concept of diabolical witchcraft there. In 1490 the Dominican order condemned Kramer for excesses in his work.[57] True, the Nuremberg city council requested Kramer's assistance in witch trials in 1491. He obliged by writing a treatise denouncing laxity in the pursuit of witches and rebuking sceptical magistrates. The aldermen, perhaps now informed about his past, refused to publish it.[58] Kramer moved yet again, to Bohemia, where he died in 1505.

The difficulties of this dishonest and tormented monk after the early 1480s raise the question of how much he ever cared about women's wickedness, as opposed to how much he sought a way of advancing his own status. Leaving Kramer's personal problems aside, Walter Stephens refuses to call writers like him 'demonolgists', insisting instead that they were theologians and 'witchcraft theorists'. The goal of their tracts was to defend the reality of demons and physical interaction with them, a subject to be explored in more depth in the next chapter. Concerning the image of women in the late medieval period, Stephens's point is that Kramer and others needed to paint a dark picture of female sexual transgressions in general in order to bolster the notion that Satan and his lieutenants could easily recruit some humans. Female lust served to facilitate the demons' quest to wreak havoc on earth.[59] Since women were already considered the weaker sex, and the devil was definitely a male figure, demonic copulation had to be overwhelmingly with females. *Incubi* is the term for demons who insert a sexual member into a human body, while *succubi* are sexually receptive figures. One scholar estimates that *incubi* appear nine times as often in works on demonology as their seemingly more feminine counterparts.[60]

Walter Stephens even maintains, in contrast to other writers, that Kramer was not especially misogynist. This is going too far. Nevertheless, the point that women became not the target but the vehicle for the monk's discussion of the devil and theology seems valid.

Yet, as we have seen, secular and church officials who knew Kramer rejected the application of his portrayal of women in court, as well as his excessive curiosity about their sexual behaviour. German authorities further ignored the witchcraft theories of the *Malleus* in favour of traditional injunctions against sorcerers in the Bamburger law code of 1508.[61] Kramer's work therefore did not provoke persecutions by itself. What it did do was to provide a handy list of reasons why women more often than men should be suspected of witchcraft. And, as noted, it was also a useful procedural manual. But it served these purposes only where other preconditions for a witch hunt had arisen.

[*]

By the early fifteenth century, the ingredients of the witch stereotype, fashioned from ancient legends and new fears, were almost all in place. Lepers, Jews, homosexuals and heretics had been characterized as anti-human, hunted down, confined, tortured and burned. Along the way, negative images of women, following the downward curve of their financial status, had become popular. From tales of Lilith fleeing the Garden of Eden to sermons by St Bernardino in northern Italy, a repulsive kind of human was identified. People of this type had become so depraved that they killed and ate babies, even their own. Disguised as ordinary Christians, they were widely active within the good society. In the late fifteenth century, the *Malleus* brought together recent thought and condemnation of women and identified their insatiable sexual appetite as the source of all witchcraft.

The legends about spirits of the dead promenading at night under the guidance of a Roman goddess had been transformed into the charge that real people are gathering in the dark to perform the ultimate in evil. Sorcerers and magicians, especially of the folk variety, had not yet been eliminated from the discourse of the elite, but the vastly more vivid image of the witch, someone dedicated to the devil's cause, had risen to overshadow the cunning people. The stage had been well set for the witch trials.

Still, the witch processes have a peculiar history of their own. Like the career of Bernardino of Siena and his views about women, or what happened to Heinrich Kramer, almost nothing regarding the witches proceeded in a simple, straight line. The next chapter details the spread and growth of witch trials from their frequent origin as political affairs to their everyday destructive presence in some, not all, of the villages.

NOTES

1. Tertullian (1974) 'De Culta Femina', in Rosemary Radford Reuther (ed.) *Religion and Sexism: Images of Woman in the Jewish and Christian Traditions* (New York: Simon and Schuster), p. 105.

2. Stuart Clark (1997) *Thinking with Demons: the Idea of Witchcraft in Early Modern Europe* (New York: Oxford University Press), pp. 9, 26, 35, 37–46, 119–21 and 132; quotation on p. 115.

3. Jack Goody (1983) *The Development of the Family and Marriage in Europe* (Cambridge: Cambridge University Press), p. 189.

4. George Huppert (1986) *After the Black Death: a Social History of Early Modern Europe* (Bloomington: Indiana University Press), p. 6.

5. Olwen Hufton (1995) *The Prospect Before Her: a History of Women in Western Europe. Vol. 1: 1500–1800* (New York: HarperCollins), p. 64.

6. Andrew Sullivan (2000) 'The He Hormone', *The New York Times Magazine*, 2 April.

7. Christiane Klapisch-Zuber (1985) *Women, Family, and Ritual in Renaissance Italy*, trans. Lydia Cochrane (Chicago: University of Chicago Press), pp. 20 and 105.

8. Goody, *Development of the Family and Marriage*, p. 19, prefers the term bridewealth to the widely used brideprice; the latter word suggests outright purchase of a bride, which did not happen in Europe.

9. David Herlihy (ed.) (1995) *Women, Family, and Society in Medieval Europe: Historical Essays, 1978–1991*, with an introduction by A. Molho (Providence, RI: Berghahn), pp. 44–9; quotation on p. 48.

10. Klapisch-Zuber, *Women, Family and Ritual*, pp. 129–30.

11. Quoted in Dale Kent, 'Women in Renaissance Florence,' in David Alan Brown et al. (eds) (2001) *Virtue and Beauty: Leonardo's* Ginevra de' Benci *and Renaissance Portraits of Women* (Washington: National Gallery of Art and Princeton University Press), p. 27.

12. Goody, *Development of the Family and Marriage*, p. 103. Often such transfers of land did not mean that it was completely alienated from the donating family, which might continue to enjoy income or rights to its use. Nevertheless, a substantial shift of outright landownership to the Church took place.

13. Herlihy, *Women, Family, and Society*, pp. 13–95.

14. Merry E. Wiesner (1986) *Working Women in Renaissance Germany* (New Brunswick, NJ: Rutgers University Press), p. 3. Wiesner's introduction discusses many other studies of women at work.

15. Hufton, *Prospect before Her*, vol. 1, p. 300.

16. Ibid., pp. 300–37.
17. Merry Wiesner-Hanks (ed.) (1996) *Convents Confront the Reformation: Catholic and Protestant Nuns in Germany*, introduction by Merry Wiesner-Hanks, trans. Joan Skocir and Merry Wiesner-Hanks (Milwaukee: Marquette University Press), p. 18.
18. Dyan Elliott (1999) *Fallen Bodies: Pollution, Sexuality, and Demonology in the Middle Ages* (Philadelphia: University of Pennsylvania Press), pp. 7 and 36.
19. Ibid., pp. 111, 34, 82 and 163.
20. R. N. Swanson (1995) *Religion and Devotion in Europe, c.1215–c.1515* (Cambridge: Cambridge University Press), p. 305.
21. Peter Biller (1990) 'The Common Woman in the Western Church in the Thirteenth and Early Fourteenth Centuries', *Studies in Church History*, 27. *Women in the Church* (Oxford: Basil Blackwell), p. 139.
22. Alice K. Turner (1993) *The History of Hell* (San Diego: Harcourt Brace & Co.), p. 113. Turner mistakenly places Berthold in the fourteenth century.
23. Quoted in Biller, 'Common Woman', pp. 139–40.
24. D. Bornstein 'The Shrine of Santa Maria a Cigoli: Female Visionaries and Clerical Promoters', *Melanges de l'école francaise de Rome: Moyen Age, Temps Modernes* 98 (1986), p. 228, quoted in Swanson, *Religion*, pp. 304–5.
25. Carlo Ginzburg (1992) *Ecstasies: Deciphering the Witches' Sabbath*, trans. Raymond Rosenthal (New York: Penguin Books), pp. 96–7.
26. Wolfgang Behringer (ed.) (1995) *Hexen und Hexenprozesse in Deutschland*, 3rd edn (Munich: Deutscher Taschenbuch Verlag), p. 25.
27. Jeffrey Burron Russell (1972) *Witchcraft in the Middle Ages* (Ithaca, NY: Cornell University Press), pp. 76–7.
28. E. E. Evans-Pritchard (1937) *Witchcraft, Oracles and Magic among the Azande* (Oxford: Oxford University Press), pp. 21–5.
29. One of the first scholars to comment on the transition from concepts and trials of sorcerers to those of witches was probably Joseph Hansen (1990) *Zauberwahn, Inquisition und Hexenprozess im Mittelalter* (Munich, reprinted Aalen: Scientia Verlag, 1964), pp. 14–15 and 235–303.

30. Carlo Ginzburg (1985) *The Night Battles: Witchcraft and Agrarian Cults in the Sixteenth and Seventeenth Centuries*, trans. John and Anne Tedeschi (Baltimore: Johns Hopkins University Press).

31. Wolfgang Behringer (2004), *Witches and Witch-Hunts: A Global History* (Cambridge: Polity), p. 54. Behringer also enumerates the various Roman and medieval statutes against evil magic.

32. Edward Peters (2001) 'Introduction', in Karen Jolly, Catharina Raudvere and Edward Peters *Witchcraft and Magic in Europe: The Middle Ages*, The Athlone History of Witchcraft and Magic in Europe, series eds Bengt Ankarloo and Stuart Clark (Philadelphia: University of Pennsylvania Press), ix.

33. Certainly magic and religion have 'shared ground', as Edward Peters puts it. For example, saints' prayers supposedly have coercive power: their closeness to God compels him to grant their requests. Peters, 'Introduction', p. 12.

34. On Lilith see Gershom Scholem (1974) *Kabbalah* (New York: Quadrangle), p. 356; and Kristen E. Dvam, Linda S. Schearing and Valarie H. Ziegler (eds) (1999) *Eve and Adam: Jewish, Christian, and Muslim Readings on Genesis and Gender* (Bloomington: Indiana University Press), p. 204.

35. Noted in Nehama Aschkenasy (1986) *Eve's Journey: Feminine Images in Hebraic Literary Tradition* (Philadelphia: University of Pennsylvania Press), p. 50.

36. Drorah O'Donnell Setel (1993) 'Witch', in Bruce M. Metzger and Michael D. Coogan (eds) *The Oxford Companion to the Bible* (Oxford: Oxford University Press), p. 805.

37. Marina Warner (1995) *From the Beast to the Blonde: On Fairy Tales and their Tellers* (New York: Noonday Press), p. 67.

38. Kirsteen Macpherson Bardell (2002) 'Beyond Pendle: The "Lost" Lancashire Witches', in Robert Poole (ed.) *The Lancashire Witches: Histories and Stories* (Manchester: Manchester University Press), pp. 109, 118.

39. On the widely varying treatment of folk magicians and healers in the period of the witch hunts, see Willem de Blécourt (1994) 'Witch Doctors, Soothsayers and Priests. On Cunning Folk in European Historiography and Tradition', *Social History* 19 (3): 293–301; and

Richard A. Horsley (1979) 'Who Were the Witches? The Social Roles of the Accused in European Witch Trials', *Journal of Interdisciplinary History* 9 (4), esp. 696.

40. Robin Briggs (1996) *Witches and Neighbors: the Social and Cultural Context of European Witchcraft* (New York: Viking), pp. 126–7.

41. Raisa Maria Toivo (2004) 'Marking (dis)order', in Owen Davies and William Blécourt (eds) *Beyond the Witch Trials: Witchcraft and Magic in Enlightenment Europe* (Manchester: Manchester University Press) pp. 10–11. Most trials of cunning folk in Finland ended in acquittals; p. 20. The conclusions I draw from Toivo's are the opposite of hers; she does find these campaigns to be ones of education by the authorities.

42. Johannes Nyder [Nider] (1971) *Formicarius*, introduction by Hans Biedermann (Graz: Akademische Druck), Book Five, Chapter 8, p. 224. In general I have relied on the translation in C. G. Coulton (ed.) (1910) *Life in the Middle Ages* (New York: Macmillan), vol. 1, pp. 210–13, but here I have changed his phrase 'witches and sorcerers' to 'magicians and sorcerers'.

43. Coulton, *Life in the Middle Ages*, vol. 1, pp. 210–13.

44. Michael Bailey (2003) *Battling Demons: Witchcraft, Heresy, and Reform in the Late Middle Ages* (University Park: Pennsylvania State University Press, pp. 102, 123

45. Edward Peters, 'Le Franc, Martin' (2006), in Richard Golden (ed.) *Encyclopedia of Witchcraft: The Western Tradition* (Santa Barbara, Calif.: ABC-CLIO), III, pp. 647–8

46. Joan Kelly (1984) *Women, History and Theory: The Essays of Joan Kelly* (Chicago: University of Chicago Press), pp. 65–95, is still the best introduction to the *querelle*.

47. Baldesar Castiglione (1967) *The Book of the Courtier*, trans. and with an introduction by George Bull (New York: Penguin Books), pp. 241–2, for example.

48. Coulton, *Life in the Middle Ages*, vol. 1, pp. 216–29.

49. The account of Bernardino's activities is based largely on Franco Mormando (1998) 'Bernardino of Siena, Popular Preacher and Witch-Hunter: A 1426 Witch Trial in Rome', *Fifteenth-Century Studies* 24: 85–118; and to a lesser extent on Ginzburg, *Ecstasies*, pp. 297–9.

50. Rossell Hope Robbins (1977) 'Introduction', in *Witchcraft: Catalogue of the Witchcraft Collection in Cornell University Library* (Millwood, NY: KTO Press).

51. Eric Wilson, 'Institoris at Innsbruck: Heinrich Institoris, the *Summis Desiderantes* and the Brixen Witch-Trial of 1485,' in Bob Scribner and Trevor Johnson (eds) (1996) *Popular Religion in Germany and Central Europe, 1400–1800* (New York: St Martin's Press), pp. 87–8.

52. Heinrich Kramer [Institoris] and James [sic] Sprenger (1969) *The Malleus Maleficarum*, trans. by Rev. Montague Summers (New York: Dover), pp. 210–35 and 43–47. Hereafter cited as *Malleus*.

53. Wilson, 'Institoris', p. 95.

54. Behringer, *Hexen und Hexenprozesse*, p. 112.

55. Wolfgang Behringer, 'Malleus Maleficarum', in Golden, *Encyclopedia*, III, p. 718.

56. Günter Jerouschek, 'Kramer (Institoris), Heinrich (Ca. 1430–1505)', in Golden, *Encyclopedia*, III, p. 613.

57. Henry Institoris and Jacques Sprenger (1990) *Le Marteau des Sorcières. Malleus Maleficarum. 1486*, trans. Amand Danet (Grenoble: Jerome Millon), pp. 18 and 35; Russell, *Witchcraft in the Middle Ages*, p. 231.

58. This section is based on Wilson, 'Institoris', and Gary K. Waite (2003) *Heresy, Magic, and Witchcraft in Early Modern Europe* (New York: Palgrave Macmillan), pp. 42–3.

59. Walter Stephens (2002) *Demon Lovers: Witchcraft, Sex, and the Crisis of Belief* (Chicago: University of Chicago Press), p. 34.

60. Vern L. Bullough (1982) 'Postscript: Heresy, Witchcraft, and Sexuality', in Vern L. Bullough and James Brundage, *Sexual Practices and the Medieval Church* (Buffalo: Prometheus Books), p. 217.

61. Behringer, *Hexen und Hexenprozesse*, p. 112.

CHAPTER THREE

THE SPREAD OF THE WITCH TRIALS

As the campaign against heresy progressed in the West, especially in France, the image of the heretic and of the witch began to overlap. As early as 1180, heretics in Besançon were accused of having made a written pact with the devil that permitted them to commit evil magic. During a trial of Cathars held in Châlons-sur-Marne in 1239, a female defendant told an inquisitorial court that she had left a demon, who had obligingly assumed her image, in bed next to her husband while she travelled to a distant gathering of her fellow heretics. The judge in this case was Inquisitor Robert 'Le Bougre', so named because he was a former Cathar who had defected to Catholicism. Visits to a sabbat of evil-doers actually attended by the devil are probably mentioned first in a trial of heretics in Toulouse, France, in 1275.[1] Thus what has been called the 'French conception' of witchcraft began to evolve;[2] this chapter will examine how it began to diffuse across Europe through trials in France and other regions.

In several places, notably Ireland, Scotland, France and Russia, early prosecutions of people accused of using evil magic often had a distinct political cast: they arose from issues of power or money at the highest levels of society. As time passed, the trials spread out socially and politically to lower social strata, until they involved overwhelmingly the commonest of commoners – the peasants. To further complicate this picture, the witch hunts often moved across space as they traversed time and society; for example, the first clearly identifiable witch trial was in southern Ireland, but no further cases in that region are known until 1578, when one person was tried.[3]

Nor can the centres of preaching and writing on the witches be linked neatly to the locations of witch trials. While there seems to have been a kind of contagion effect at work in many cases, as the elite imported notions of witchcraft from a nearby area or even across oceans, it is frequently not possible to find close connections between the 'experts' on the subject and the eruption of new persecutions. To some degree this is because those hunters who left statements of their activities often wrote towards the end of long careers. But it seemed to require a particular set of circumstances before the treatises on the danger of witchcraft were taken seriously in the first place. And, new studies suggest, demonology was not necessarily what it seemed.

Whatever their origins, the fires eventually claimed many victims. How many has long been a subject of sharp debate, one laden with political implications for male–female relations today. On this topic some comparisons and a frank discussion of the issues are in order.

This chapter, then, deals with the spread and scope of the witch hunts. Appropriately enough for our complicated story, we begin not with a trial of witches, and not with females, but with French trials of heretics and supposedly errant knights.

MONARCHS, MONEY AND ENEMIES WITHIN

Among the biggest problems that European monarchs faced into recent centuries was lack of money. Medieval kings usually had little power to tax the main sinews of a country, its land and labour. The chief sources of income for these rulers were taxes and levies from the territory they controlled directly, like any other noble, and from customs duties. For the most part monarchs paid their followers by allotting parcels of land to them, in return for which the latter were supposed to render service to the crown.

The kings of France provide perhaps the best example of this situation. When Hugh Capet was elected king of France in 987 by the bishops and high nobles of a loose agglomeration that could hardly be called a country, he could count on income from only a small area in the centre of his realm, Île de France. Hugh's successor Robert II (the Pious) attended and approved the trial of heretics at Orléans in 1022, after his wife's confessor was implicated in the accused group's activities. This persecution remains obscure, although certainly high figures in the Church were defendants. Did Robert want to break the power of a faction within the Church? Did he want to confiscate the property of the accused?

In any event, the trial at Orléans marked not only the first execution in Western Europe of heretics since the fourth century, but featured several charges that later became standard parts of the witch stereotype: that members of a sect held orgies involving sex even with close relatives, worshipped a demon and killed and ate children. It is hard to imagine that King Robert accepted these accusations as valid. Apparently the church court that tried the case, in Robert's presence, did not readily agree that the defendants were guilty, for the king pre-empted the tribunal by personally pronouncing a sentence of death. It may be that Robert, a staunch supporter of the mainstream Church, feared any sort of unapproved reform or excessively spiritual movement within it. After all, the clergy were already a mainstay of royal rule in that they administered large areas, provided educated personnel for the government, and kept the lower classes in line by preaching loyalty to the crown. But there was also a steady tendency for the Church to acquire too much land and power. Thus Church–state relations required constant attention from the monarchy. The Orléans group is said to have been especially zealous in its faith and to have gone to the stake laughing, possible indications that its members had overstepped the desired bounds of organized religion, devoting their attention too much to spiritual matters and not enough to the powers on earth. In any event, the main point is that under the direction of a king of France, a group active within the realm was condemned to death on charges of anti-human behaviour. This would not be the last such case.

As the discussion of the Cathars' fate showed, French monarchs were quite willing to apply images of ultimate depravity to heretics. In the campaigns against the Cathars in southern France (called Albigensians there), which began in the early thirteenth century, not only did the same charges used at Orléans reappear, the dissenters were also tarred with the ideas that they flew out at night to their meetings, where they had sex with each other and with the devil. He often appeared to them in the form of a goat, receiving from his adherents a ritual kiss on the anus. The repulsive power of these images helps explain why ordinary French soldiers slaughtered thousands of men, women and children in villages in Provence and other regions.

The kings of France turned south mainly to bring new territories under their control, not to combat heresy for the glory of Christianity. Much preoccupied with disputes with the popes and by war in the north against the English and the Flemish, the French rulers needed money more than ever. Eventually they turned their greedy eyes on one of the most important and wealthy organizations in all Europe, the Order of the Knights Templar. Taking their name from the Temple in Jerusalem, this order developed after about 1118 to protect pilgrims on their way to the Holy Land. Within a few years the knights became a permanent army, and in 1128 were recognized as a fighting order of monks, announcing their devotion to God and dedication to chastity. Paralleling the acquisition of land by many arms of the Church, the Templars quickly built up their holdings by accepting gifts of property from various sources, including, ironically, the kings of France. The military monks went into many a business, especially banking, and by the mid-twelfth century had erected a substantial 'temple', in fact a massive castle, in Paris itself. This building now became the 'centre of European finance',[4] and the Templars developed into a powerful international organization.

The reader should be able to guess what happened then to the Templars. But before discussing the destruction of the order, one short detour needs to be taken. Philip IV (the Fair), who ruled France from 1285 to 1314, had severe financial difficulties. His policies of imposing heavy taxation and debasing the currency of the realm produced great discontent; at one point he had to flee an enraged mob in Paris, taking shelter, naturally, in the Templars' headquarters. How could he improve his finances? The Jews presented an obvious target for Philip; since by now they had been repeatedly defamed as devil-worshippers and practitioners of various filthy and disgusting acts, it was relatively easy for Philip to turn on them, murder and torture many, and order the survivors to leave France. In July 1306 the monarchy seized all their goods and property. But the wealth harvested from the Jews proved inadequate to sustain Philip for long, and little more than a year passed before the king turned to the fattest goose of all, the Templars. On the morning of 13 October 1307, royal officers arrested members of the order throughout France.

Philip had attacked an organization not under royal, but under papal jurisdiction. No matter; the current pope, Clement V, was a Frenchman living in France during the 'Avignon captivity' (1305–78) of the papacy. Philip's candidate for the papal throne to begin with, Clement was not in a position physically or politically to resist the will of the French king.

Philip had prepared a long list of familiar charges against the Templars. They were supposedly required to commit sodomy with each other, to give the devil (this time appearing as a large cat) the ritual kiss beneath the tail, and to worship an idol, which they lovingly anointed with the fat of murdered, roasted infants. Once the royal torturers had begun their work, the knights, along with servants and shepherds who worked for the order, began to confess; however, several recanted or made public protests about their treatment. At times Clement openly expressed misgivings about the whole procedure. Given these problems, the affair dragged on until 1314. Finally the grandmaster of the order, Jacques de Molay, was burned, and virtually the entire wealth of the Templars reverted to the French monarchy. All this, incidentally, did not solve the financial difficulties of the French kings, which continued until the Revolution of 1789 removed the problem, after a fashion, by removing the monarchy.

During the attack on the Templars, Philip took extraordinary steps to make sure that their villainy would become known throughout the land. In May 1308 he convened the Estates General, an assembly of representatives of the church, nobility and common people. The third group alone sent more than 700 delegates. To this meeting Philip's officers read out a document condemning the Templars and treating their alleged offences as fully proven. Meanwhile, Franciscan and Dominican monks, eager to curry royal favour, aided the king's men in spreading tales of the Templars' behaviour throughout France.

It hardly seems necessary to state that the charges against the order were overwhelmingly, probably completely, false. Philip wanted to weaken the Templars and seize their wealth. He accomplished this by using a combination familiar from the third, twentieth and other centuries: smearing his targets while forcing them through torture to confess to the charges. The whole affair was arranged to suit the king's political and financial purposes.

The accusations against the Templars fell just short of the witch stereotype. Molay confirmed, after torture, that the whole order had succumbed to the devil's control. But no defendant said that the knights flew out at night to murder livestock and babies, cause storms and so on. Nevertheless, the trial of the Templars is a pivotal event in the history of the witch persecutions. We have no idea whether ordinary people believed the charges made against the order, although writers into the twentieth century accepted at least their partial validity, but the trial was a key factor in spreading the idea in Western society that people who appeared to be normal and beneficent on the surface could be secret agents of the devil carrying out his anti-human will.

It took almost no leap of the imagination, and only a small one of geography, from the destruction of the Templars to what is commonly recognized as the first real witch trial in Europe. This was the case of 1324 against Alice Kyteler, a wealthy and well-connected woman living in Kilkenny, southern Ireland. The link between the French events of 1307–14 and the Kyteler case is clear; it was personified by Bishop Richard Ledrede. Born in England sometime between 1260 and 1275, Ledrede became a Franciscan and completed his theological training in France. He had a knack for impressing popes, and because of that ability and the happenstance that he was in Avignon when the Irish bishopric at Ossory became open, he received an appointment to the post in 1317. Thus upon his arrival in Ireland, ruled then by the English, Ledrede was a complete outsider whose only source of political support, albeit an important one, was the pope.

Ledrede certainly brought with him knowledge of the Templar affair; it would have been odd indeed if a well-educated person living in France at the time of the trial had been ignorant of it. The new bishop also had to be aware of the political possibilities in charges of witchcraft as well as of the fact that Pope John XXII (1316–34), still living in Avignon, had prosecuted members of the papal court for sorcery in 1318. Two years later, the pontiff specified offences regarding magic to be prosecuted by the Inquisition, whose main task of course was to pursue heresy.

It is difficult to sort out what happened and why in the Kyteler affair on the basis of the few contemporary sources available to us.

The accused was from an important merchant family; she first married in 1280, so that by 1324 she was probably over 60 years old. She had outlived three wealthy husbands and was on to her fourth at the time she was accused of witchcraft.

In the main, the charges Ledrede laid against Dame Kyteler replicated those against the Templars. The only original account of the case, written from Ledrede's point of view, says that he discovered 'very many heretical sorceresses (*haeretici sortilegae*)' who met at night, denied Christ and practised various black arts. The group of eight women and four men mentioned in Ledrede's indictment allegedly cut living animals into pieces and scattered them at crossroads as offerings to a demon 'from the humbler levels of the underworld'. Why they could not conjure up a more prestigious spirit remains a mystery.

Their ritual purportedly involved putting animal parts and hairs from dead bodies into the skull of a decapitated robber. Kyteler and her followers used spells and lotions obtained during their rites, the charges continue, to murder some of her husbands and to make sure that their heirs turned over all their property to Alice. The sect 'afflicted' the bodies of other Christians, which probably meant that they caused impotence. Kyteler had a personal demon with whom she had sexual intercourse. Sometimes this hell's agent appeared as a large cat, sometimes as a dog and occasionally as a black man. The only points of the full-blown witch stereotype missing from the case are an actual pact with the devil, flying and a large recruiting effort. These are important gaps, and it would therefore be better to see the Kyteler episode not as the first of the fully developed witch trials but as another major step in the transition to them.

It seems that Alice's case led to court proceedings, but without the chief defendant, who must have fled. However, one of Kyteler's servants, Petronilla, was seized by the bishop's men and whipped until she produced all the details given above. After that she was burned, despite the lack of any provision in English law for the execution of heretics before 1401.

As fragmentary as the basic document on the case is, it reveals that Alice had important supporters in the area. Although the bishop had his way in regard to a trial and the execution of Petronilla, he was excommunicated by the bishop of Dublin, his superior in Ireland, in 1329, and had to flee to France. Four years later he returned to Ireland, but there he continued to have intermittent trouble with the English authorities until his death in 1360. Certainly there was no quick and easy acceptance in Ireland, or for that matter in England, of the idea that noxious heretics/witches were roaming about the land and had to be exterminated. The sources refer to complaints about Ledrede as a 'foreigner' who 'comes from England and says we're all heretics and excommunicates, on the grounds of some papal constitutions that we've never even heard of'.[5] This was not an auspicious beginning for a large-scale witch hunt in Ireland, and indeed none occurred in that land then or later.

The case grew out of a local power struggle. Ledrede attacked Kyteler's whole family, some of whom held prominent offices: eleven others close to her, either family or friends, were also accused. Of the twelve mentioned in the indictment, eight were female and four were male, but this ratio in all likelihood reflects only the composition of people close to Alice. Probably the bishop singled her out as leader of the sect because she was the matriarch of the family, three of her husbands had died, she had once been accused of homicide, and only lastly, if at all, because she was a woman. The chief contemporary source on the case does not even refer to the negative images of females recently purveyed by the Church. Had the head of the Kyteler family been male at the time, the charges would probably have closely echoed those against the Templars, except that the sodomy with men could have been replaced by acts with a male demon.

In ways reminiscent of the Templar affair, the Kyteler trial 'shows how the issue of witchcraft became the occasion for a major confrontation between secular and ecclesiastical authority and law. The political nature of [early] witchcraft accusations . . . was part of the larger struggle between church and state.'[6] It is possible that Ledrede was insulted and opposed by some of Alice's influential kin before he made his accusations of witchcraft against them; in any case, he picked up familiar devices for use against an enemy in the form of the charges he had heard in France.

Kyteler's trial helped effect the transfer to witches of images earlier attached to Jews, lepers and heretics. Yet, as noted, the case was not followed by similar affairs in Ireland or England involving men or women. Only several centuries later is there evidence of other witch persecutions in either place. We must shift back to the Continent to follow the trail.

THE EARLY WITCH TRIALS

Between Alice Kyteler's trial and about 1500, prosecutions of witches in Europe assumed more than a sporadic character in only a few areas. Little significant action against witches has been found in the records before about 1375; until then, cases rarely involved charges of devil worship. Instead, they repeated ancient accusations of sorcery. Pope John XXII, who kept a magic snakeskin to detect poisoned food and drink, prosecuted sorcerers several times at his court at Avignon. In 1326 he issued a bull which alleged that many Christians 'make a covenant with Hell' and employ objects to bind and use demons. Despite the mention of a pact, John's warning still fits with traditional denunciations of sorcerers. Nor did he draw upon the Kyteler trial or other sources to bring stereotypical witches to justice.

At Carcassone, France, some 200 kilometres (130 miles) from Avignon, trials were held in 1335 that involved old-style charges of magic, *maleficia* and heresy. In Toulouse, less than 100 kilometres away from Carcassone, a trial of malefactors in 1353 mentioned night meetings and a witches' dance. In 1390, two women accused in Paris of using evil magic added under torture that they had called up the devil. By this time two key aspects of the early modern witch hunts – inquisitorial procedure and torture – had become established practice.

As these trials went on, a number of new books, including inquisitors' manuals, referred to witchcraft as a danger and a heresy. An example is a work by Nicholas Eymeric, inquisitor in Aragon and Avignon, entitled *Directorium Inquisitorum* (1376). But this wave of writing did not mention the sabbat, flying or committing harm at the devil's order; such works remained largely within the old framework of invoking the devil or worshipping him. In 1398 the theological faculty at the University of Paris deliberated the question of whether *maleficia* entailed idolatry and apostasy if the evil deeds were conducted through a pact with the devil. The answer was yes, and witchcraft was declared a heresy.[7]

What seems to have happened was that the emphasis on witches as a heretical sect quickly began to merge with older conceptions of the activities of heretics and sometimes magicians. At the beginning of the fifteenth century, Nicolaus von Jauer contributed the view that demons could 'assume bodies', including the forms of old women, using which they stole children at night, 'tearing them and cooking them with fire'.[8] The French conception of the witch was developing steadily.

By the end of the 1420s, judge Claude Tholosans had tried more than 200 witches in Briançon, Dauphiné,[9] a mountainous region of France close to Italy and not far south of Switzerland. It appears that some of the old heretics, especially the Waldensians, had either taken refuge in the mountains or had made converts there. At any rate, armed with the new idea that witchcraft was a heresy, the inquisitors now sought out the dissidents and put them on trial.

From the Dauphiné, trials of witches/heretics spread north into Savoy and from there east into Switzerland.

From 1394 to 1406, many trials of Waldensians and Jews for heresy were held in an area bounded by Strasbourg, still part of the Holy Roman Empire, and Basel, Bern and Fribourg, Switzerland. Two Dominican preachers, Johannes Mulberg and Vincent Ferrier, had been active in the region in denouncing heretics and probably played a major role in bringing about the first large trial of Waldensians, held in Fribourg in 1399. A number of trials of magicians (*Zauberer*) took place at virtually the same moment in Lucerne and Basel, Switzerland, as well as in Freiburg im Breisgau, farther north and at the time part of the Empire. These cases were set in a context of nearby fighting against the Turks, drought, and the sighting of a comet, in the early modern period always a cause for anxiety. A number of witches were accused, tried and burned at Simmenthal, near Bern, between 1395 and 1405.

At this point much of modern Switzerland was already independent from the Empire except in the most nominal fashion. Several towns in the north-east were beginning to establish their own judicial systems outside of the old feudal system. Trials of heretics and later of witches may have been part of the municipalities' efforts to expand their exercise of law; in the same era Swiss towns began on their own to prosecute crimes such as murder for the first time. In the north-western part of Switzerland the number of witchcraft cases began to decline well before 1500,[10] further suggesting that the accusations had been related to the establishment of new judicial organs and procedures. At least, in such cases and a number of later ones as well, it seems that a local jurisdiction was determined to maintain its judicial independence. Sometimes the expression of that goal came through prosecution of witches. Here, then, is a limited argument for function in the hunts.

The modern German word for witchcraft, *Hexerei*, derived from a Swiss dialect of the language, appeared in trials at Lucerne and

Interlaken from 1419 to 24.[11] In the same period, just across the Alps, Bernardino of Siena was preaching extensively against witches. The modern conception of witchcraft was put into final form by the Church Council of Basel, back on the other side of the mountains, in the years 1431–49. The Council was attended by Johannes Nider, who wrote his *Formicarius* around 1435–37. Its secretary was Martin Le Franc, who produced *Le champion de dames* in 1440–42; in it he reported on more witch trials conducted by Judge Tholosans in Valpute, Italy. Le Franc's character Defender denied the reality of witches' flight, as Nider had done, but a copy of *Le champion* dated 1450 depicted them riding on brooms to the sabbat. The original work describes in any event how the evil ones met the devil, who appeared to them as a cat or ram, and kissed his behind. From Satan the witches received powders and other materials and then went out to do evil. Le Franc reported that 10 000 witches had gathered in a place in Italy then called Valpute.[12] By now the French conception had begun to triumph in an area including northern Italy, south-eastern France, parts of Switzerland and southern Germany. Finally complete, the stereotype of the witch assumed its deadly career in courtrooms.[13]

Meanwhile another short text on heretics, witches and the devil, only about six printed pages long, appeared around 1435. This work, *Errores Gazariorum* (Errors of the Cathars) surfaced in north-western Italy, not far from Basel and Valpute. Probably written by Ponce Feugeyron, it is subtitled 'those who have been convinced that they ride a broomstick or a rod'; that is, to the sabbat. Although the *Errores* thus began by referring to the medieval view that people are victims of satanic illusions rather than actual participants in evil gatherings, the author nevertheless maintained for the first time since Alice Kyteler's trial that a sect of heretics/witches existed.[14] They did fly out to meet their master, copulate and receive orders to commit *maleficia*. Complete with a detailed description of the unguents and powders used by Satan's recruits, the *Errores* circulated widely because of its brevity and detail. Even though the text began by focusing on the Cathars, it provided an easy means of transferring their iniquities to witches.

In north-western Switzerland, the number of cases that increasingly adopted the lines of witch trials rather than heretic accusations rose slowly but fairly steadily during the fifteenth century, peaking at more than 30 between 1477 and 1496. From this heart of persecution the witch stereotype spread, both through a flood of new writings on the subject and through men who had been at the Council of Basel and then went elsewhere to take up new assignments in the Church.

The witch concept appears, for example, in a trial of 32 defendants in Arras, now part of Belgium. Begun in 1459 as an illegal process against heretics – that is, without the approval of higher authorities – the case turned into charges that they were Satan worshippers who flew out at night to commit evil.[15] Details like the devil's mark, a place on the body where the master scratched a new recruit, supposedly leaving it insensitive to pain, flying on brooms and small animals such as cats that were regarded as demons sent to help the witch, were added in other cases of the same period.

By this time many jurists, theologians and other members of the elite had come to reject the *Canon Episcopi* and its admonition that night flying and processions of spirits were merely fantasies. To reach this conclusion scholars had only to refer to Aquinas, Augustine or the Bible itself to find material pointing in another direction: that the forces of Satan were real and were out in force. A raft of works now argued that the witches were something new and that any sane person could not deny their existence.

In 1486 the *Malleus Maleficarum* expressed rather than developed the new witch stereotype, including flying and the sabbat, at length. The book provoked a negative response in some quarters, as we have seen, and it did not lead to an increase in trials in Switzerland, where in fact a decline in numbers occurred after the appearance of the book. But in some areas it fell on fertile soil, possibly helping to spark witch trials in places like Cologne in 1487 and 1491 and Trier in 1497 and 1501.

Yet it is often hard to trace any clear chronological line in the development of the witch hunts. Like the Kyteler affair, the early trials in Germany and Italy, for example, were not necessarily followed quickly by other witchcraft cases in the same regions. Indeed, Italy, although home to several of the early calls for alarm about witches, remained relatively free of prosecutions. Sometimes four or more decades passed before other cases came to court in the same area, while in Cleves, for example, new influences halted trials for a long period by the mid-1500s. In Spain, the Inquisition cautioned against believing everything in the *Malleus* in 1538.[16]

It took a long time for witch trials to become 'systematic' even in Germany, quite close to the scene of early charges. 'Systematic' means only that cases began to figure regularly in the records instead of their highly sporadic appearance in the fourteenth century. In this sense there were witch hunts in Germany only from about 1480 onwards, and in some regions only from 1580. In the Basque country of France, the old sorcerers and sorceresses predominated in the courts until late in the sixteenth century. It required new tensions between local authorities and important families to make the new witch stereotype appear in the region with any frequency, and large hunts began only in 1609.[17] Franche Comté, today an area of eastern France that in the late medieval period was autonomous and nominally a unit of the Holy Roman Empire, witnessed no persecutions until the Austrian archdukes issued an ordinance in 1604 calling for the arrest of witches. Trials did not occur on a significant scale in Scotland before the 1590s, and in England their erratic progress was marked by several waves, particularly in the 1560s–1580s, 1612 and mid-1640s.

In general, the height of the European persecutions was the relatively short period between about 1580 and 1630. Thereafter the number of trials and executions, already on the wane or finished altogether in some areas, fell quickly. A few final outbreaks occurred, for example in the 1670s in Sweden and in 1692 in Salem, Massachusetts. The last known execution in Europe for witchcraft was carried out in Switzerland in 1782. However, rural folk in particular continued to fear that their neighbours wielded evil powers. Villagers attacked suspicious malefactors in France and Germany as late as the 1970s; in 1997 two Russian peasants murdered a woman and seriously injured another, as well as four children, because they believed that a whole family practised evil magic. These twentieth-century assaults, of course, were aimed at the traditional figure of the magician/sorcerer, not the witch of the early modern period.

WITCH HUNTS: PRESENT AND ABSENT

After the early 1400s, witch hunts spread out from the central zone described above. In some areas within or close to this core area, notably in Germany and part of France, the hunts also reached their greatest intensity and lasted a relatively long time. Similar to the way that an epidemic or new innovation spreads, although often much more slowly, the prosecution of witches moved across Europe from this region. Although there was no hard and fast rule about how or if the hunts reached the periphery of the Continent, generally this took a long time. In Sweden, for instance, the sabbat is mentioned only around 1600; in England it arrived, through French Catholic demonology, in 1613. Mass burnings occurred in Sweden rather late, between 1668 and 1676, when they were ended by royal order. In Finland, then a province of Sweden, the hunts peaked in the 1670s.

Even in central Europe, witch trials did not always spread quickly. Hungary was only a short distance away from the core zone and was quite open to outside influences because of the elite's use of Latin. But the witch stereotype made a tardy entrance in Hungary; it first appeared in areas close to Germany or Austria, and early accusations of witchcraft in the country were often made by German soldiers. 'Regular persecution' of witches began in Hungary only in the 1560s and 'mass persecution' only at the end of the next century, when trials were disappearing in western Europe. Under the influence of extensive references to witch hunting in Austrian law codes and the late seventeenth-century manual for judges written by Benedict Carpzov, both introduced into much of Hungary after 1711, prosecutions peaked there in the first half of the eighteenth century.[18]

Sometimes the importation of the witch stereotype and its accompaniment, trials, occurred suddenly and deliberately because of decisions in the highest strata of society. This happened in Alice Kyteler's case, although perhaps the clearest example concerns Scotland. The realm adopted a Witchcraft Act in 1563, but the statute led to few trials and fewer convictions until 1590. In the previous year, King James VI had sailed to Denmark to claim his bride, Anne. James had spent the winter relaxing, hunting and hearing about witchcraft. Although the Danish government had taken steps to regulate witch trials carefully, for example requiring in 1576 that all local courts' sentences of death had to be appealed to higher instances, perhaps 2000 people were tried and 1000 executed in the country in the sixteenth and seventeenth centuries. James would have had much opportunity to think about witches.

Before he travelled to Denmark, his bride had made one attempt to cross the North Sea to reach him, only to be driven back by storms. Belatedly gallant, James then went himself. As the couple tried to return to Scotland in 1590, they encountered more foul weather and had to turn back. By now James, a nervous man who could not stand summer heat and who as an adult washed at most his fingers and neck, behaved as though he believed witches were out to destroy him.

We will never know whether he cynically adopted this pose in order to strengthen his somewhat shaky power at home or whether he sincerely feared witches; in any event, upon returning to Scotland he immediately heard reports of new witch arrests in Denmark and rumours that at home the devil's lieutenants were trying to attack him personally. The case began in North Berwick, some 20 miles from the capital at Edinburgh. There a servant woman was tortured by local citizens, apparently illegally; she confessed to witchcraft and implicated others in the area and in Edinburgh. James now had several of the suspects brought to his own chambers, where they regaled him with stories of sabbats, storms raised along the coast and other evil acts. The king responded by appointing royal commissions to hunt witches; the new boards naturally found what they sought. Although previously torture had been limited in Scotland to important cases and had required approval by the Scottish Privy Council or Parliament, in 1590 James recommended its use more widely. He was particularly interested in linking the Earl of Bothwell, a powerful nobleman, to the witches, but a jury failed to provide the necessary connection when it refused to convict one of Bothwell's acquaintances of consorting with witches. Nevertheless, Bothwell prudently fled the country, as it became clear that the king wanted to gather more material against him. In June 1591 Bothwell was outlawed for conspiring against his sovereign and consulting with witches.

In 1590–91, perhaps up to 300 people were tried in Scotland for witchcraft, though only 59 names are known. James published a ringing endorsement of persecution, entitled *Daemonologie*, in 1597. Nevertheless, in the same year he 'showed signs of anxiety about prosecutions'.[19] He revoked the standing commissions on witchcraft and required all evidence for a case to be submitted to the Privy Council, which then *might* authorize a trial. The king was certainly worried that witch hunting had got out of the central government's control, as any landowner had been able to set up his own court and convict witches, with the aid of torture.

But James was cooling towards the whole idea of witch persecution; after he ascended the throne of England in 1603 as James I, he did not pursue the matter vigorously. Indeed, in one large trial he intervened and brought proceedings to an end. His action came after nine witches were convicted on the testimony of a single 'possessed' boy. All nine were hanged at Leicester on 18 July 1616. A month after the executions, James happened to be in the area on a royal 'progress', a sort of public relations tour outside of London made popular by Elizabeth I. Six more accused persons were languishing in the Leicester jail, awaiting prosecution in the autumn, as James arrived. Although he spent only about 24 hours in the area, he ordered the star witness of the July trial, one Smythe, about 12 or 13 years old, to be brought to him. After questioning the boy for a while, the king pronounced him a fraud. Five of the indicted witches were then released without trial; the other had already died in prison. James also reprimanded the presiding judges for accepting faulty evidence. In the nine remaining years of his reign, only five other known executions for witchcraft occurred in England.[20]

The broader story of the witch hunts in that country provides an excellent illustration of how chequered the trials could be, even within one relatively uniform, centralized political entity. To begin with, the English law codes on witchcraft were enacted in fits and starts. The first such statute was adopted under Henry VIII in 1542, more than a hundred years after systematic trials of witches began in Switzerland; before then, 'the general impression is that prosecutions [in England] were scarce'.[21] To the extent that witchcraft or sorcery was punished earlier, it was apparently under the articles against heresy. 'The Bill ayest [against] conjuracons & wichecraftes and sorcery and enchantments' of 1542 spoke of people pretending to be able to find treasure under crosses, an 'infinite nombre' of which had supposedly been 'dygged up and pulled downe . . . wtin this Realme'. The law also made it illegal to 'provoke any persone to unlawfull love' or to harm anyone through 'wichecraftes enchauntments or sorceries'. These activities were felonies punishable by forfeiture of property and death.[22]

But this statute appears to have been little used, and it was repealed under the boy king Edward VI in 1547 as part of a blanket repudiation of all new felony legislation adopted during his father's reign. The legal status of witchcraft reverted to its earlier vague situation.

Then in 1563, Parliament under the young Elizabeth passed a bill 'agaynst Conjuracons Inchantments and Witchecraftes'. This law lamented the presence of 'many fantasticall and devilishe persons' who had been allowed to remain at liberty after 1547. Such people had caused much harm to subjects of the queen. However, the punishments specified for a range of acts, including claiming to know the location of buried gold and silver, love charms and bodily harm, were lighter than in Henry's law. Convictions for employing witchcraft to search for treasure or to injure people or property carried a sentence of one year in prison for the first offence and a life sentence for a second conviction, with loss of property. In the heart of the European Continent, such leniency would have appalled judges.

By 1604, James had ascended the throne; Parliament now adopted a new witchcraft measure in place of the Elizabethan law. But this was not a 'king's bill'. Thoroughly discussed in both Lords and Commons, it took a long time to pass. There is no evidence that James showed any particular interest in seeing the new statute enacted. It was certainly harsher than the law it supplanted; a first conviction for using witchcraft to find treasure brought a life sentence, while a second incurred the death penalty. Injuring people or property by witchcraft was a capital crime even for the first offence, while removing dead bodies from graves for any reason also merited execution.[23]

Even in this final law, which was not repealed until 1736, the English clearly had not fully abandoned the old concepts of sorcery and cunning in favour of the new witch stereotype. All three of the statutes mentioned enchantment, charms and incantations alongside witchcraft, and the laws appeared to put all of these enjoinments of the supernatural on an equal level. Nowhere was the devil mentioned, and therefore no pact with him figured in the legislation. Witchcraft was not defined except by reference to using the aid of any 'evill and wicked Spirit'.

Nor were these laws widely applied. Alan Macfarlane estimates a total of 300 executions for witchcraft in all of England between 1542 and 1736,[24] a sharp reduction from the old commonly accepted figure of 1000 offered in 1929 by C. L. Ewen.[25] The population of England in this period has been estimated at, on average, 4 million. Accepting this figure and Macfarlane's estimate of the death toll would put the annual rate of execution at .04 persons per 100 000 population,[26] not a large ratio. Using James Sharpe's vaguer estimate of 'probably less than 500 executions' makes little difference.[27] Certainly persecutions on such a scale would not have made English people widely fearful either that hordes of witches were loose in the land or that anyone might be the next victim of a trial.

Moreover, the witch hunts in England were bunched geographically and chronologically, rather than being more or less evenly distributed across the country. Between 1560 and 1680, the span in which the hunts amounted to something more than extremely sporadic affairs, there were 473 indictments for witchcraft in Essex, but 132 in Kent, 71 in Surrey, 63 in Middlesex and only eight in Hertfordshire. In the rest of the country, data are thin indeed, but it appears that few trials took place.[28] It may well be that Essex, lying as it does on the south-eastern coast of England, was more open to continental influences than was the rest of the country.

Even in Essex, indictment by no means resulted in conviction. Of the 291 people accused at the county assizes (superior circuit courts) for witchcraft between 1560 and 1680, 151 were found not guilty or had the charges dismissed; 129 were convicted, and of those 74 were executed and 55 imprisoned. Except for the years

1645–46, in the midst of the country's Civil War, only three jail terms and one capital sentence were imposed on Essex witches after 1620.[29] Thus the English hunts, bad as they were for the people caught up in them, were not in general systematic, extensive or particularly lethal.

Had the country remained politically stable, witch prosecutions would largely have ended by the 1620s. Any witch trial held after about 1625 was 'likely to fail' because of 'the exposure of the accuser as a fraud, insufficient evidence, or a natural medical explanation'.[30] But the Civil War (1642–46) opened unfortunate cracks in the English legal system through which fell a number of accused witches. These events will be discussed below.

Chaos in England reverberated in Scotland, as the two countries had been united under the same crown since the time of James I; the new level of anxiety arising from the Civil War contributed in 1649 to the first large wave of witch trials north of the Scottish border since the 1590s. Although the restoration of the monarchy in 1660 did not lead to a substantial increase in trials in England, it did allow local Scottish courts to revert for a time to their old independent ways. The result was another round of witch trials north of the border in 1660–61. In both this era and in 1649, some 200–300 cases were tried per year in Scotland, which still permitted the use of torture. Certainly the role of James VI in the 1590s in spreading the continental concept of witchcraft, as well as the greater autonomy of Scottish tribunals compared to their English counterparts, made the hunts more serious in Scotland. But there too the number of victims was not overwhelming; altogether 'probably well under 1500' executions for witchcraft took place in Scotland, and named individuals number only 599.[31] Trials in that land fed on local tensions and fears but assumed large proportions only when the central authorities also became deeply alarmed.

In a few areas, one person wielding authority, with the encouragement or toleration of higher officials, produced large hunts. A terrible example is the activity of Balthasar Nuss in Fulda, Germany, between 1603 and 1605. Using 'unheard of tortures' and 'formless investigations', he was responsible for the deaths of some 250 persons convicted of witchcraft. But the death of the Prince-Abbott Balthasar von Dermbach in March 1606 removed Nuss's permissive supervisor and sponsor. The new prince-abbott had Nuss arrested; after 12 years in prison, during which the authorities heard many complaints about his persecutions, Nuss was beheaded in 1618.

This especially gruesome episode sprang from a complicated set of circumstances in which von Dermbach, exiled from his abbacy for many years, unleashed Nuss on his enemies and their families. Fulda is often cited as an example of persecution of one faith by another, in this case Catholicism. Yet a close study of the evidence shows that the issue of religion was 'only in the background'. In fact, Nuss's punishment strongly undermined a common Catholic argument about witch trials, that God would not allow the innocent to be condemned.[32]

In the nearby prince-bishoprics of Würzburg and Bamberg, some of the Catholic rulers supported mass witch hunts beginning in 1616. These persecutions, which killed more than 1500 people, reached their peak in both places in 1628–29. Then strong pressure from other Catholic authorities, especially Bavarian and imperial ones, succeeded in ending the witch burnings.[33] These cases from the realms of German 'spiritual princes' suggest not a concerted effort to control any part of the population or to enforce certain norms among it; instead, these were outbreaks of witch fear compounded by religious fanaticism,[34] sadism and the lack of any restraint from more central authorities. When the persecutions went too far, influential Catholic rulers brought strong pressure on the local Catholic fanatics to mend their ways, and witch hunts in these jurisdictions came to an end. 'Articulate, rigorous, and vociferous opposition to the witchcraze existed in the Society of Jesus, in the

Catholic universities, and even at the Bavarian Privy Council, the highest organ of government in the leading Counter-Reformation state.'[35]

If some Catholic rulers in Germany became intense advocates of witch hunts, other similar figures did not. In the seventeenth century Germany's two most prominent and equally devout Catholic brothers, Maximilian and Ferdinand of Bavaria, adopted opposite positions on witch hunting. After some hesitation, Maximilian halted them while he was the ruling duke of Bavaria 1597–1651. Ferdinand arranged the largest individual hunt in European history while he ruled as archbishop and elector of Cologne from 1595 to 1650.[36] Both brothers had been educated to believe in witches and the necessity of destroying them; Maximilian's tutor, the Spanish Jesuit Gregory of Valencia, had even made his young charge spend numerous days watching suspects being tortured. But Maximilian never became comfortable with the evidence offered in court to convict witches, a point to which much attention will be devoted below.

No executions occurred in the abbey of Kempten, the Swabian Imperial Cloisters, and the Bishopric of Regensubrg, for example. Catholic jurisdictions, reflecting the great differences of opinion among the theologians of that Church, mounted no steady offensive against witches.

Across the religious divide, the Calvinist Palatinate of northern Germany had few trials and, 'for reasons of principle, absolutely no witches were executed'. The area's rulers 'developed official methods intended to nip any attempts at prosecution in the bud, refusing to admit accusations of witchcraft in their law courts'.[37] The Protestantism of the Palatinate may have had something to do with this attitude, yet the large number of trials in other Calvinist areas only a short distance away suggests that other influences were at work. Individual decisions by the elite, Catholic or Protestant, determined whether witch persecutions would occur.

Attention to witches, as the Scottish cases demonstrate and as the Templar affair in France comes close to showing, could begin as a political affair and radiate outwards from the capital of a country. But in these same instances, central authorities were also quick to assert their control over the hunts and to examine charges of witchcraft carefully. Persecutions in countries characterized by strong central supervision of cases rarely achieved the scale of the more autonomous parts of Germany, Switzerland and France. This difference suggests that if there was occasionally a political function to witch trials, broad social or behavioural goals usually did not play a large role in them. Had such ends been the object of the persecutions, surely the highest male authorities of any realm would have widely promoted, not blocked, the charge of witchcraft.

This issue is thrown into sharper focus by events in the Saar region of west central Germany, extending around the city of Trier, where a particularly bloody dynamic characterized the witch hunts. The Saar in the sixteenth and seventeenth centuries was divided into Catholic and Protestant areas and into dozens of legal jurisdictions with little if any supervision by higher courts. Here the incidence of the persecutions, which involved 591 known trials ending in 467 executions and only 23 acquittals, was probably twice as deadly per capita than in south-western Germany, and eight times more lethal than in the south-eastern German lands.[38] In Trier the authorities proved especially willing to listen to the complaints of local peasants and to give them a leading role in prosecutions. The witch hunts thus proceeded 'from below' in social terms, with the elite acting mostly as the facilitators of action by the peasants, who formed village committees to find and prosecute witches.[39] 'The population's initiative was . . . merely channelled' from above.[40] The local committees tended, moreover, to *start* with torture when villagers levelled accusations of witchcraft against their neighbours rather than to undertake an initial, careful gathering of testimony about the alleged crime. A study of three committees in the Saar shows that they almost invariably convicted the people they arrested: of 73 cases begun between 1595 and 1659, only 12 were halted in the early stages of investigation.[41]

But all this occurred in a context of 'dogmatic witch teaching in the social, religious, economic and mental relations of village society' conducted for a long time by the elite.[42] The witch stereotype was laid over the peasants' traditional views about sorcerers and their evil deeds. Villagers then enacted their tensions, antagonisms and fears on the bodies of their neighbours.

A recent investigator of the hunts in the Saar, Eva Labouvie, sees them as 'multifunctional'; they were 'explanatory, supervisory, and channelling' devices used by the community to strengthen itself.[43] Yet clearly the familiar combination of pressure from below and teaching from above, emphasized by the same author, prompted villagers to depart for a certain period from the ways in which they had traditionally handled the problem of alleged *maleficia* by their neighbours. Labouvie's own work provides an example. In 1630 Mattheis Bart, a 55-year-old peasant with his own house, was accused by neighbours of witchcraft, specifically of appearing at their bedsides and trying to make them ill. His wife had been executed as a witch the year before. The accusations against Bart can be termed 'functional' only if one assumes in advance that, in the sociological or anthropological sense, any village accusation fits under that rubric. Taken by itself, however, the material presented on his case indicates that deep suspicion fell on him because of his wife. Therefore if any of three conditions had been absent – the general background of teaching and frightening people about witches; the readiness of the local elite to allow witch prosecutions or, more precisely, its inability to contain them; or the earlier execution of Bart's wife – it seems doubtful that he would have been accused. A better explanation for his case is that other villagers were deeply scared of witchcraft and pointed to a new suspect not because he was marginal or disruptive to the community, but because they felt that Bart was committing a real crime. Chapter 5 will explore further the distinction between functional control within a community and suppression of perceived crime.

The difficulties of village life alone had long produced some lynchings of purported evil sorcerers, as happened in Freising, Germany, in 1090. Peasants burned three female 'weather makers' despite the protests of the Catholic Church, which referred to the victims as martyrs.[44] As noted, killings of this sort occurred occasionally in Europe into the 1990s. But even without the disapproval of the authorities, such actions would never have amounted to the scale of the witch hunts; they were too severe and disruptive to village life. Small communities needed other ways of handling their internal tensions.

Witch hunts were different from occasional lynchings; to produce a sustained persecution, the witch stereotype first had to be brought to an area by its elite. Following that arrival, the secular and clerical authorities might or might not permit hunts to take place, or they might be too weak to oppose them effectively. 'With encouragement from above, the lower classes can supply an almost unlimited number of suspects', Christina Larner wrote, generalizing from the witch hunts in Scotland.[45] But this would have been so only for a time, as the arrests would soon have become destabilizing and tension-inducing (Chapter 5 explores this subject further). Counter tendencies would quickly have arisen, as ultimately happened in the Saar. Before and after the witch hunts, peasants found means to deal with suspected perpetrators of evil magic in their midst that included counter-spells and community pressure but rarely extended to execution.

In several countries of eastern and western Europe, witch hunts by the definition used here did not occur or were at most rare events. Russian executions for maleficent magic can be described as concerning witches only if the term is stretched almost beyond recognition. In 1467 Tsar Ivan III said that his first wife had been killed by magicians; in 1497 he ordered his current wife drowned for consorting with them. Ivan IV (the Terrible) likewise blamed the death of his first wife in 1560 on the evil arts and accused some of the highest nobles, who held the rank of *boiar*, of murdering her through diabolical connections. In 1638, Russian officials used torture to obtain confessions from a court seamstress and those connected to her, following a denunciation of her use of black magic by two of her co-workers. Another high service noble was convicted of endangering the tsar's life in 1689 and was executed. But such incidents were by no means common. Accused sorcerers had been put to death in Russia for centuries, as they had in Germany, but their numbers appear to have been small. Few if any such cases are recorded after the eleventh century, while more modern documents for the period 1622–1700 count only 161 persons tried for *maleficia* in Russia. Scattered trials occurred thereafter; it seems that only one found thus far involved the charge of making a pact with the devil, as opposed to invoking his aid in the way that magicians hoped to do.

Russian culture was one of the most patriarchal and misogynist in Europe. But Russian priests are allowed and encouraged to marry, nullifying one of the prominent factors in medieval Western attacks on women, the despised Catholic priest's wife or concubine. Besides this crucial difference, the Russian elite never learned to fear witches the way that the upper strata of the West did. Russian culture contains extensive references to the devil but has not produced one large and terrifying satanic figure, although the Orthodox Church uses the Christian Bible. Russian icons, derived directly from Greek medieval art and sometimes actually painted by Greeks, present numerous scenes of devils tormenting saints. But such pictures are set around the margins of the main illustration, and they fail to portray the large Western devil.

The Russians never developed the 'demonological view of the universe' necessary for the big Western witch hunts.[46] In part this relates to Russian resistance to Western ideas. Whatever the reason, references to diabolical connections are only peripheral in known Russian trials, which concentrate overwhelmingly on *maleficia*. Nor did the torturers elicit testimony about sabbats, night flying or personal appearances by the devil as a goat or other creature.[47] The Russian episode therefore sounds more like old European trials of sorcerers than encounters with the fearsome, well-travelled witch of Western persecutions. And trials of sorcerers anywhere in Europe did not expand into the mass hunts that witch processes could produce.

The eastern part of the Continent was in general not hospitable ground for the witch stereotype, and not necessarily because of religious or linguistic differences. Educated Poles, almost solidly Catholic after a brief attraction to Protestantism, also read Latin in the early modern period and might have been expected to absorb the new concept of the witch; nevertheless, the transition from sorcerers to witches in Poland was incomplete at best.[48] There, too, the trials, if they may even be called processes against witches in the western European sense, reached a zenith in the early eighteenth century. Even in the German-speaking 'eastern Alpine region', close in area to present-day Austria, a pact with the devil was rarely mentioned before the end of the 1500s.[49]

But resistance to the witch concept was by no means a pattern peculiar to eastern Europe. In the West, besides the low number of trials already noted for Italy and Spain, Portugal provides a good example of this omission. There 'the religious elite rejected the influence of the European witch craze';[50] few trials occurred, and altogether seven people were executed, all in 1559. In the independent northern Netherlands, clerics, jurists and other officials of the sixteenth and seventeenth centuries likewise did not accept the new witch stereotype. While some Dutch writers argued for the pact with the devil as the key to witchcraft, others did not go that far, and the ideas of flight, the sabbat and sex with the devil did not figure in Netherlandic trials. The result was a low incidence

of cases in which diabolical magic played a role; given our definition, they were not witch trials. It will be no surprise that Dutch
executions for sorcery ended early, generally before 1600.[51]

Where the elite of any area did not absorb the witch stereotype,
prosecution on the charge of performing *maleficia* was uncommon.
A feeling among a nation's leading strata that they were not Germans
or French and did not do things the way those people did was
probably important at times in blocking the arrival of the new
ideas. However, the dominant figures of Poland and Hungary often
eagerly borrowed cultural patterns from the West and might have
been expected to follow suit regarding witches. The Dutch and
Portuguese were westerners but not great witch hunters.

It appears that in the central core of the persecutions, publishing, preaching and university specialists dedicated to finding witches
tended to reinforce each other and to propel the hunts, although it
must always be borne in mind that even in the heart of Europe the
trials did not appear steadily and indeed did not arise at all in some
regions. Outside of the core zone, the full apparatus created for
finding and trying witches did not materialize, leaving much more
room for rejection of the stereotype. Finally, many influential Europeans across the Continent simply refused to take the witch scare
seriously.

'CAUSES' OF THE HUNTS

If it is sometimes possible to see how witch hunts started or, con-
versely, were never allowed to begin in a particular area, the question
of why in general the number of persecutions generally rose after
1400 still requires discussion. As noted, the peasant rebellions of
the fourteenth century, localized in parts of France and England,
cannot be taken as a direct cause.

On the other hand, new judicial practices clearly contributed
to the spread of the hunts. Richard Kieckhefer points out that

inquisitorial procedure, which came into wide use by the 1300s, made it possible for courts to accept charges from the general populace.[52] In the old accusatorial courts, anyone making a criminal charge who could not prove it was liable to the punishment normally meted out to a person convicted of that crime. For example, if the penalty for theft was having a hand cut off, someone who charged a neighbour with theft but could not prove it might have his or her own hand severed by court order. Called talion, or *lex talionis* (the law of retaliation), the principle meant that few would dare to lodge a serious charge without substantial evidence, and probably not without important social or political support. The change to inquisitorial law meant that responsibility for making criminal charges passed out of the hands of private individuals into the hands of officials. In short, the impersonal state now took on the role of accuser and prosecutor, often combining these roles in the early period with that of judge.

Politics, personal or on the state level, played an important role in the creation of demonology. Heinrich Kramer's disturbed mind produced the *Malleus*, as shown, in reaction to personal troubles and courtroom defeats. Walter Stephens argues that the texts of the 'witch theorists' provide 'strong evidence' that they did not 'even usually' believe that their ideas 'corresponded to reality'.[53] Johannes Nider appears to have been more concerned with heretics and reform within the Catholic Church than with condemning witches when he wrote in the 1430s.

In a fascinating dissection of the major French writers on witchcraft, Jonathan Pearl describes their work as a 'genre of religio-political literature'. The authors were strongly attached to a zealous faction, the Catholic League, at the height of the French wars of religion in the 1580s and 1590s. Their books were chiefly concerned with the country's violent internal divisions. Once more, writing about satanic acts was not so much directed at the danger from witches as it was about a struggle between humans.

The French demonologists, among them Nicholas Rémy, Jean Bodin and Henri Boguet, largely offered propaganda about witchcraft directed against their fellow Catholics, especially the 'politiques', who wanted to reach an accommodation with the French Protestants. Vehement Catholics reacted by portraying the Protestants as 'polluted vermin', but also by maintaining that moderate Catholic judges were soft on witches and thus formed part of a great satanic conspiracy. Most of the French demonology produced in the late sixteenth and early seventeenth centuries, Pearl continues, was written in part to tie Protestants to the devil but also in response to the moderate policies of the Paris Parlement, essentially an appeals court, toward witchcraft cases. The stance of this court will be examined in some detail in Chapter 5. For the moment, it will be enough to note two points about this Parlement: first, when it applied torture in witch cases it did so with considerable moderation. In contrast to the results obtained in other parts of the Continent, the Parlement judges received a confession from exactly one of the 185 people they ordered to be tortured. The technique used was to force water into the victim's mouth – horrible enough when done to an extreme, but obviously not something that the Parlement's employees put their hearts into. Second, the last use of torture in a Paris witchcraft trial was in 1593, long before the huge waves of persecutions swept through Germany in the seventeenth century.

Certainly the French demonologists did not direct French courts, except for the years 1588–94, when members of the Paris Parlement were closest to the Catholic League. It was no accident that in that span the proportion of death penalties handed down in the appeals cases heard by the Parlement rose to its highest level, 27 per cent.[54]

Politics and the witch hunts therefore affected each other on multiple levels and at various moments. And earlier the campaigns against heretics, using the same images fastened by the 1430s on witches, obviously had the political goal of cementing the good Christian community. But none of that meant that any hunt was deliberately organized to extirpate a specific type of person. In fact, to reiterate a point, France – excluding French-speaking areas like Lorraine that in the early modern period were part of the Holy Roman Empire – had an extensive demonology but relatively few witch trials. As France recovered from the chaotic revolt of the 1540s known as the Fronde, then again from the wars of religion that lasted into the late 1620s, it did not prove necessary in any sense for officials to use witch trials to attain their political ends. The hunts were not functional in France in the sense of taming women or marginal people.

The coincidence of the rise of inquisitorial procedure and witchcraft cases has led various authors to postulate that the prosecution of witches was an inherent part of state-building. This hypothesis seems upside down. State-building *facilitated* the prosecution of witches because in the new courts, most of all in Germany, the possibility that accusers would be severely punished if the prosecution failed had largely disappeared. People could now come forward to make charges against others much more confidently than before, as happened in the Saar.

Many courts in Europe maintained a kind of dual judicial system long after inquisitorial courts appeared, in which talion continued in some instances. Moreover, individuals making a charge of witchcraft were not completely safe, as courts in Europe and North America sometimes found such accusers guilty of slander. In Russian procedure, it was not rare for the accusers, the arrested and witnesses all to be tortured. Nevertheless, inquisitorial procedures did accompany the growth of new state structures in western Europe, providing as they took hold a more favourable arena for witchcraft charges than had the old tribunals.

But there is little if any evidence that 'witches' or, for that matter, traditional folk healers or untutored magicians presented a grave, growing threat to the 'new states' and therefore had to be liquidated to smooth the way for innovative administrative structures. Certain early witch cases involved high-born people, although monarchs desperately needed the nobility in general to help hold their realms together. At the other end of the social structure, the immolation of peasants, on whom many old and effective controls were already in place, did not usually help cement a state. Why an attack on old women would strengthen a political system is unclear. And there was no reason why authorities should have preferred the charge of witchcraft above all others as a pretext for eliminating obstacles to their rule. In any event, trials after the early, politically coloured processes were seldom directed by central authorities, and witch persecutions did not occur at all in many areas. Nor can an urban assault on village ways be demonstrated. Not only were the witch hunts far too erratic to support such theses, they usually occurred in places where central power was and remained weak during the actual hunts. Witch prosecutions were the product of a different confluence of events.

Some authors have pointed to the sixteenth-century Reformation and the zeal to tighten ranks that it provoked among all the major Christian religions as the essential factors in the expansion of the witch persecutions. Joseph Klaits, for example, argues that 'the missionary thrust of religious reformers was crucial to the advent of witch trials on a massive scale. In seeking to spread their messages to previously untutored rural Europeans, the reformers [of various faiths] engaged in a vast struggle against popular religious practices, which they interpreted as satanic in origin.' The new zealots 'were prepared to cast ordinary folk as devil worshipers and witches'.[55]

Several objections to this neat scheme have already been offered here, and others will follow. For the moment, a few more points may be raised. First, peasants' ordinary folkways were not the focus of attack in the witch persecutions; rather, defendants were charged with allying with the devil and carrying out repulsive crimes (Chapter 5 will treat this problem in detail). Nor does the chronology of the witch stereotype and early trials, which began well before the Reformation, support Klaits's assertion. True, the massive hunts occurred after the religious splits in the West, but usually some 30 or 40 years later, and sometimes as much as 100 years after Luther began his protests against Catholic practice. To say that the religious schism in western Europe raised tension and fear, for instance in France, is obviously correct, but in earlier centuries deep anxiety had been equally or more pronounced. As noted, any number of jurisdictions in the central zone of witch hunting were immune to it. If in Germany Rottenburg saw many cases, Rothenburg had very few. Catholic Bavaria essentially stopped executions in 1600; although southern Austria was a Catholic region with a fair sprinkling of Protestants in the sixteenth century, Heinrich Kramer's abysmal failure to convict witches in 1485 precluded any further trials in Brixen. Such a list could go on and on, for both Catholic and Protestant areas. Finally, whatever impact the new religious strife had on the witch hunts was in the direction of enhancing cultural trends that already dated back 500 or more years in Europe. For all these reasons, the Reformation may have worsened the witch hunts for a time in certain areas, but it was not a central factor in producing them in the first place.

Some historians have assigned considerable weight in the background to the persecutions to the 'Little Ice Age' that occurred at the beginning of the early modern period. In the sixteenth century, winters became longer, shortening the growing season and diminishing harvests. Particularly in the Alps, where glaciers increased in size and the margin of existence for the peasants was not large to begin with, it may have been easy to identify 'witches' as the cause of local problems.[56] Yet this thesis should not be carried too far, as persecutions of witches took place only in some parts of the Alps. In other regions of Europe characterized by many trials, climatic change appears to have played little or no role in the hunts. Nor is there reason to think that at the apex of the persecutions, for example in various parts of Germany in the late 1620s, weather problems were especially acute.

Generally, other factors seem more important in the rise of witch persecutions from the early 1300s to the middle of the sixteenth century. Above all, the witch stereotype had to be in place, and it had to become widely accepted. It had to overcome traditional scepticism about night processions and to overwhelm the positive aspects of women's image. The elite had to become educated in a new way about witchcraft; this was not necessarily easily accomplished, as the story of Maximilian of Bavaria shows. In the many regions where the new stereotype was accepted, misfortunes of various kinds could be ascribed to witches. The plague of the fourteenth century was not blamed on them because other classic villains, the Jews and heretics, were then much more prominent. By the mid-sixteenth century, plague could be and was assigned to the realm of the devil's minions. Price rises, fluctuations in the incidence of poverty, disease, famine, poor weather and a vast array of other problems had occurred for centuries. While any combination of these could figure in the immediate background to a given witch hunt, they led to persecution only when a ready image of the witch had become fixed in a region's culture. Disaster and image were both necessary to produce a witch hunt. Even so, mass trials did not tend to take place during moments of crisis, but just after them, as though society needed breathing room to 'speculate' about the causes of its problems.

We cannot say precisely why the witch stereotype began to replace the stock images of heretics in France and Switzerland in the fourteenth and early fifteenth centuries. If eye-catching, titillating ingredients are provided by writers and artists, someone will surely make a dish of them. Here the plague, so broad and deadly that people could well imagine a vast conspiracy behind it, was also of great importance. The idea of such a plot, which deeply enhanced the idea of an attack from the outside on western European

Christians, was much more important in the witch hunts than the specific charge of spreading the plague. That accusation appears in relatively few cases.

Of course, slaughtering Jews did not stop the epidemics, and neither did their expulsion from various countries, which began before the plague struck. Remaining western European Jews were now confined to ghettos and closely regulated in their contact with Christians; all Jews were known to local authorities and were often required to wear special badges or clothing that immediately identified them to the general population. This situation actually protected Jews to a degree, as they were not in a position to do much harm to the Christian community. In particular, Jews did not live in villages, the locus, as we shall see, of witchcraft accusations.

One group remained that could prove handy as a focal point for general fears about a plot to undermine the good Christian society: the heretics. Forced underground in the twelfth and thirteenth centuries, they might still be trying to spread their doctrines, now depicted, as we have seen, as anti-human. Apparently some communities of heretics remained in mountainous areas, outside the reach of traditional authorities. But as the grasp of the new states expanded, bringing with it the inquisitorial courts, civil authorities close to the mountains set out to try and to execute people whom they probably genuinely regarded as loathsome enemies of humanity. As they did so, the French conception of the witch made the accused even more noticeable and compelling. Whether the authorities at first believed in the stereotype of the devil's helpers will remain unknown. But it seems likely that the more that members of the elite repeated the witch images to each other, the more these pictures caught on as an explanation of misfortune.

In the shift from the figure of the sorcerer or heretic to that of the witch is another clue as to why women so outnumbered men in most trials after the late fourteenth century. Kieckhefer estimates that in the cases judged before 1500, about two-thirds of defendants whose sex is known were female, but that this percentage climbed as the fifteenth century wore on.[57] In the Jura region of France and Switzerland, men predominated in witchcraft trials in the early period; in Neuchâtel, 29 of 36 accused witches in the fifteenth century were male. This proportion probably related to the way in which heresy and witchcraft quickly blended into one charge there.[58] Women may have been in a distinct minority among heretics, or at least the ones identified by inquisitors; among Cathars tried at Montauban in the thirteenth century were 71 males and 28 females. Yet the church regarded women as the ones who 'opened the door to heresy'.[59] Perhaps as heresy became witchcraft and vice versa, the elite could not resist attaching to women aspects of the hatred for them developed millennia earlier and compounded by the clerical celibacy campaign of the twelfth century. Given the new contempt for females retailed by the elite, the common people then added charges that women had caused illness and the deaths of babies and domestic animals.

HOW MANY VICTIMS?

On one level, any discussion of the number of victims of the witch hunts completely misses their essence, which was the suffering inflicted on flesh-and-blood individuals. On another level, the numbers mean everything. An estimate of 9 million dead women, for example, imparts a completely different character to the hunts than does a figure of 40 000 of both sexes executed. The first toll lends itself readily to the notion that the persecutions were a particularly vicious part of a male war against women. The second number suggests that the hunts were not necessarily a fundamental aspect of male–female relations in early modern Europe and North America.

Almost any discussion of the number of victims in a mass persecution is fraught with politics. Without suggesting that cynicism reigns in any choice of an estimate, it seems clear that political inclinations are often conducive to the selection of a 'high' number. The word 'high' in this sense is taken from controversies over the impact of slavery and of communist terror. When in 1969 Philip Curtin examined the number of Africans landed in the Americas as slaves, he opened a sharp, even antagonistic controversy. On the basis of extensive archival and secondary research, Curtin offered an estimate of just over 9.5 million in place of the previously accepted range of 15–25 million for the entire period of the slave trade, roughly 1500–1890.[60] Writers of African origin accused Curtin, who is white, of belittling a great tragedy and of playing fast and loose with the numbers. For Joseph Inikori, higher estimates explained Africa's underdevelopment, which was a direct result of the human devastation wrought by the slave trade.[61] Curtin, obviously stung by the attacks on his work, replied that any grand total 'has no meaning at all for the morality of the slave trade, which has no defenders in any event. . . . For myself, no possible figure from five million to fifty can make the evils of the trade any less than they were, or any more.'[62] Nevertheless, the political implications of the removal of 5 million Africans by Europeans are vastly different from the picture suggested by the export of 50 million. Rightly or wrongly, a sense of outrage and blame changes with the estimates.

The same arguments, with some of the same implications, have raged over attempts to calculate the number of witches put to death in Europe. When feminism was struggling to become established as a respectable academic approach and as a world view for women, some female writers offered 'high' numbers for the victim toll. In 1974, Andrea Dworkin, more a publicist than a historian, but whose influence was large for a time, put 'the most responsible estimate' of women's executions from the late fifteenth to the late seventeenth centuries at 9 million. This astonishing figure was first offered by the German anti-cleric Gottfried Christian Voight in 1784. He had looked at archives of the abbey of Quedlinburg for some periods, then extrapolated to derive a figure for victims there during the whole span of the witch hunts, then extrapolated further from that point to reach a total for all of Europe, assuming that the persecutions had everywhere and always been constant.[63] Dworkin, who used the *Malleus* but little else as a source for her remarks, sees the witch hunts as a vast campaign to control women; she terms them 'gynocide as a strategem of social control'.

But Dworkin made it clear that she was on a mission in her writing: 'This book is an action, a political action where revolution is the goal. It has no other purpose. It is not cerebral wisdom, or academic horseshit, or ideas carved in granite or destined for immortality. It is part of a process and its context is change. . . . commitment to ending male dominance . . . is the fundamental revolutionary commitment.'[64]

It may be that no book about history, or no estimate of victim tolls, is without a political agenda, and that Dworkin was merely being more frank than the rest of us. However, detailed research into archival records, now compiled in a great stream of case studies, suggests that fewer than 100 000 trials took place. Typically less than 70 per cent of those charged were executed, though in some places the death rate was closer to 25 per cent. Scholars have lately suggested tolls as 'low' as 40–50 000.[65]

Scotland in the sixteenth and seventeenth centuries is a well-researched case that demonstrates how the victim toll has been reduced by mainstream scholars. Prior to the work of Christina Larner and her associates,[66] estimates of the number of executions for witchcraft in Scotland ranged from 3500 to 30 000. But after Larner's team combed available court and other records, they determined that the total could have been no more than 1500.[67] Many of these, moreover, occurred during 'intensive outbreaks [of prosecutions] in confined areas',[68] which would have left large sections of the country relatively unscathed by either persecutions of witches or fear of them. On the basis of these findings, the general impact of the witch hunts on Scotland must be reduced substantially compared to earlier treatments. A smaller example concerns a hunt in the Basque-speaking Pays de Labourd in France during the early seventeenth century. Earlier writers believed that 600 'witches' were executed, but recent research shows that probably only 80 fell victim.[69] An old legend that in the convent lands of Quedlinburg, 133 witches were executed in a single day in 1589 must be discarded, as no documents surviving from that period support such a figure.

An estimate of 15 000 dead in Poland was offered by the historian Bohdan Baranowski in 1952 and was long repeated in other works. But only two years after publishing his figure, Baranowski confused it drastically. Without providing any further explanation, he announced in the postscript to a book by another author that 'a few [thousand] or 10–20 000 persons' were executed in Poland. The trials were 'only sporadic'.[70] Baranowski's first estimate had also been made through extrapolation from a few records, a risky procedure.

The newer, lower calculations for Europe as a whole strongly suggest that the impact of the witch hunts on the populace, particularly on women, was greatly exaggerated for a time in the literature. But the fight over numbers is not over. In response to recent estimates, Anne Barstow rejects 'exaggerations' of the death toll which put it at 3 million or above. However, she argues that many records must be lost, while other deaths at the hands of mobs and in confinement were not recorded. She therefore prefers figures of 200 000 accused and 100 000 put to death.[71] But Barstow offers no specific evidence for increasing the numbers.

Surely Barstow's depiction of the witch 'craze' as a massive disaster for women in general is related, consciously or unconsciously, to her raising of the estimates. Her treatment sounds much like many discussions of the Stalinist regime in the Soviet Union,[72] as she maintains that the witch hunts constituted a 'reign of terror' against women. Females became atomized, although Barstow does not use the term. A woman:

would guard her lips with her neighbors – because any woman could be a witch, she must not be associated with any of them. The women's subculture of the Middle Ages . . . began to dissolve under the terror of witch hunting. The new cult of individualism that cultural historians write about in connection with the sixteenth century was based not only on capitalistic competition or Renaissance idealism; it was, in the case of women, based on fear.

One of the 'dehumanizing effects of this campaign on women' was that they 'began to fear to speak up for themselves'. The impact of all this continued into the nineteenth century, Barstow believes; through violence and the lesson it transmitted to women about acceptable behaviour, males achieved a great degree of control over females.[73]

Like Joseph Inikori, Barstow stresses the long impact of one group's victimization of another. She is careful to say that women were 'victims and . . . agents of their own fates'. They were 'both strong and persecuted'.[74] But such thoughts appear early in her book, are given almost in passing, and all but disappear below the theme that men as a bloc persecuted women as such.[75]

The higher the numbers, the more plausible this picture becomes. If 100–110 000 people were tried over a span of 300 years across all Europe, and 40–50 000 of them were executed – figures that should be high enough to evoke profound revulsion and condemnation in any person – it is much more difficult to sustain an analysis like Barstow's than it is using estimates almost twice as large. This is not the place to argue in depth with her conclusions about women's behaviour after the hunts ended; suffice it to say that considerable evidence indicates they were not terrorized at any time into silent submission. Moreover, the witch hunts, to repeat a fundamental point, were far too erratic to have had any one specific impact across Europe.

Are we therefore doomed to a situation in which women writers argue for high death tolls and grumpy males open fire on their work? No – some of the strongest criticism of 'high' estimates in recent years and of the analytical framework based on them has come from women. Diane Purkiss finds that 'radical feminists have needed a Holocaust of their own'. They had to reject history and argue that the witch hunts represented 'the way things *always* are', in order to depict women's constant suffering at the hands of men. 'Witches became crucial to the effort to make men and especially women *believe* in women's oppression.' Purkiss maintains that the traditional story (or 'myth') of the witch persecutions has a set of clear oppositions, good and bad, oppressed and oppressor, that tries to teach women 'how perfect our lives would be without patriarchy and its violence'. Purkiss's angry rejection of a cursory approach to the numbers question is evident throughout an early section of her book, especially in the phrase 'history indeed becomes hystery when the unspeaking body is the only site which can be recollected'. That is, some feminist historians have depicted the witch hunts only as an assault on the female body, which ironically deprives women of any voice at all.[76]

Since the extant records of witch trials are so spotty, the question of the victim toll will never be definitively resolved. A few new studies have found previously unknown witch trials, involving a few hundred persons at most. But the 'low' estimates have emerged over a period of decades based on painstaking archival research, and they are not likely to be displaced by extensive troves of information that still lie hidden in obscure collections. Meanwhile, the numbers fight is only a symptom of the larger struggle over the meaning of the witch hunts as a whole.

[*]

Several hundred years elapsed between the critical events of the eleventh century, for example the rise of the papacy and the elaboration of new heresies, and the first witch trial. Then another two centuries had to pass before the witch hunts became more than occasional, and still more decades went by before the hunts reached the periphery of Europe, if they ever did. This slow geographical spread from the core area of the witch fear, a zone no more than a few hundred miles on either side of a line from south-eastern France through Strasbourg to north-central Germany, was outpaced by the social expansion of the hunts. In various places they began at the higher levels of the populace, then largely sank down among the peasantry, only to rise spasmodically during the great panics to touch people of virtually any social status.

Social dislocation, rising prices, falling standards of living, wars, bad weather, that the herring failed to spawn in their usual place and other perceptible changes in the way people lived did not necessarily kindle witch hunts. Certainly such connections do not appear in any systematic way. It is equally true that regions characterized by great social and economic change, for example parts of England, Italy and Spain, witnessed almost no hunts. Scotland, on the other hand, underwent no striking changes in the economy or social structure during the sixteenth and seventeenth centuries, yet did have witch persecutions. No clear patterns have emerged from the efforts of many researchers to relate the coming of the hunts to any combination of social alterations.

The rending of the western European Christian community with the Protestant Reformation increased tensions in many areas and led the various sides to accuse each other of being the devil's followers. Yet at least several decades elapsed between the emergence of Protestantism and a significant rise in the number of witch hunts. When this finally occurred, Catholics hunted each other as readily or more so than they hunted Protestants, while the latter persecuted their co-religionists just as quickly. Members of the various faiths sometimes brought strong pressure on each other to end hunts.

Likewise, the debate about numbers of victims has often produced more heat than light. The 'low' estimates of recent detailed research do not admit the clarity about the hunts that 'high' numbers once afforded, at least to their adherents. Still, estimates of 40–50 000 dead point to another firm conclusion: that there was not much of a campaign character to the hunts – they had no particular functional goal.

Were the witch persecutions therefore merely episodes peculiar to a few parts of Europe? The general clustering of the trials between roughly 1550 and 1680, with a peak from around 1580 to 1630, obviously suggests otherwise. The next chapter examines several local persecutions in detail in order to probe more deeply into the questions of why hunts occurred and what, if anything, they may have been intended to accomplish.

NOTES

1. Joseph Hansen (1964) *Zauberwahn Inquisition und Hexenprozess im Mittelalter*, Neudruck der Ausgabe München 1900 (Aalen: Scientia Verlag), pp. 239 and 234–6.

2. Andreas Blauert (1989) *Frühe Hexenverfolgungen: Ketzer-, Zauberei- und Hexenprozesse des 15. Jahrhunderts* (Hamburg: Junius Verlag), pp. 28–32.

3. Patrick F. Byrne (1967) *Witchcraft in Ireland* (Hatboro, Penn.: Folklore Association), p. 28. No witchcraft literature was published there until the early nineteenth century. See also St John D. Seymour (1996) *Irish Witchcraft and Demonology* (New York: Barnes and Noble), who finds that the Irish folk widely believed in witches and demons, but again that almost no trials occurred.

4. Norman Cohn (1975) *Europe's Inner Demons: An Enquiry Inspired by the Great Witch-Hunt* (New York: New American Library), p. 77.

5. L. S. Davidson (1993) 'Introduction', in *The Sorcery Trial of Alice Kyteler: A Contemporary Account (1324) together with Related Documents in English Translation, with Introduction and Notes*, L. S. Davidson (ed.) and J. O. Ward (Binghamton, New York: Medieval and Renaissance Texts and Studies), pp. 2, 27–30, 62–3 and 48.

6. Ibid., p. 2.

7. Richard Kieckhefer (1976) *European Witch Trials: their Foundation in Popular and Learned Culture, 1300–1500* (Berkeley: University of California Press), p. 22.

8. Nicolaus von Jauer, *Tractatus de superstitionibus*, 1405, quoted in Henry Charles Lea, compiler (1957) *Materials Toward a History of Witchcraft*, ed. Arthur C. Howland, introduction by George Lincoln Burr, 3 vol. (New York: Thomas Yoseloff) [hereafter Lea, *Materials*], vol. 1, p. 132. Von Jauer was active in Prague and Heidelberg, where he wrote his book.

9. Lea, *Materials*, vol. 1, p. 250 mentions what must be the same man: Claude of Toulouse, *consiliario dalphinali, judice maiori Brianchonesii*, as holding a trial in Briançon in November 1437.

10. This argument is made by Blauert, *Frühe Hexenverfolgungen*, p. 116. For the decline of cases in the area, see p. 18. Helfried Valentinitsch (ed.) (1987) *Hexen und Zauberer: Die grosse Verfolgung–ein europäisches Phänomen in der Steiermark* (Graz: Leykam-Verlag), p. 257, provides a table that indicates 162 trials in Fribourg from 1607 to 1683, but in that span only 33 per cent of the accused were convicted.

11. Though see Wolfgang Behringer (ed.) (1995) *Hexen und Hexenprozesse in Deutschland*, 3rd edn (Munich: Deutscher Taschenbuch Verlag), p. 66, for the use of *hecse* (pronounced the same as *Hexe*) in a German source from the early fourteenth century.

12. Lea, *Materials*, vol. 1, p. 177.

13. Much of this section is based on Blauert, *Frühe Hexenverfolgungen*, pp. 20–34.

14. Stuart Clark (2002) 'Witchcraft and Magic in Early Modern Culture', in Karen Jolly, Catharina Raudvere and Edward Peters *Witchcraft and Magic in Europe: The Period of the Witch Trials*, The Athlone History of Witchcraft and Magic in Europe, series eds Bengt Ankarloo and Stuart Clark (Philadelphia: University of Pennsylvania Press), p. 233.

15. On this case and other early trials, see Eva Labouvie (1991) *Zauberei und Hexenwerk: Ländlicher Hexenglaube in der frühen Neuzeit* (Frankfurt am Main: Fischer), p. 23.

16. Edward Peters, 'The Medieval Church and State on Superstition, Magic and Witchcraft', in Jolly, Raudvere and Peters, *Witchcraft and Magic in Europe: The Middle Ages*, p. 240.

17. François Bordes (1999) *Sorciers et sorcières: procès de sorcellerie en Gascogne et Pays Basque* (Toulouse: Privat), pp. 22–3, 43 and 86.

18. Gabor Klaniczay (1993) 'Hungary: the Accusations and the Universe of Popular Magic', in Bengt Ankarloo and Gustav Henningsen (eds) *Early Modern European Witchcraft: Centres and Peripheries* (Oxford: Clarendon Press), p. 219; and Gabor Klaniczay (1990) *The Uses of Supernatural Power: The Transformation of Popular Religion in Medieval and Early-Modern Europe*, trans. Susan Singerman, ed. Karen Margolis (Princeton: Princeton University Press), pp. 152–4. For a sample of Carpzov's extreme pro-persecution and pro-torture views, see Lea, *Materials*, vol. 1, pp. 813–16, drawing from Carpzov's *Practica Rerum Criminalium*, Wittenberg, 1670.

19. Christina Larner (1984) *Witchcraft and Religion: the Politics of Popular Belief* (London: Basil Blackwell), pp. 28 and 17.

20. George Kittredge (1929) *Witchcraft in Old and New England* (Cambridge, Mass.: Harvard University Press), pp. 322–23.

21. Alan Macfarlane (1999) *Witchcraft in Tudor and Stuart England: A Regional and Comparative Study*, 2nd edn, introduction by James Sharpe (London: Routledge), p. 14.

22. C. L'Estrange Ewen (1929) *Witch Hunting and Witch Trials: the Indictments for Witchcraft from the Records of 1373 Assizes Held for the Home Circuit A.D. 1559–1736* (London: K. Paul, Trench, Trubner), pp. 13–21, provides the original text of all the English laws on witchcraft.

23. A table summarizing the main points and punishments of the 1563 and 1604 laws is in Macfarlane, *Witchcraft in Tudor and Stuart England*, p. 15; the statutes themselves are in Marion Gibson (ed.) (2003) *Witchcraft and Society in England and America, 1550–1750* (Ithaca, NY: Cornell University Press).

24. Ibid., p. 8.

25. Ewen, *Witch Hunting and Witch Trials*, p. 74.

26. John Putnam Demos (1982) *Entertaining Satan: Witchcraft and the Culture of Early New England* (New York: Oxford University Press), p. 12.

27. J. A. Sharpe (1996) *Instruments of Darkness: Witchcraft in Early Modern England* (Philadelphia: University of Pennsylvania Press), p. 125.

28. James Sharpe, 'Introduction', in Macfarlane (1999), *Witchcraft in Tudor and Stuart England*, 2nd edn, p. 22.

29. Macfarlane (1999), *Witchcraft in Tudor and Stuart England*, 2nd edn, pp. 57–60. Macfarlane does not explain what happened to the other 11 people.

30. Malcolm Gaskill (2005) *Witchfinders: A Seventeenth-Century English Tragedy* (Cambridge, Mass.: Harvard University Press), p. 32.

31. Larner, *Witchcraft and Religion*, p. 28.

32. Gerhard Schormann (1991) *Der Krieg gegen die Hexen: Das Ausrottungsprogramm des Kurfürsten von Köln* (Göttingen: Vandenhoeck & Ruprecht), pp. 116–20.

33. Ibid., pp. 122–23.

34. See the comments by Wolfgang Behringer on the Prince-Archbishop of Cologne, Ferdinand of Bavaria (ruled 1612–50). Ferdinand was a member of the first generation of clerics 'seriously confronted with enforced sexual segregation and celibacy'. He operated with a 'gloomy world view' and practised self-flagellation. This psychological state, Behringer argues, inclined him, as it did other 'spiritual princes' in Germany, to see sin, witches and the devil everywhere. Wolfgang Behringer (1996) 'Witchcraft Studies in Austria, Germany and Switzerland', in Jonathan Barry, Marianne Hester and Gareth Roberts (eds) *Witchcraft in Early Modern Europe: Studies in Culture and Belief* (New York: Cambridge University Press), p. 88.

35. R. Po-Chia Hsia (1989) *Social Discipline in the Reformation: Central Europe 1550–1750* (New York: Routledge), p. 160.

36. William Monter (2002) 'Witch Trials in Continental Europe 1560–1660', in Jolly, Raudvere and Edward Peters, *Witchcraft and Magic in Europe: The Period of the Witch Trials*, p. 22.

37. Behringer, 'Witchcraft Studies', p. 75, citing the work of Bernd Thieser and Jürgen Michael Schmidt.

38. Labouvie, *Zauberei und Hexenwerk*, p. 68.

39. On the Trier accusation committees, see Rita Voltmer and Herbert Eiden (2000) 'Rechtsnormen und Gerichtspraxis bei Hexereiverfahren in Lothringen, Luxemburg, Kurtrier und St. Maximin während des 16. und 17. Jahrhunderts', in Rita Voltmer and Franz Irsigler (eds) *Incubi/Succubi: Hexen und Ihre Henker bis Heute. Ein historisches Lesebuch zur Ausstellung* (Luxembourg: Luxembourg City: Publications scientifiques du Musée de la Ville de Luxembourg, tome IV), pp. 56–77.

40. Walter Rummel (1991) *Bauern, Herren und Hexen: Studien zur Sozial-geschichte sponheimischer und kurtrierischer Hexenprozesse 1574–1664* (Göttingen: Vandenhoeck & Ruprecht), p. 42.

41. Ibid., p. 79.

42. Labouvie, *Zauberei und Hexenwerk*, p. 261.

43. Ibid., pp. 260–5.

44. Behringer, *Hexen und Hexenprozesse*, p. 12.

45. Christina Larner (1981) *Enemies of God: the Witch-Hunt in Scotland*, foreword by Norman Cohn (Baltimore: Johns Hopkins University Press), p. 1.

46. Russell Zguta (1977) 'Witchcraft Trials in Seventeenth-Century Russia', *American Historical Review* 82 (5): 1205.

47. W. F. Ryan (1988) 'The Witchcraft Hysteria in Early Modern Europe: Was Russia an Exception?' *The Slavonic and East European Review* 76 (1): 56–74, finds that the concept of demonic magic was known in Russia, but that many cases 'can hardly be called witchcraft trials at all'. Ryan provides various examples from eighteenth-century cases of charges that individuals had devils at their command, which is vastly different from the Western witch stereotype, but exactly one instance of a purported pact with the devil. It is also significant that in Russian there is no single, specific term corresponding to 'witchcraft'.

48. Bohdan Baranowski (1952) *Procesy Czarownic w Polsce w XVII i XVIII Wieku* (Lodz: Lodzkie Towarzystwo Naukowe), pp. 174–5.

49. See the tables in Valentinitsch, *Hexen und Zauberer*, pp. 257, 286–8, 300 and 302.

50. Francisco Bethencourt, 'Portugal: a Scrupulous Inquisition', in Ankarloo and Henningsen, *Early Modern European Witchcraft*, p. 405.

51. Marijke Gijswijt-Hofstra (1991) 'Six Centuries of Witchcraft in the Netherlands: Themes, Outlines, and Interpretations', and Marcel Gielis, 'The Netherlandic Theologians' Views of Witchcraft and the Devil's Pact', in Marijke Gijswijt-Hofstra and William Frijhoff (eds) *Witchcraft in the Netherlands from the Fourteenth to the Twentieth Century*, trans. R. M. J. van der Wilden-Fall (Rotterdam: Universitaire Pers).

52. Kieckhefer, *European Witch Trials*, p. 17.

53. Walter Stephens (2002) *Demon Lovers: Witchcraft, Sex, and the Crisis of Belief* (Chicago: University of Chicago Press), p. 10.

54. Jonathan L. Pearl (1999) *The Crime of Crimes: Demonology and Politics in France, 1560–1620* (Waterloo, Ontario: Wilfrid Laurier University Press), pp. 4 ,16, 17, 21, 27, 32, and 68.

55. Joseph Klaits (1985) *Servants of Satan: the Age of the Witch Hunts* (Bloomington: Indiana University Press), p. 4.

56. Wolfgang Behringer (2000) *Hexen: Glaube, Verfolgung, Vermarktung* (Munich: Verlag C. H. Beck), pp. 47–8, 53–4.

57. Kieckhefer, *European Witch Trials*, p. 96.

58. E. William Monter (1976) *Witchcraft in France and Switzerland: the Borderlands during the Reformation* (Ithaca, NY: Cornell University Press), pp. 23–6.

59. Peter Biller (1990) 'The Comman Woman in the Western Church in the Thirteenth and Early Fourteenth Centuries', *Studies in Church History*, 27. *Women in the Church* (Oxford: Basil Blackwell), pp. 156–7 and 139.

60. Philip D. Curtin (1969) *The Atlantic Slave Trade: a Census* (Madison: University of Wisconsin Press), p. 268.

61. J. E. Inikori (1982) 'Introduction', in J. E. Inikori (ed.) *Forced Migration: the Impact of the Export Slave Trade on African Societies* (New York: Africana), pp. 51 and 53. J. Suret-Canale (1977) 'La Senégambie à l'ère de la traite', *Revue Canadienne des études africaines/Canadian Journal of African Studies* 11 (1): 130, makes a similar argument.

62. Philip D. Curtin (1976) 'Measuring the Atlantic Slave Trade Once Again', *Journal of African History* 17 (4): 595–6.

63. Wolfgang Behringer (2004) *Witches and Witch Hunts: A Global History* (Cambridge: Polity), p. 157.

64. Andrea Dworkin (1974) *Woman Hating* (New York: Dutton), pp. 130 and 191, quote on p. 17. Wanda von Baeyer-Katte (1965) 'Die historischen Hexenprozesse: Der verbürokratisierte Massenwahn', in *Massenwahn in Geschichte und Gegenwart*, herausgegeben von Wilhelm Bitter (Stuttgart: Ernst Klett), p. 222, speaks of numbers 'bordering on millions'. See Behringer, *Hexen*, p. 67, on the story of the 'often named figure of "nine million witches"'.

65. Robin Briggs (1996) *Witches and Neighbors: The Social and Cultural Context of European Witchcraft* (New York: Viking), p. 260, estimates 40–50 000; Sharpe, *Instruments of Darkness*, p. 5, offers a figure of

'probably less than 50 000 executions' for witchcraft in all of Europe from 1450–1750.

66. Christina Larner, C. J. H. Lee and H. V. McLachlan (1977) *A Source-Book of Scottish Witchcraft* (Glasgow: SSRC).

67. Larner, *Witchcraft and Religion*, pp. 26–30.

68. Ibid., p. 30.

69. Gustav Henningsen (1980) *The Witches' Advocate: Basque Witchcraft and the Spanish Inquisition 1609–1640* (Reno: University of Nevada Press), pp. 23–5 and 480–1.

70. Bohdan Baranowski (1963) 'Posłowie', in Kurt Baschwitz' *Czarownice: Dzieje procesów o czary* (Warszawa: Państwowe Wydawnictwo naukowe), p. 430.

71. Anne Barstow (1994) *Witchcraze: a New History of the European Witch Hunts* (San Francisco: Harper), pp. 21–3.

72. For an introduction to these discussions and to the debate over the number of victims under Stalin, see Robert W. Thurston (1996) *Life and Terror in Stalin's Russia, 1934–1941* (New Haven: Yale University Press).

73. Barstow, *Witchcraze*, pp. 157–9. Dworkin also sees the witch hunts as a vast campaign to control women and describes them as 'Gynocide as a strategem of social control': *Woman Hating*, p. 191; and see Baeyer-Katte, 'Die historischen Hexenprozesse', p. 221, who speaks of 'socially disintegrating groups' and 'terror' in connection with the witch hunts.

74. Barstow, *Witchcraze*, p. 10.

75. Ibid., pp. xiii, 5, 16 and 29, among many pages.

76. Diane Purkiss (1996) *The Witch in History: Early Modern and 20th-Century Representations* (New York: Routledge), pp. 8–17.

CHAPTER FOUR

VICTIMS AND PROCESSES

For the witch hunts or any mass persecution, the question of what the trials were all about hinges to a great extent on an identification of the victims by sex, social background, behaviour before arrest or religion. To note that women constituted the great majority of accused witches is essential. But probably 80 per cent or more of those arrested in the Soviet 'Great Terror' of the late 1930s were male, as were the targets of white southern lynch mobs in the United States. With good reason, no one argues that males as such were the targets of lynching or of Soviet terror. Gender would be only one of several important topics in explaining the rise, dynamics and fall of mass persecution in both the USSR and the American South.

Earlier parts of the book have looked at a broad range of factors in the coming of the European witch trials. This chapter concentrates on who the victims were. Sometimes no more than glimpses of the defendants are visible, but even scant information often makes it possible to look at the trials from the inside out, considering what is known about the accused against the backdrop of the deeds and words of the men who prosecuted them. This approach brings us closer to understanding what the persecutions were intended to accomplish.

The setting, in the broad sense of the word, was always crucial to the hunts. Therefore this chapter relates two case studies, one whose details are well known but whose meaning is hotly disputed, and another, newly discovered series of trials. National and state boundaries counted for little in these two instances: Salem, Massachusetts in 1692–93 and Ban de la Roche in 1607–30. Witch beliefs and fears could cross oceans, mountains, valleys and political boundaries, and in these two spates of witch killing such movements can be traced with some assurance. Especially in Salem, the rise of a panic and then its quick retreat is evident. A closer look at these persecutions will provide a better platform for assessing the hunts in general in western Europe and North America.

Before plunging into the case studies, it is necessary to take a brief look at people's attitudes towards and beliefs about witchcraft.

WHAT DID 'WITCHCRAFT' MEAN TO WESTERNERS?

Into the fifteenth century, and possibly to the end of the hunts, witchcraft appeared to mean different things to the elite and to the common people. The latter thought more in terms of *maleficia*, while the elite – or rather, some portion of it – added the pact with the devil and insisted that this was the worst crime. Probably this attitude migrated across Europe through the Church, as it did in Alice Kyteler's case. In English ecclesiastical trials for witchcraft in the early modern period, 54 per cent mention diabolism, while only 11 per cent of secular cases refer to it. References to alliances with the devil appear much more often in records kept in Latin than in vernacular documents.[1]

The common people thus had a sense of witches as individuals who carried out specific acts of harm against other individuals. Believers in witchcraft among the elite, on the other hand, argued for a general anti-human conspiracy led by the devil. Peasants rarely spoke of the sabbat or night journeys unless prompted to, often under torture, by the officials examining them.[2] With the emphasis on flying, which could supposedly allow vast numbers of witches to cross any distance in an instant, witchcraft could be discussed as a threat to every Christian community at any time. Diabolism also explained the witches' purported general desire to kill infants; their bodies were needed for the infernal rites of the sabbat.

Such gatherings did not take place. No serious researcher now argues that there was a great sect of fertility worshippers across Europe who went out at night to conduct their services. Carlo Ginzburg has found many stories of night processions, journeys to the land of the dead and transformation of humans into animals among various European and Asian peoples. But while there are widespread indications that ordinary Europeans accepted the possibility of night marches and fights between humans and spirits over the fertility of the land,[3] there is no credible testimony that any large gatherings of would-be witches ever occurred. Moreover, left to their own devices, peasants did not link the notions of flying or night battles to the witch stereotype.[4]

No practices or beliefs drew together witches of the type hunted and convicted for *maleficia* and diabolism, for the reason that no such witches existed. What people convicted for witchcraft shared was instead victimhood, for they were found guilty of doing the impossible. The witch heresy existed only in the minds of contemporary educated Europeans who feared that a vast cult of devil worshippers was sweeping over the land.

Certainly ordinary people, especially the 'wise' or 'cunning' folk, tried to practise magic. 'Every village had a healer', an English account of the seventeenth century suggests.[5] For this type of person, magic was a business 'for which some paid the ultimate price'. Some victims of the witch trials, John Swain argues, were 'not innocent'.[6] But this is only to say that some common people, and for that matter some well-off astrologers, tried to use magic for good or evil. These practitioners may have been central to peasant life and economy, but they were in no way guilty of producing actual harm, except perhaps through the power of suggestion. 'Low' or popular magic was not what the witch hunters sought to uncover, for the most part; they cared about it when it could be blown up, in a context of fear, into the pact with the devil and the witch stereotype.

Yet some people who were not tortured confessed to witchcraft. Eliminating those aware that they would be tortured unless they admitted to crimes leaves a relatively small group who confessed without coercion of any kind. Some of those were surely senile or mad. Of the rest, it is possible that they had at some point called on the devil for help and had later come to feel deep guilt about the request. When Europeans widely prayed to specific saints about various problems, why should they not have turned occasionally to another powerful being they had heard much about, the devil? In eighteenth-century Sweden, many men apparently took exactly that course and tried in some fashion to make an agreement with Satan. He 'was someone they could do business with'.[7] Rather, these men *hoped* to traffic with the Prince of Darkness; it must have been difficult to find him at the moment people wanted him most. Still, they sought him out of desperation: starvation was often the only cure for poverty, while disease and loneliness drove people to seek aid on many fronts. Once the devil became deeply embedded in popular consciousness, his name was invoked frequently; certainly this happened among the Salem villagers.

It became evident as the trials in that locale went forward that confessing witches would not be executed, obviously a powerful incentive to admit to the charges. But at the height of the Salem hunt, the mere accusation of witchcraft was apparently enough to make some family and community members bring 'unbearable pressures' on female defendants to confess. Accused women, so one argument runs, had not met the community's expected stand-ards of behaviour and were expected to apologize in the form of a confession. Women might also internalize Puritan ideas 'of their abiding sinfulness and guilt', which for some meant that they 'needed little provocation to believe they had succumbed to the devil'.[8] Such cultural pressure must have existed in many other locations, Catholic and Protestant alike. Taking these factors together, there is not much mystery about why a few Europeans and North Americans confessed to diabolical crimes they could not possibly have committed.

However, 53 residents of the nearby town of Andover signed a petition during the Salem hunt in favour of five accused women, citing exactly such pressure as a major problem in the trials.[9] Once again, there is no simple course through the trials to an understanding of their meaning.

But these educated speculations have not pushed the analysis much deeper. It is necessary to look closely at what happened; case studies are the way to do that.

THE WITCH HUNTS IN BAN DE LA ROCHE

As the Introduction noted, Ban de la Roche, or Steinthal in German, is a French commune which lies in the Vosges Mountains about 60 kilometres (40 miles) to the west of Strasbourg. The Ban, about 49 square kilometres in area, encompasses nine villages situated close to each other; it is only about 6 kilometres between the two that are farthest apart. Indeed, the inhabitants had to walk up and down steep slopes to reach some of the other settlements; at 855 metres above sea level, Belmont (Schönenberg in German, both meaning 'beautiful mountain') is the highest of the villages, while Rothau is far lower, at 387 metres. Several of the hamlets were roughly at the same elevation and were easily reached from one another by a system of trails. Thus the residents of Steinthal, always fairly few in number, often knew at least the outlines of each other's lives. They had plenty of time and opportunity to gather such information; the concept of privacy in Europe dates only from the eighteenth century and in any case rarely applies to peasant existence anywhere. For the reasons discussed in Chapter 1, peasants want and need to know what is happening in their neighbours' lives. In a relatively small, secluded and self-contained environment such as Ban de la Roche, the pressures to know and the habit of enquiring into others' business were even more highly developed.

The people of the Ban were poor compared to the elite of the seventeenth century, but they were not necessarily badly off. As data on the property left behind by executed witches show, it was possible for local commoners to amass some wealth, although not in land, which they held by tradition but did not own outright; rather, their property consisted of goods, money and livestock. Even though houses in Steinthal were often partly dug into the steep sides of the hills in order to conserve warmth and fuel during the long winters, they were frequently substantial dwellings. The rich carvings, cloths and other folk art of the area testify to a relative degree of prosperity among at least a significant portion of the Ban's population.

The villagers, who possessed old and well-established forms of self-government, were far from serfs. Established inhabitants who paid a minimum of taxes to the landowner had the status of 'bourgeois'. Immigrants to the Ban could also achieve this distinction after a year of residency, provided they met the other qualifications. That the people were not destitute and that the area was attractive enough to draw immigrants is confirmed by demographic information. The number of inhabitants grew overall, though not without ups and downs caused especially by visits from the plague. In 1489, Steinthal had a total of 73 houses and 383 members of bourgeois families; by 1578 there were 164 dwellings with 860 bourgeois. As noted, despite more vicissitudes, in 1630 the registered inhabitants probably numbered about 1200.

Alsatian villages had long since proved sufficiently resilient and financially secure to establish a body of traditional rights. Following the practice found in many parts of Europe, a seigneur or lord, who was usually a noble but also could be a church institution or sometimes even a merchant, owned the land. But the peasants had the right to farm more or less as they wished on the terrain they occupied, to bequeath it, or to travel in search of other work. In Alsace by the seventeenth century, if not long before, the lord could usually demand no more than a token payment of cash or one animal each time peasants inherited land. Of course, there were more severe restrictions on the sale of land; if this happened at all, it was generally conducted on a large scale and solely by the seigneurs.

At the district or sometimes the village level, Alsatian adult male peasants elected a leader called the *Schultheiss*; this official served as both the representative of the area to the lord and as judge for local disputes. However, more complicated cases went immediately to a tribunal comprised of the seigneur's representatives. There was no police force, jail in the modern sense of the term, or bureaucracy at the disposal of the rulers in Steinthal. This was the situation virtually everywhere in early modern Europe. By today's standards, the villagers were undergoverned, and months or years might pass before they even saw anyone from the outside or from the seigneur's family who might wield authority over them.

Ban de la Roche changed hands several times in the Middle Ages and the early modern period, passing by purchase from one seigneur to another. But whoever the local ruler was, he bore responsibility for security and the administration of law. The district was part of the Holy Roman Empire, that loosely organized hotchpotch of large and small political units, most of which had certain rights to autonomy. As a responsible figure in what is usually called the feudal system, the seigneur owed allegiance to the Holy Roman Emperor. This fact was important in wartime, when local lords were expected to contribute men and money to the army. But usually the only practical effect of owing fealty to the Emperor was that in special circumstances, when a point of law was contested and the dissatisfied party had enough money to hire a prominent lawyer, decisions of the local court could be appealed to imperial tribunals. This was a rare event for any part of the Empire; in Steinthal it was unknown. In short, the nine mountain villages comprised an almost wholly autonomous judicial district, from which there was effectively no appeal, and this legal position in a weak state with little tangible central authority played a large role in determining the course of the witch hunts. It was this kind of location on a border, or far from central authority possessing a strong, hierarchical judicial structure, that could make a real difference in allowing the hunts to go forward. The next chapter will clarify this point by examining the effect that higher or appeals courts could have in dampening witch persecutions.

If the people were left alone on a day-to-day basis and the lords were few, what kept the ordinary folk in order? Often the two sides reached the kind of compromise reflected in traditional Alsatian political arrangements. But at other times the most important factor in obtaining compliance was fear of retaliation from the upper classes for any serious resistance to their will. In 1525 a peasant war broke out in southern Germany and Alsace, especially Lower Alsace, the downriver and less elevated portion of the region. Sparked by poverty, fluctuations in prices, increasing debts and new demands on the peasants by the lords, Alsatian peasants rose in revolt and killed some seigneurs and their officials. Few actions of this type succeeded for long in Europe; the combined wealth, training, monopoly of effective weapons and of the most powerful contemporary factor in combat, the horse, usually brought peasant uprisings to a quick end. The German peasant war was no exception, and in six weeks the rebels had been crushed. Savage reprisals followed; troops of the Duke of Lorraine slaughtered some 12 000 people at Saverne in May 1525, and 6000–7000 more at Scherwiller several days later.[10] Summary trials held later in the year led to the execution of 600–800 peasants at Ensisheim, while financial exactions were levied on many villages.[11] It should be noted that, as in other pacification campaigns of the period, no charges of witchcraft were lodged against the peasants. In the minds of the elite, the problems of witchcraft and of rebellion were almost invariably separate issues.

Although the peasant war and its aftermath occurred close to Steinthal, they had little immediate impact in the mountains, where no fighting took place. Of course, the villagers would have been sensible to their likely fate if they ever tried to revolt against the social and political structure. This realization gave them another powerful incentive to show loyalty to their ruler, yet they must have considered the peasant war an event that concerned other people. In the Ban, the more remote setting and the less direct and onerous rule of the local lords, at the time the Rathsamhausen family, gave the peasants more autonomy in the first place.

This relative freedom was enhanced by a broader set of cultural influences than was normally found in European villages. During the sixteenth and seventeenth centuries, and for a long time after, Steinthal straddled the linguistic frontier between French and German. The names of the inhabitants then and now have come from both languages, and records of witch trials from the early seventeenth century may proceed for a few pages in one tongue, then switch for no apparent reason to the other.

Thus the area, if not each and every one of its inhabitants, was truly bilingual in the early modern period. But there is no indication that this border status by itself had anything to do with the arrival of the witch hunts in Steinthal. The fact that two languages were used there does not necessarily mean that somehow tension arose between those who spoke French and those who spoke German, and that this antagonism became expressed in witchcraft accusations. Rather, what seems important about the use of two languages is that it opened the region to cultural influences, including writings about witches and news of their trials, from two pools of sources.

After 1584, the Ban was also a Protestant region, one virtually surrounded by Catholic areas. That year a German nobleman, the Count Georg von Veldenz, purchased the Ban, with all its agricultural land, ore mines, timber and villages, from the previous owners, the Rathsamhausens. Veldenz's homeland was between Trier and Koblenz, where witch hunts had already reached a fever pitch. The family was Lutheran and, following the usage of the day, Veldenz simply informed his new subjects that henceforward they too would follow his faith. After a while a pastor arrived to replace the priest, and the old saints disappeared from the churches. The villagers could now read the Bible in the vernacular, but otherwise relatively little changed in their spiritual lives; they held weddings and funerals in the same churches they had used previously, and at home they continued to mix many old attitudes and practices with the formal religion brought to them from the outside.

Here, too, great care is necessary in discussing what the area's liminal religious status might have meant. Having changed their religion on orders from their seigneur, the Ban's inhabitants did not engage in a recorded witch trial until more than 20 years had passed. And none of the surviving documents indicate that members of one religion harassed adherents of the other under the cover of witchcraft charges, or for that matter on any other pretext. On the contrary, residents of the Ban, all good Lutherans, accused each other.

Although Steinthal is usually described as isolated, in fact it was hardly insulated from major economic or cultural activity in the late medieval and early modern periods. To begin with, the region lay adjacent to the road from Strasbourg to Lorraine. This route, which followed the valley of the Bruche River and thus skirted Ban de la Roche, constituted the major passage through the mountains between the Rhine, with its fertile plains and foothills, and the towns and villages lying on the western side of the Vosges. Merchants, soldiers, nobles of the ruling families and their servitors, priests and later pastors, musicians, tinkers and others were only some of the types who passed through the Ban or at least travelled along its edge. After about 1525, mining activity in the mountains attracted both unskilled workers and those technically skilled.

Literacy was surely not widespread among the people, but neither was it unknown. In 1598 the bourgeois of Steinthal produced a 'sermon' to their current lord, 'Count Georg Gustav de Veldenz', written in decent French. In the document they renewed their pledge of loyalty to him, in return for protection of their 'ancient rights and customs'.[12] From the migrants and visitors to the region, as well as from the preaching they heard and the books they read, the people of Ban de la Roche must have heard a great deal about witchcraft. And, of course, their lord was already attuned to the possibility that the devil was active on earth.

Attention to witches in the region was all the more likely considering that Strasbourg was a centre of speaking and publishing about them. The *Malleus Maleficarum*, mentioned earlier, was printed in the city in 1487. Another important work on witches and their acts appeared in Strasbourg in separate editions in 1510 and 1511; this was Ulrich Tenngler's *Neuer Layenspiegel* (New Mirror for Lay Persons). It drew heavily on the *Malleus* but went beyond it to discuss the presence of dragons, gryphons, witches, sorcerers and so on in the world. Tenngler, himself a German judge, succeeded in his aim of providing a handbook for officials; it is possible that for the conduct of witch trials, the *Layenspiegel* had greater importance than its more notorious predecessor. At least 13 editions of Tenngler's book were printed in various cities by 1560, and it was widely kept in libraries of town administrations.[13]

In roughly the same period, Strasbourg also became a site of sermons on witches. During the late fifteenth and early sixteenth centuries, Simon Brandt and Johan Geiler von Kaysersberg, for example, spoke regularly in the city on the dangers of *maleficia* and pacts with the devil. Geiler warned that those who practised sorcery and 'weather making' would end up on Judgement Day in live coals in a lion's mouth. He was also deeply anti-Semitic and regularly mentioned Jews and witches in the same denunciations.[14] A book of his collected sermons, called *Die Emeis* (The Ants), was published in Strasbourg in 1516 and again in 1517. These sermons referred to witches and other women who joined the Furious Horde to march out at night around Christmas. Several woodcuts appeared in the book, including one of witches in which three women offer pots of malevolent brew to the sky while a demonic figure urges them on from a perch in a tree.[15]

Visual arts produced or displayed around Strasbourg in the high Middle Ages and early modern period often depicted the devil and his henchmen or other enemies within society. Witches do not appear in the *Isenheim Altarpiece*, created around 1512–16 by Matthias Grünewald for a hospital south of the city, but demons play a large role indeed in the magnificent work. The *Altarpiece* shares several characteristics with other northern European art of the same period: it leaves in doubt the contest between even the most saintly humans and the devil, demons are depicted as highly threatening, and Jews or their culture are associated with excrement.[16] The many patients at the hospital and a large number of other visitors would have seen Grünewald's work.[17]

However, both publications on witches and hunts for them declined in number in many parts of western Europe by the 1520s, only to resume with greater strength by the 1570s–1580s. Indicative of this second wave of publishing was Johann Fischart's *Vom Aussgelasnen Wuetigen Teuffelsheer* (On the Unleashed Furious Devil's Horde), first issued in Strasbourg. One edition appeared in 1581, another in 1586. This book was a translation into German, with a commentary, of Jean Bodin's *De la démonomanie des sorciers* (On the demonomania of sorcerers), which itself appeared in many editions beginning in 1580.

Bodin's manual became one of the most widely known works of all on witchcraft. To the author, witchcraft was such a grave matter that a judge should use 'all means that he could imagine to drag out the truth'.[18] Writing a few years later, men like Henri Boguet and Pierre de Lancre cited Bodin approvingly. Boguet's book was published in Strasbourg in 1602; there were several later editions.[19] The city's printers issued another major work on witches, by Martin del Rio, in 1611. De Lancre's vividly illustrated contribution to the subject appeared in Strasbourg in 1612; it was later reissued numerous times in various cities.[20]

Probably the most important work of this type in contributing to Alsatian witch hunts was Nicholas Rémy's *Demonolatry*. Like Boguet and De Lancre, Rémy was a jurist; eventually he rose to become prosecutor-general of Lorraine, then part of the Holy Roman Empire, in large part because of his previous services in trying witches.[21] Rémy claimed to know of more than 900 'capital trials' of witches in Lorraine in the 15 years prior to the appearance of his book in 1595. Although he added little to the existing stock of lore about the devil and his minions on earth, the wealth of detail, the vividness of his writing and the sheer number of cases Rémy discussed must have contributed to the popularity of his book, which was widely reprinted and cited in other works. From the court records he drew 'actual facts, not a visionary dream'. Moreover, like the author of the *Malleus*, Rémy supported his claims about witchcraft's ubiquity and durability by citing many old legends and remarks of ancient writers, from Homer to Apuleius.[22]

Thus by the early seventeenth century, Ban de la Roche was ringed by printed and visual suggestions that warned of hideous enemies at large in the world. Such images would have been brought to the Ban by the wanderers and immigrants who arrived there. The Rhine, at most two days' journey away, was a major information highway of its day, carrying people, goods, books and tales from Switzerland to the North Sea and back. Some local residents would have been able to read the witch hunters' manuals and to relate their contents to neighbours.

Another major factor in heightening a sense of the witch danger among the mountain villages was the ever-closer approach of other witch trials. Nearby prosecutions occurred, for example, in Geneva in 1545 and 1568–69; in Ensisheim 1551–1622; in Thann 1572–1620;[23] in Basel 1570; and in Molsheim, probably in 1575 and certainly in the 1590s, with another round in 1619–20.[24] St Dié, not far away in Lorraine and lying directly on the road through the mountains, witnessed numerous trials in 1593–94 and again in 1618.[25] As noted, most of Rémy's cases are from Lorraine. It appears that news of witches travelled through knowledge of other trials, as the same names for the devil are used in Boguet's and Rémy's books, in witch prosecutions in Lorraine, and in Ban de la Roche.[26] The devil was also depicted similarly, as a terrible cheat and miser who gave money to anyone he ensnared, only to have the coins turn to leaves or dung when the dupe returned home. Not just any such material would serve, however; in each instance oak leaves and horse dung predominated.

Perhaps the usual question about why witch persecutions arose should be reversed: how could Ban de la Roche have escaped witch trials in such a context? Despite the occasional sceptical voice, images of the devil or his sworn followers at work and news of their disgusting and harmful acts reached the villages of Steinthal from every side and in multiple realms of culture. After about 1570 a steady transmission of fear to the region took place, just as it did among the elite for the first large Scottish witch hunt. Southwestern Germany, only a few days' travel away, supplied news of 20 towns holding trials in 1616 alone, and of 31 separate regions 'seized by the panic' in 1629.[27] In the Vosges, witch fear touched elite and common people alike.

This background helps explain why the charge of witchcraft appeared on a remarkable scale in Ban de la Roche. Available records show that at least 174 people were accused of witchcraft in the villages between 1607 and 1630; a minimum of 83 of those were executed. This is a high toll given the area's population of perhaps 1200 in 1630. Close to 15 per cent of the entire population were accused of witchcraft, while 7 per cent were put to death on that charge. These figures suggest that it would be wrong to speak of an attack in the Ban on women or deviants in the form of a witch hunt; the violence was too broad and inclusive to permit that conclusion. But it was also too erratic and concentrated when it did strike, as we shall see.

A close look at the gender distribution of victims in Steinthal also points to the likelihood that something other than a campaign against women occurred. Altogether 114 females, or 66 per cent of the total, were accused of witchcraft between 1607 and 1630. However, men comprised 39 per cent of those convicted, a proportion that does not suggest an overwhelming preference for killing women (there is only one mention of an exiled witch). The hunts in Ban de la Roche took place, as they did in many other areas, in several waves. During one of these (1621–22), it is especially doubtful that females were singled out. In those two years, 21 males and 27 females, or 44 and 56 per cent respectively, were convicted of witchcraft. At this ratio the persecutions cannot be characterized as a campaign against women; the percentage of men is simply too high. Finally, testimonies extracted under torture often mentioned local women *and* men as attending witches' sabbats.[28] The interrogators did not guide their prisoners to name only women, which would have been logical if the goal had been repression of females.

The Steinthal persecutions also do not lend much support to the argument that witch trials functioned or were intended to clarify social boundaries. One executed man's estate was estimated at 372 florins. He owned four oxen, ten 'big and small steers', five milk cows, two calves, two pigs and five horses. A married couple both burned for witchcraft left an estate of over 2200 florins. These families were well off by the standards of the day. But the documents list a range of property left behind, down to nothing at all. Occasionally occupations or social designations are mentioned, among them charcoal burners and carters but also farriers, weavers and even one *Schultheiss*. To remove a village's farrier, who usually doubled as blacksmith, was no light matter. Victims of the hunts in Ban de la Roche sometimes left behind small children, which likewise suggests that the persecutions did not settle social issues but instead caused social disruption.

Thus there is really no pattern of victims in Steinthal according to position in society. Only a few simple observations about who was tried can be offered: first, all the defendants and those accused but apparently never formally judged were more or less ordinary villagers; that is, they were not newcomers to the region, were not limited to the poorest strata and were not of an alien religion. However, they were not from the clergy, let alone from the ruling Veldenz family. We must speak instead of a fairly broad cross-section of the village population.

The first witch trial in the Ban, held in 1607, involved charges of illicit sex, petty theft and possession of a 'little book', apparently of spells, while the devil figures in the case only peripherally. The defendant was a man, Christman Dietrich, accused by several of his neighbours of a range of crimes. In sworn testimony, four men said that Dietrich had committed adultery with the wife of another man. Dietrich had also supposedly given the little book to a cuckolded husband. Dietrich denied the charges and responded in kind, saying that one of his accusers had been stealing and selling wandering livestock he caught in the forest. Other men came forward with more stories of Dietrich's sexual activity with married women. Apparently he had had one lover, called only Mansiat in the sources, for 18 or 19 years. The disjointed record also mentions a man thrown from his horse through magic, although Dietrich is not identified as the culprit.

The devil enters this tale of what appears to be mostly ordinary sin and petty crime midway through the testimony, when one of Mansiat's neighbours reported that once she had come into his house and complained that her husband had beaten her. Mansiat allegedly said that she 'did not want to have God' and that she had called on the devil for help. According to other testimony, she had 'given herself' to the devil in the hope that he would help her flee from her husband, had taken and sold a towel she was supposed to deliver to someone else, and had wished that Dietrich's house would burn down.

Unfortunately, the documents do not say what happened to any of the villagers involved in this tangled story.[29] Overall, the affair gives the impression that mundane quarrels and tensions among neighbours, especially over Dietrich's history of sexual misconduct, eventually gave rise to charges of witchcraft. But there were no accusations of especially heinous crimes or serious incidents, the sort that surface in records from the Ban a few years later. Finally, the jumbled account of this first witchcraft case in the area does not provide any indication that the accused were coerced into giving testimony. What the 1607 trial did accomplish was to establish the idea that the devil visited Steinthal; in the right circumstances he might be able to entrap other villagers. It seems highly likely that this notion was imported from the surrounding culture and from nearby witch trials.

The next indication of witchcraft in the Ban is not dated, but its position among the documents puts it in 1620 or 1621. Now the charges became much more serious. The defendant was Georgette, wife of Jehan Le Neuf, bourgeois of Rote (Rothau). Accused of sorcery, Georgette supposedly gave testimony 'freely and voluntarily' at her examination; whether she feared torture if she did not confess is unclear. At any rate, by now this woman, at least, had absorbed all the standard elements of the witch stereotype. She lost no time getting to the heart of the matter; 12 years after she came to Rothau, she had been out gathering wood when the devil appeared to her in the form of a man with horned feet and hands. She had sex with him, and because she was poor he gave her a coin. But when she returned home the money turned out to be horse dung.

Although the Steinthal records do not expressly say so, documents from other areas, as well as various witch hunters' manuals, affirm the contemporary view that once a person had intercourse with the devil or a lesser demon, the pact with the evil one was sealed. The new witch could not ordinarily break free from her fateful relationship with her master and lover. Only the help of a saintly intercessor sometimes ended the infernal obligation.

This did not happen to Georgette. The devil returned to her for sex several times, once in the form of a gentleman. It is likely that the woman may have been interjecting some of her personal fantasies here, as demons rarely appeared in this guise, and he came in this way to Georgette only once. As her relationship with the devil went on, she said, he made her promise not to invoke the name of God or to go to church. He gave her a sign of her status as his servant by pinching her on the forehead, apparently leaving a permanent mark, which must have impressed the judges as an indication that she told the truth. In return, the devil promised not to forsake her for her whole life. Her master's name was Piercin, variants of which appear in trial records from other locations. Piercin then assigned her to another demon lover, Joly (from the French *joli*, pretty or handsome).

At first Georgette received minor tasks to fulfil; for example, on several occasions she had to keep the sacramental church wafer in her mouth and not eat it. Then she delivered the wafers to Joly. Georgette does not say what he did with them. Her demon transported her to a sabbat held on the lands of a 'Count Rhingraffe', presumably the elector of the Palatinate. Georgette recalled – this point is written in the margin of the text, which suggests that it may have been added in response to a leading question – that 'Nicolle, widow of Musler, and others whom it is not necessary to mention' were also there. All who attended the sabbat ate black flesh (of what is not stated) and black rice 'cooked and also boiled with black milk'. After dinner they danced to the tone of a horn and fornicated. Then they prepared a 'venomous grease' and each took some away, she in a black bottle supplied by Piercin.

Soon she used this unguent to kill a neighbour's pig. Twelve years later she rubbed the grease on a loaf of bread, with which she tapped two bulls belonging to another man; they, of course, died. Then she advanced to the murder of a man, using the same material. About eight years later she poisoned five piglets but for some unexplained reason cured one with a different grease; where that came from she did not say. After another four years went by, she blinded a girl in one eye by touching her with a finger dipped into the venomous mixture. Thus at least 24 years had elapsed between Georgette's first meeting with the devil and this incident. One can see the strong memories of the peasants at work and understand something of the grave significance that the death of two bulls or even four piglets would have for a rural family.

But Georgette's confession grows worse. With Piercin, she told her interrogators, she entered the house of Philipe Mareschal and removed an infant that had not been baptized. The witches and their mentors had the custom of dividing such babies into four pieces and eating one, mixing the rest with 'spiders and yellow venomous beasts' to make a deadly grease. They disinterred buried infants, even a baptized one, for this purpose. Georgette provided the year of excavation and the name of one such child.

All of these details – exactly four dead piglets, and one saved – with the approximate dates of human deaths and the girl's blindness, which her neighbours would have remembered, provided a framework for the confession that must have given it some ring of truth. Wouldn't the judges and the neighbours have nodded their heads at such words, finding in them an explanation of various misfortunes over a long span of years? At least, the villagers would probably have reacted in that manner as long as the witch hunts did not claim too many victims (but that is a subject for the next chapter).

With the talk of murdered or disinterred infants, Georgette's confession abruptly ends. The documents say no more about her, but it is difficult to believe that she escaped execution. In her story we encounter the full-blown, anti-human witch. She claimed to have had sexual intercourse with a creature who was part animal and pure evil and to have blinded and killed for him. She had committed the ultimate crime of murdering a baby and eating its flesh. This is the creature that the King James Bible had in mind in admonishing Christian society that 'Thou shalt not suffer a witch to live'.

After Georgette's tale, the other confessions from Ban de la Roche in the years 1621–22 and 1629–30, when the last wave of witch hunts swept over the area, seem almost ordinary. Claulin le grimp ('the climber') of Neuville was one of the male witches of the area. He received a female as his demon lover, but otherwise his story sounds much like Georgette's. He claimed to have killed animals and a man, though not babies, and he also received horse manure instead of money from his master. The interrogation record states that Claulin was not tortured, but in the end he was executed.

Sometimes the Steinthal witches flew to the sabbat, sometimes they rode on animals like a black dog or a male goat, and one travelled on a pitchfork. The assembled demons and witches ate cat or horse flesh. Several other men mentioned receiving female lovers; both male and female witches noted that intercourse with devils, often in a front to back position, was cold, 'like ice'. The demonic names Piercin and Joly or cognates thereof recur in the documents. Evil acts at the devil's bidding continued in several cases for decades, the accused said. They claimed that the devil beat them if they failed to carry out his orders. Sometimes they did fail, but often they reported success; stories of animals and babies done to death figure over and over in the transcripts.

The men who tried the cases of 1621–23 were headed by Monsieur Jehan Wilhelm Stam, a university graduate with a degree in law, who was 'councillor and commissar for criminal affairs of H[is] M[ajesty]', that is, of Count Veldenz. Other members of the tribunal were Monsieur Marmet, Minister of Rothau, and 'deputies of justice'.[30] Who the last men were is not specified, but at a nearby witch trial in 1620 the panel consisted of the seigneur's bailiff, a doctor of law, the *Schultheiss*, a notary and local bourgeois.[31] Marmet (or Marmett) again served on a Steinthal tribunal in 1629. Whatever the exact composition of these courts, it is clear that Veldenz took time, trouble and expense in the judicial procedure.

It was also necessary to pay the torturer/executioner, one Meister Bernhardt. The title of 'master' implies both that the man had a reputation for expertise in his field and that he could not be hired cheaply. In 1621–22 he received one florin for each session of torture, and 10 florins for burning someone after conviction. Thus when he 'hoisted' the daughter of Gutt Clauss six times, he billed the count for six florins. How anyone could have withstood even one session of this torture is difficult to imagine. Yet Catharina Ringelspach was 'put to the question' in 1629 as many as eight times.

Altogether, Meister Bernhardt's fee in 1621–22 came to 130 florins,[32] a considerable sum, but this probably represented money paid only for his activities, not his travel and maintenance expenses. More money had to be spent to cover the costs of other tribunal members. Thus it is highly unlikely that the witch trials in Ban de la Roche were a money-making proposition. One-tenth of all goods of convicted persons reverted to Veldenz as a fine, but too many of the defendants were poor to make judging them a profitable operation. The same was true in many other witch trials, for example those held in nearby Molsheim during the 1590s.[33] On the other hand, the do-it-yourself processes in Trier, in which village committees apparently attacked leading peasant families and sometimes exacted large sums from them as trial costs, for food and drink, and as fines, were profitable affairs,[34] at least in the short run. But this activity 'from below' was the exception in the witch hunts.

In considering what the witchcraft cases in Ban de la Roche were all about, their clustering must also be noted. The trials occurred in three sets: the single process of 1607 and then two large groups, one in 1620–22 and the other in 1629–30. This concentration of the prosecutions suggests that the trials had no function, as it is usually described, in the villages. Instead, a kind of panic must have descended upon the inhabitants and the officials, making them eager to find the alleged witches and eliminate them. Sometimes, as in Trier, this kind of fear combined with greed and social tension between villagers in an explosion of violence largely from below.

The Dutch theologian Cornelius Loos, teaching at the University of Trier in the 1590s, was appalled at the actions of the village committees and especially at the burning of Dr Dietrich Flade, a jurist and former rector of the university who confessed to witchcraft under torture in 1589. Flade, the highest-ranking European to be convicted of witchcraft, had served as a judge in witchcraft cases with some reluctance. Accused himself, perhaps because of his moderate stance, perhaps because of personal antipathy towards him on the part of other elite men in the city, Flade attempted to flee but was captured. Loos, teaching at the University of Trier in the 1580s and 1590s, then wrote a manuscript highly critical of the hunts; but before he could publish it, his work was seized by the archbishop of Trier and he was imprisoned. Eventually he had to apologize to a church congregation for his views. Yet his scathing criticism of the madness in Trier became well known. The persecutors, he wrote, had themselves become magicians, who with their 'new alchemy' had found ways to 'spin human blood into gold and silver'.[35]

Further waves of witch hunting swept through Trier in 1626–30 and, in a smaller phase, 1650–60. Extremely hard to control from above, the killing accomplished nothing positive; no purpose that might give some greater meaning to the deaths, even in terms of furthering an oppressive system or hatred of women, can be discovered.

THE WITCHES OF SALEM, MASSACHUSETTS

Between mid-June and late September of 1692, accusations of witchcraft cost the lives of 20 people in Salem; 19 were hanged as convicted witches while one, Giles Cory, was pressed to death under heavy stones. Cory had refused to enter a plea before the court, so the ancient English practice of *peine forte et dure* (strong and hard pain) was imposed upon him in an effort to make him speak. Over the course of two days, more and more stones were placed upon a board lying on his chest, but he would not plead before the judges. Altogether 185 people were accused of witchcraft during the Salem hunt, although only 59 were tried.

All-male juries found the condemned persons guilty of allying with the devil and harming individuals and the community as a whole. The witches, who were not outsiders but local residents and Puritans, had supposedly tormented many good citizens by appearing in spectral form – that is, as floating, perhaps translucent spirits separated from the witch's body – and choking, pulling, pricking and hitting them. Spectres could appear anywhere, even while the bodies they came from were awake and active in another place. Animals, adult humans and a number of babies had all supposedly died as a result of the defendants' actions. Witnesses brought up incidents that had occurred as long as 30 years earlier.

Almost as quickly as it began, the Salem affair ended. In October the governor of Massachusetts Colony, Sir William Phips, ordered the operations of the special Court of Oyer and Terminer, as it was called, to be temporarily suspended. Although the Court reopened the next January and condemned three more witches, they were never executed. One of the last major spasms of witch-killing in all Europe and North America was over.

Of the 19 convicted witches, five were males. Thus among those put to death at Salem, women comprised 70 per cent of the toll. Once again, the proportion approaches the 75–80 per cent proportion of female victims traditionally given for the witch hunts as a whole.

The events at Salem have been explained in recent decades in several different ways. One interpretation argues that the Puritans of the area found it convenient to remove social deviants by labelling them 'witches' and prosecuting them.[36] A second view is that the patriarchal, God- and devil-fearing Puritan society condemned deviant women as witches. Females whose legal situation as widows or daughters blocked men from receiving an inheritance, or who had demonstrated their contentiousness in quarrels or court cases, were especially likely to be identified in Salem as the devil's helpers, this second argument continues.[37] A third study maintains that the major source of witchcraft charges was a long-simmering dispute between people in Salem Town, which was fast becoming a commercial port, and Salem Village, a farming community nearby. The hostility between these two different economic communities worsened as people from both divided over a recently arrived minister, Samuel Parris,[38] who began to preach in Salem Village in late 1689.

Parris had tried his luck at business several times but had repeatedly failed. He was a bitter man who saw enemies in all who seemed to thwart his economic advancement. Probably because of his own sense of failure and conspiracies against him, he stressed that the colony and the village in particular were under attack by evil forces. By December 1689, Parris was regularly mentioning the devil and witches in his sermons, a common theme in contemporary Massachusetts churches. Given the broader difficulties of the colony at the time, surely many of his parishioners were receptive to the message.

A new study by Mary Beth Norton argues instead that the chief factor in bringing on the Salem hunts was panic about Indian attacks on the Maine frontier, imported into Massachusetts by several girls who were refugees from the northern fighting. A sense of near despair about the future of the colonies in Massachusetts and Maine was heightened by the suspicion that some Puritan leaders had engaged in treason with the Indians and their French allies. In Salem the traumatized populace was primed to listen to accusations from 'afflicted' teenaged girls.[39]

It may well be that problems of Indian attack, deviance, division and the situation of some women helped to precipitate the hunt. But none of the studies that emphasize such themes explain exactly how such fears or resentments towards one group or another were transformed into charges of witchcraft. Why was that accusation employed to attack the targets? It is much more important to emphasize the broader set of conditions that contributed to the killings in Salem; first among these were the streams of culture and fear that together helped produce witch hunts in Europe.

Massachusetts in 1692 was, after all, an outpost of Europe and its culture. The worst local disputes imaginable would simply not have led to a witch hunt in the colony if its leaders' outlook had not been shaped by events across the Atlantic. No European witch hunts, no Salem witch hunt, regardless of the Indian wars or what any Puritan ever said about a minister, a neighbour or the female sex. This connection should be obvious on the face of it, since the proceedings against the Salem witches already sound familiar to those who know something about trials in Europe. The timing of the Massachusetts persecution was also crucial; the hunt there occurred somewhat late in the history of all Western witch trials and would have been unthinkable even a decade or so after 1692; that is, if much more time had elapsed after the end of the vast majority of European persecutions, the weight of educated public opinion in New England would have turned much more solidly against putting alleged witches on trial in the first place. The argument made earlier about the spread of the witch stereotype applies as well to its end; criticisms of witch persecutions also emanated from the core area of the pyres and took some time to reach the periphery of Europe, which in the seventeenth century included Massachusetts as well as areas like Sweden. As it was, important figures in Boston and the surrounding region objected to aspects of the prosecutions almost from the moment they began (these last two points will be discussed further in the next chapter). And, as already noted, the Salem outbreak was virtually the last process against witches in North America.

Direct links existed between European and New England charges of witchcraft. Increase Mather, a leading minister, president of Harvard College, and one of the most influential men in the colony, had spent the years 1689–92 in London, and had just returned to Massachusetts as the outcry about witches was gaining strength. Increase and his son Cotton, almost equally well known and respected in New England, were keenly aware of a mass witch hunt that had occurred around Mora, Sweden, in 1668–76. Cotton Mather discussed the Swedish hunt with approval in his *Wonders of the Invisible World*, published in Boston in October 1692. He was convinced that in Sweden 'the **Devils**, by the help of **Witches**', had drawn 'hundreds' of children into an evil plot to harm their neighbours.[40] The Mathers must have known that the Swedish trials ended in the freeing of many prisoners, the result of scepticism brought to the scene by royal commissioners sent from Stockholm, but Cotton did not bother to convey that outcome to his readers.

Beyond the point that the European connection and example were crucial to the Salem persecutions, the trials there would not have taken place in normal political circumstances. Only a unique set of events, starting with the Glorious Revolution of 1688 in England, which displaced King James II and installed William and Mary in his place, allowed the Massachusetts witch hunt to proceed in the way and on the scale that it did. Before 1692, witchcraft cases in New England had usually involved only one or two defendants. Most accusations of witchcraft did not lead to a trial; those that did usually ended in acquittal. Juries were reluctant to convict for witchcraft in the first place. If the initial panels returned a guilty verdict, magistrates who took witch convictions on appeal often exercised their right to overturn the decision. Before 1692, there were 93 defendants altogether in witch cases in New England; only 16 of those were executed.[41] Moreover, there had been no death sentence for witchcraft in the region since 1663, except for a case in Boston in 1688 personally managed by Cotton Mather. Witch hunting, especially on a large scale, was decidedly not the norm in North America before the Salem hysteria struck. Therefore any assessment of the 1692 events must emphasize the exceptional circumstances that facilitated their outbreak.

Late the previous year what had 'begun as fearful curiosity was turning to sharp panic' among a group of Salem girls trying to forecast their own futures.[42] The girls began to assume odd postures, make strange noises, lie rigid in bed for many hours and so on. Within a few months adults were speaking of 'fits', and a local physician announced that he feared the 'Evil Hand' was at work.[43] Rumours of witchcraft began to circulate in the area. Adults questioned the girls closely about the causes of their affliction, soon termed possession by evil spirits. Finally, the girls named three women, Sarah Good, Sarah Osborne and a West Indian slave, Tituba. They were arrested at the end of February. Tituba quickly confessed and supplied a description of the devil as a tall man with white hair, dressed in black.[44] She escaped death, but Sarah Osborne died in May in the Boston jail; she and others who perished in the same way should in fairness be accounted victims of the hunt.

At this point Massachusetts had little in the way of a functioning government. After the Glorious Revolution, the previous governor had been ejected in a popular, bloodless demonstration. The new governor, Phips, virtually hand-picked in London for the post by Increase Mather, arrived in Boston in May. He brought with him a new charter for the colony.

Phips sailed into a situation in which the colonists, especially those around Salem, had grown increasingly nervous about the possibility of witches in their midst. The court system had come to a halt by 1692, so that in the early stages of the uproar about possession, the local authorities had no choice but to throw suspects in jail and await the new governor. Meanwhile, the girls had been busy denouncing people and had found a ready audience in their elders. By the time Phips arrived, the jails were overflowing. Tension among the residents of Salem must have reached a high pitch as they waited for trials to begin.

Phips, under the influence of Increase Mather and wishing to deal promptly with what by now was a great backlog of cases, appointed a special court to hear them; this was the Oyer and Terminer tribunal mentioned earlier. Its archaic name meant that it was to hear and determine cases. This panel, now created in Essex County, Massachusetts, was the re-creation of one in the county of Essex, England during an earlier political crisis, the English Civil War. Both of these courts operated outside the usual judicial structure, specialized in hunting witches, operated only for a short span of time, and quickly became discredited.

Members of the Massachusetts Oyer and Terminer Court were drawn from the governor's advisory council, and its chief justice was William Stoughton, the lieutenant-governor. Thus this body was already highly unusual in its assignment and composition.

Unlike the courts that had previously handled witchcraft cases in New England, it was supervised only by the governor, not by superior magistrates.

The period of the early 1690s was already one of 'extreme and pervasive anxiety in New England'. Besides the constitutional crisis and all its attendant uncertainty, the times were marked by wars and epidemics. It seemed to many people that there was a 'general movement of Divine Providence against the region'.[45] The situation of the whole colony was still perilous; it was perched, so the white inhabitants felt, on the edge of civilization. Beyond it lay savagery, which could unleash death from the forest at any time in the form of Indian attacks. Yet another war between the English and their Indian allies on one side and the French and their native partners on the other was under way, and Phips departed Massachusetts shortly after his arrival to personally direct the English military effort in Maine. The Court of Oyer and Terminer was left without higher supervision.

If the immediate zone of fighting had been pushed west and north from Salem, it was still not far away, and the village lay at the southern end of a region of marsh and woods open to attacks by the French and their allies. Norton is certainly correct in pointing to similar fighting in Maine as a strong factor in increasing general anxiety around Salem. A number of girls living in the village in 1692 had recently been orphaned during Indian forays in Maine; some had witnessed the slaughter of their families.

This fluid, dangerous situation added greatly to the tension over witchcraft charges in the village, and perhaps only such a context could have prepared the ground for a sympathetic response to the girls' claims in the first place. It was certainly unusual for adults, let alone a court, to give such credence to the testimony of children and adolescents. The new court began its work in Salem in early June, in the heart of the witch panic, and empanelled juries of respectable male residents. One such body promptly found Bridget

Bishop guilty; she was hanged on 10 June. A group of five convicted witches was hanged on 19 July. Six more were executed in mid-August. Giles Cory died under the stones on 19 September, and on 22 September eight more convicted men and women perished. The girls taunted one, Samuel Wardwell of Andover, as he choked on smoke from the hangman's pipe while trying to make a last statement. The devil was hindering Wardwell, the girls shouted. There seemed to be no limit to the humiliation they could produce.

In England and its colonies, torture as such was normally used only in cases of alleged treason. However, there are indications that 'neck and heels' binding was practised in Salem; this involved tying a person for long periods with the legs drawn up tightly beneath the chin.[46] Incarceration in a filthy hole of a jail for months, without adequate food, heat, or ventilation, might have broken many a strong person. But in Massachusetts the judiciary did not aim to force defendants to confess; as mentioned, those who did were not executed. Apparently the Puritans thought that a confessing witch might be redeemed and returned to the community. But for a God-fearing member of the faith, it was often too much mental anguish to confess to abhorrent deeds in order to save one's life. Surely God would punish those who lied by admitting to witchcraft, and the stigma of having acknowledged oneself a witch might never disappear.

The Salem jury returned guilty verdicts on the basis of testimony given by local residents, especially the afflicted girls. Pacts with the devil played a relatively minor role in the trials; witnesses instead referred repeatedly to *maleficia*, including physical harm and the killing of animals, adult persons and children. Fear of evil acts by witches was so great that a 4-year-old girl, Dorcas Good, daughter of an accused woman, was held in chains in Boston prison for nine months. She was never the same again. If she was not an unruly female when she went into jail, she was when she came out.

Plate 1 The devil presenting the demon pact to Theophilus. Illumination of c.1210 from the Psalter of Queen Ingeborg of Denmark in the Musée Condé, Chantilly. © 2005 TopFoto/Fortean Picture Library, UK.

Plate 2 Knights Templar: Jacques de Molay burned at the stake with Geoffrey de Charney, 14 March 1314. © 2005 TopFoto/Fortean Picture Library, UK.

Plate 3 Limbourg Brothers, Hell, from *Les Très Riches Heures du Duc de Berry*, *c.*1413. Musée Condé, Paris. The Ancient Art & Architecture Collection.

Plate 4 'The Four Witches' with a demon. Engraving by Albrecht Dürer, 1497. © 2005 TopFoto/Fortean Picture Library, UK.

Plate 5 Four English women hanged as witches – original caption begins 'many poor women imprisoned'. © Bettmann/Corbis.

Plate 6 'Witches' Sabbat' by Hans Baldung Grien, 1510. Note the pseudo-Hebrew letters on the witches' pot, once again making the link between various enemies of Christianity and humanity. © Bettmann/ Corbis.

Plate 7 Anonymous drawing of witches at work from Johann Geiler von Kaysersberg, *Die Emeis,* 1517. Cornell University Library.

Plate 8 Pieter Brueghel's *Dulle Griet (Mad Meg)*, (c.1515–69). (GIR325) Museum Mayer van der Berg, Antwerp, Belgium. The Bridgeman Arts Library, London/ Getty Images. Meg, powerful and unfeeling, has emerged from hell bearing her loot. Other women wait for a demon to scoop money to them from his behind.

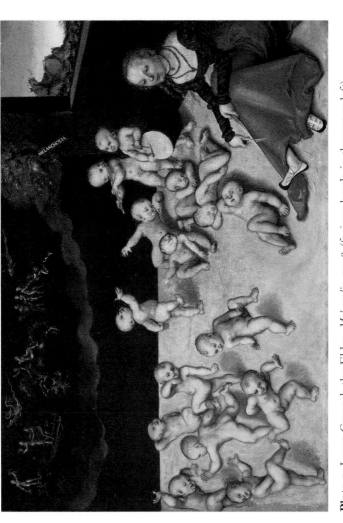

Plate 9 Lucas Cranach the Elder, *Melencolia*, 1528 (furious horde in the upper left). Columbus, Ohio Museum of Art. © Christie's images/Corbis.

Plate 10 A witch feeding her 'familiars' (imps). © 2004 TopFoto/Fortean Picture Library, UK.

Plate 11 Man being prepared for the strappado. © 2005 TopFoto/
Fortean Picture Library, UK.

Plate 12 The North Berwick coven, 1591: members drink in the cellar, one takes down the words of the devil preaching from the pulpit, others boil up a cauldron to create a storm and sink a ship at sea. The large figure of a man reclining in two places is surely meant to represent the Earl of Bothwell. © 2005 TopFoto/Fortean Picture Library, UK.

Plate 13 Frans Francken (II the Younger), *The Witches' Sabbath*, 1606, Victoria & Albert Museum. © Stapleton Collection/Corbis.

Plate 14 The witch house at Bamberg. © 2003 Charles Walker/ TopFoto.co.uk.

Plate 15 Artemis/Diana with her bow and arrow. The Furious Horde is no longer to be seen. From Tooke's *Pantheon*, 1659, p. 208. Mary Evans Picture Library, London.

Plate 16 The witches' sabbat. A typical image from the period of the hunts, although a bit late in their history. Note the ritual kiss of the devil's posterior, here depicted as a goat. From Gottlief Spisseln, *Die Gebrochne Macht der Finsternuss*, 1687. © TopFoto/Fortean Picture Library, UK.

Although the trials and executions continued, by October the dissidents had grown in number and influence, and they were able to persuade Phips to suspend the court's operations. The governor was certainly influenced in his decision by the fact that more than a few leading citizens of the colony had been accused of following the devil, including prominent merchants, military men and his own wife. The next chapter will return to the end of the Salem trials.

The scale of the events there places them in a category of their own among all New England witch persecutions. Why this happened may be summarized as follows: the political and military position of the colony was uncertain and tense in 1691–92. Already deeply troubled by that situation and by recent waves of disease, the inhabitants of Salem were unusually willing to listen to bizarre tales of witchcraft and possession from young girls, a source in which they would not have put great stock during calmer times. Increase and Cotton Mather, influenced by the recent mass witch hunt in Sweden, at first strongly promoted the Salem trials. Cotton interfered directly in the prosecutions, announcing that George Burroughs, a former minister in Salem who had been brought back from his residence in Maine to stand trial, was the chief conspirator behind the devil's plot to destroy the colony. Thus many currents set the stage and continued to provide a receptive atmosphere for the girls' claims of possession and for the adults' reaction to them.

It is possible to categorize some of the Salem victims in certain ways: several of them were highly quarrelsome and had frequently taken their neighbours to court. Some of those hanged were involved in a long and complex dispute between two prominent families. A number of the executed women had inherited or stood to inherit considerable property, keeping it out of the hands of men. But it seems odd to suggest that such factors, which have been common in human affairs in many places, found expression in the particular form of witchcraft accusations. Moreover, those charges found a ready response for less than ten months. Besides the fact that no direct link between these social frictions and the charges has been discovered, it was not Puritan practice, or typical of English jurisprudence in general, to use the courts to take lives in this way.

Functional arguments ignore the European background of the Massachusetts hunt. They imply, but never make the case clear, that colonial leaders, judges, juries and witnesses all participated in a plot to destroy inconvenient neighbours, then for unexplained reasons changed their minds after six months and twenty killings.

It is only possible to write about the Salem witch hunt as a purge of undesirables if little attention is paid to the central concern of the colony's ministers and judges during the trials – evidence of witchcraft. Finally, if we remove any of the truly major factors in the picture – Reverend Parris, the Mathers, the political and legal hiatus as the suspicion of witchcraft grew, the anxiety related to war and epidemics, or the European connection – it seems unlikely that a mass hunt would have developed in Salem.

DEVIANCE, CRIME AND WITCHES

Neither the trials of 1621–30 in Ban de la Roche or the Massachusetts cases of 1692 suggest that male officials suddenly found it necessary to liquidate women or deviants in order to discourage others from behaving similarly. Of course misogyny existed in both places; it had been promoted throughout the regions' culture for many centuries. But males' antipathy towards females did not lead to a sustained, comprehensive campaign against them under the guise of witchcraft charges or, for that matter, any other accusation. Many cultural and legal mechanisms dedicated to that task were in place already. If anything, trials of witches should be seen as the breakdown of regular social control, not expressions of it.

It is necessary for our purposes to try to distinguish between 'deviance', as sociologists use the term, and more serious problems that will be called 'crime'. 'Deviance' refers to any kind of behaviour that does not conform to prevailing social standards. Various dances and forms of dress, for example, have been deemed lewd and unacceptable by many societies and have been designated as crimes. Crime is always deviance by this definition, in that it is socially unacceptable conduct. But, for the sake of clarity, 'deviance' here indicates those social offences that are not directly harmful to other human beings or their property. Of course, dancing or dressing in the wrong way has often been considered injurious to community standards, or, more precisely, to community solidarity. Ruptures in that solidarity can be dangerous indeed, as peasants have often felt around the world. Nevertheless, deviance is socially situated and determined; as long as you cover a minimal area of breasts and genitalia, you can now wear virtually anything you please on the streets of New York, London and many another place. In Saudi Arabia, you will need more coverage to avoid arrest.

Many sanctions for deviance existed in early modern Europe and North America, ones which usually made clear the type of infringement involved. For example, quarrelsome women in parts of Germany were made to wear large, uncomfortable wooden 'neck violins' in public for a day, while drunkards might be made to walk about wearing a huge barrel symbolizing their transgression.[47] Peasants usually quickly brought serious misfits back into line through community pressure, including mockery and beatings, as the case of Martin Guerre shows. It is true that villagers frequently appeared afraid to discipline witches, fearing their powers, but it is also clear that when witches went on trial, it was not merely for possessing those powers but for using them in the cause of evil.

Witchcraft, as everyone knew at the time, was a matter far more serious than deviance. Allying with the devil and following his orders involved committing heinous crimes which caused tangible harm to property, crops, animals and humans. The alleged ceremonies that marked adherence to Satan's cause were taken seriously by officials, but the real problem was the results of making a pact with him. The difference between wild dancing and killing a cow or a child was obvious to all. During periods of extreme tension about witches, when a hysterical atmosphere gripped entire communities, the belief that a follower of the devil made beer or butter go bad – which represented serious dietary or economic loss for peasants – may have been enough to lead to the charge of witchcraft, but for the most part the sources speak of grievous injury inflicted by the accused. While improper dancing, drinking and so forth might be an indication that a person was more open than others to the devil's snares, wrong day-to-day behaviour by itself does not appear in the sources as grounds for conviction on the charge of witchcraft. Even sexual misbehaviour, including adultery and the birth of illegitimate children, did not serve in this way.

When deviant conduct was mentioned during witch proceedings in Ban de la Roche or Salem, it was to establish the general reputation of an accused person clearly being questioned above all about specific actions with physically harmful consequences. In short, the issue central to witchcraft cases was not deviance but 'the constant core of crimes', offences that 'are criminal almost everywhere'.[48] Actions like murder, theft or rape committed against free citizens are punishable crimes in virtually every known society.

Of course, removing a person who is considered a dangerous criminal from any society will reduce tension and make the remaining respectable people feel better. In this sense suppressing crime is functional. However, this is the same as saying that if I pull a thorn out of my finger, I have performed a useful function for myself. The sociological/anthropological approach to functionality mystifies why people were prosecuted as witches by suggesting that they were deviants. In the trials, reputation alone served only as a general consideration or an indication of connection to a deed. The courts then weighed charges of serious crimes.

Prominent contemporary authors of treatises on witches referred to deviance but linked it to perceptible harm, their major concern. It is horror at the witch conspiracy to destroy human morality and society that emerges so clearly in the work of Henri Boguet (1602), for example.[49] His book is much less misogynist and mentions men as witches much more than does the *Malleus Maleficarum*. Boguet's attention is fixed much more on crime than on gender. In *Memorable Providences* (1688) and in *Wonders of the Invisible World*, published during the Salem trials, Cotton Mather repeatedly refers, following and citing the court hearings themselves (which are no longer extant), to the harmful actions of witches. Along the way, he has almost nothing to say that would suggest women were more inclined to commit diabolical evil than men were.

When a society became primed to fear the immediate presence of witches, suspicion did fall much more frequently on women than on men. This inclination resulted in part from the general prejudices of the patriarchal society against women. Females were accounted more mysterious than men, and possibly more closely tied to the supernatural, owing to their ability to transform substances: semen into babies, raw food into cooked dishes, dirty laundry into clean clothes. In Baden-Baden, near the epicentre of the German hunts, almost half of all women charged with witchcraft had something to do with food preparation: they were innkeepers, bakers, butchers and food merchants. So were the men accused in the duchy; probably both sexes suffered in this instance because of their purported opportunities to cause harm through poisoning food.[50] This picture diverges, of course, from the usual one of peasants accusing each other, but it does indicate the deep suspiciousness about *maleficia* that could surface in a small community.

In all likelihood women's usual 'social position and power', not gender per se, put them more at risk than men for the accusation of witchcraft. Women were the 'co-ordinating element in village society . . . it was their curse which was most feared'.[51] Women's specialized occupations and social roles, including midwifery and service as 'lying-in maids' who assisted new mothers,[52] put them in close contact with infants susceptible to illness and death. Lyndal Roper points out that, 'as the ones who gave birth, women had access to a treasure trove of potentially magical [in contemporary lore] bodily substances: cauls, dead infants, navel-cords, afterbirth. The division of labour in sixteenth-century Germany assigned the most intimate work of care for the body to women' in connection with birth, mourning and preparing the bodies of the dead for burial.[53] Women took care of livestock around the house as men went to work in the fields or other activities at a distance. Thus females were more likely to be near the scene of animal or human deaths that could not be explained at the time other than by reference to supernatural forces. However much gender may be socially constructed, it should be considered separately from what women actually did in a society.

In recent studies, the picture of the typical witch as an old woman has been questioned. Of all prisoners held on the charge of witchcraft in Thuringia, a much larger jurisdiction of central Germany in the early modern period than today's state of the same name, 87 per cent were female. But they were not necessarily old, poor, or marginalized; the most common type among them was a married woman between the ages of 20 and 50.[54] At Trier, two married women, one aged 26 or 27 and the other 36, were accused.[55] In the area around Mainz, 55.84 per cent of known female victims were married, while only 6.85 per cent were widows.[56] For the Catholic prince-bishopric of Würzburg, one of the deadliest regions of the hunts, 1200 or more executions took place, perhaps 900 of them between 1625 and 1630. Of the victims, the ages of only 255 are known. Subtracting the 55 men, we know that 140 women were over the age of 40 and 112 were more than 50 years old.[57] But between 1627 and 1629, 17 children under the age of 15 were also burned.[58] A study of Alsace, which overlooked the trials in Ban de la Roche, found that two-thirds of the females accused were married, one-quarter were widows, and one-ninth were single. Seventy per cent of those whose ages are recorded were between 30 and 45.[59] In general, it appears that 'while middle-aged and older women were over-represented amongst witchcraft suspects, females and males of all ages were vulnerable to witchcraft accusations'.[60]

One of the difficulties in deciding who were the female targets lies in determining who was 'old'. When life expectancy was 40 or less, especially for women, who died so often in childbirth or from infections following it, 50 was obviously a somewhat rare age. But it does not follow that women were widely considered repulsive or dangerous creatures simply because they had attained a certain age. They could still be productive members of a community. Social roles and occupations, in the regions where witch fear took hold for other reasons, seem more important in determining the fate of female victims.

BURNING MEN

Some areas of Europe, for example Russia, Iceland and Normandy, do not fit the standard gendered model of the witch persecutions to begin with. In these places men outnumbered women among victims.[61] Of the 161 persons tried in Russia for witchcraft between 1622 and 1700, just over two-thirds were male. Perhaps more Russian cases lie undiscovered in the archives, but judging by the several sets of evidence found so far, the gender balance in the country's witch prosecutions will probably not be revised. Why were Russian men more liable than women to the charge? The country's men commonly blamed their physical troubles on other males, not on the vicious and insatiable women of the Western tradition. Apparently only men attempted to heal impotence in Russia, and so may have opened themselves to charges of black magic instead of the helpful white variety. The argument has also been made that women were more tightly tied to their communities in Russia by serfdom and the high degree of centralization of the regime; perhaps this hampered their ability to attempt magic of any sort.[62] However, village women elsewhere, for example in Scotland, were also bound to their communities, yet charges of witchcraft arose against them. A better explanation is the almost complete absence of the witch stereotype in Russia, which denied the sexual motifs that purported to explain women's fondness for the devil a large role there.[63]

Another male majority case was the Salzburg 'Zauberer-Jackl-Prozess', or sorcerer-Jake-trial, so called because the ringleader of the gang of thieves around whom the episode revolved was named Jacob. Dragging on from 1675 to 1690, the affair counted 198 people tried for crimes such as theft, harming adults and animals, flying, making pacts with the devil and ritual child murder; 138 were convicted and executed, and several died during investigation or were exiled. Only 36 of those executed were females; they ranged in age from 11 to 80. Of the 102 executed males, 77 were under age 21; 56 of those were between the ages of 9 and 16.[64] Austria, too, as mentioned, was relatively free of the witch stereotype in actual trials, as opposed to the relevant law codes; it is indicative in this regard that the Salzburg affair was called a *Zauberer* trial, not a *Hexenprozess*. The Jackl episode further illustrates the point that gender usually figured less the longer any hunt went on; at the height of a mass persecution, on the order of 20 or more accusations, virtually any-one of either sex or any social standing was open to the charge of conspiracy with the devil. Austria again departs from the norm in the case of Kärnten, in the Alps. More men were accused of witch-craft than women there except for short periods in 1590–99 and after 1730, when the number of victims tailed off greatly.[65]

In Normandy during the second half of the sixteenth century, men formed a sizeable majority among accused witches (who were in fact charged with compacting with the devil), and males were almost exclusively the defendants in the province after 1625. About three-quarters of the 380 known accused were men. The typical witch in Normandy was a male, either a teenager or an old man, who worked as a shepherd. Those who had any kind of writing with spells on it, or who took sacramental wafers from a church, usually in the hope of curing a sick animal with them, were almost certain to be convicted. The relevant Parlement, at Rouen, took witchcraft especially seriously precisely because so many of those charged were men, William Monter argues. He also notes that the gender imbalance among defendants made it difficult to emphasize the sabbat in trials;[66] the usual sexual geometry did not make as much sense as it did when women were involved.

Adult women were also not the focus of several other large hunts. Towards the end of the seventeenth century, more trials were held in which children played prominent roles as accused and accusers, for reasons we may only guess at. It may be that as persecutions became more unusual, it took a higher level of panic to ignite them in the first place. A fear that Satan was attacking the heart of a community by using its children in some fashion could have induced particular anxiety, enough to lead to trials in settings that ordinarily did not feature them. Certainly in Salem children had centre stage, and charges of witchcraft spread far and high in society.[67]

In the willingness to try children or to accept their testimony to convict anyone of witchcraft, it is difficult to see any anthropological or social function. Raw fear must have been the key. Ban de la Roche and Salem underwent no noticeable changes in form of administration, level of cultural or political pressure to conform, or criminal statutes during or following the witch hunts there.

If the persecutions had the function of state-building or legitimization, it should have been carried out in a systematic fashion in a given locale. Obviously that did not happen in either of the case studies presented here. On the contrary, the Salem story indicates that the hunt there erupted when the state apparatus was weak; the English Revolution of 1688 had disrupted the regular administration and court system. The same is true of the hunts of 1645 in England itself, which proceeded locally at a time when the Civil War had greatly disrupted central authority and the normal procedures of justice.

Much of the recent scholarship that emphasizes function in the persecutions centres on Germany, particularly for the region of the Saar and the electorate of Trier. 'Electorate' in German history refers to a territory ruled by a prince (in Trier and several other places a prince-bishop) who voted in elections of the Holy Roman Emperor. The struggle over legal jurisdiction in this part of the Empire was especially convoluted because rights overlapped, borders were unclear, and Catholics, Calvinists and Lutherans lived next to each other. One argument maintains that the Catholic prince-electors (Kurfürsten) of Trier used death sentences for witchcraft in the period 1590–1630 to demonstrate their authority and discipline their subjects. The main goal was to present princely authority as the correct, legitimate office for dealing with any violation of religious or social norms.[68] Witch hunts in Trier served to express and strengthen the rulers' interests. Rita Voltmer, the leading scholar taking this position, finds that the hunts led to the 'instrumentalization' of a new legal order. But this awkward word can refer only to the end and aftermath of witch hunts, not to their internal dynamics or original purposes. In Luxemburg and Trier the persecutions may have paved the way for a 'modernizing' and 'bureaucratizing' process,[69] but that was clearly a reaction to the great disorder and even contempt for established judicial authority that characterized the hunts in those areas. Voltmer also refers to the 'terrible social and economic consequences of the massive witch persecution' in Trier.[70] It is difficult to see a coherent political goal in the hunts conducted in the imperial abbey of St Maximin, part of the electorate located just outside the city walls; some 500 victims perished, of a population that averaged about 2200. If we really wish to speak of bureaucratization in this slaughter, it would be the bureaucracy from hell.

As Catholic officials acted to further witch prosecutions after 1623, they were proceeding against the wishes and attitudes of the papacy. In that year, the papal investigator Giulio Monterenzi wrote an instruction to inquisitors that reflected his own experiences with trials since 1593. Although the document is standard for the period in maintaining that *maleficia*, compacting with the devil, flight by witches and the sabbat were possible, it was also highly sceptical about finding practical proof for any of those acts. Monterenzi, then a consultant for the Suprema, the highest office of the Roman Inquisition, had been instrumental as early as 1596 in bringing a trial to an end. He and other papal investigators who looked at the case, in Bitonto, Italy, concluded that testimony about the sabbat from accused witches was not worthy of belief. Monterenzi's instruction of 1623 was dispersed widely within the Church by 1628 at the latest, and other documents of the same type were also sent to inquisitors.[71]

In 1636 Cardinal Francesco Albizzi travelled through Germany on a diplomatic mission to Cologne. Ten years later, he commented on the 'horrid spectacle' outside the towns and villages of 'innumerable stakes on which are fastened the poor and altogether unfortunate women who are carried away as witches by the flames'.[72] The villages of Ruwer and Eitelsbach were virtually emptied of inhabitants during the hunts of the 1580s and 1590s. In Ruwer, with 37 households, 32 women and 15 men were burned; eight people fled; and 42 other people were at least charged with witchcraft.[73] Such destruction of the local economy and human life was utterly dysfunctional.

The consequences or reaction to a profoundly disruptive set of events are not at all the same as the motivation for them. Recent studies of the witch hunts often find that they were pushed from below, by the peasants in particular, but with the agreement – or sometimes the helplessness – of the authorities. Where conditions above and below in society were conducive to the spread of witch fear, prosecutions could result. By contrast, in the villages under the jurisdiction of the imperial city of Rothenburg during the sixteenth and seventeenth centuries, both officials and villagers seemed relatively unconcerned about witches, even when soldiers encamped in the area suggested that a hunt was in order.[74] Salem had its large hunt in 1692, but it failed to spill over into Connecticut, where only five people, all women, were arrested after a teenaged girl denounced them. The local population remained dubious, and 76 townsfolk signed a petition defending one of the accused. All the suspects were eventually freed.[75]

In any number of hunts, the financial costs of incarceration, trial and torture, and of actually burning witches became so high that they alone forced a rethinking of the whole process. To burn a human body requires a sustained source of high heat. When wood was already a carefully regulated and expensive item in much of Europe, using a great deal of it to immolate a witch could quickly create problems. In July of 1627 two villages under the jurisdiction of Cologne were unable to deliver more wood for witch burnings.[76] The fires sometimes required additions such as pitch, so that the rare English execution by flames of a woman – for murdering her husband, not witchcraft – in 1645 cost the impressive sum of £3 3s 6d. Today that might be £250. In Germany special burning huts were sometimes constructed for victims.

The cost of employing a torturer was substantial, as were the expenses of maintaining people in jail, no matter how primitive the conditions inside were. At Ipswich, England in 1645, jailing one witch cost as much as £50 a month.[77] Simply removing a productive member from peasant communities, so often on the edge of subsistence in any event, could be highly disruptive.

In some areas, notably Lorraine, the expenses of witch hunts were low. But in the villages around Trier, the cost of trials was so high that 'accusation committees' formed to share the costs. These groups drained their own resources and then fell to squabbling – and to accusing their own members of witchcraft. In Thuringia the public had to cover the expenses of trying poor victims, while in the cities of Bamberg and Coburg expensive new buildings were put up in the 1620s to house all the accused. The staggering cost of supporting Matthew Hopkins in his insatiable quest to discover witches helped turn public opinion against his operations in Essex, England in 1645. The town council of Hagenau in Alsace protested against the high cost of trials to the archduke of Austria in 1607,[78] to cite one of many such examples.

As the Introduction noted, 'function' has proved all but unusable in the discipline of sociology. However, it remains well entrenched in regard to the past, for lynching and the Soviet terror as well as for the witch persecutions. Marianne Hester repeats the theme in characterizing 'the witch hunts' as 'part of, and one example of, the ongoing mechanisms for social control of women within a general context of social change and the reconstruction of a patriarchal society'.[79] This explanatory device remains handy for some historians precisely because it can never be directly proved or disproved. Social change is often a vague concept, and the alleged need of the undoubtedly patriarchal society for even more than the usual violence against women cannot be identified. Hester's point must be taken on faith; nowhere did the electors of Trier, for example, announce that they were working to bolster their authority through the use of witchcraft accusations. This goal is always deduced from officials' actions.

In Trier the tangle of overlapping legal and judicial institutions was extreme even by the standards of the Holy Roman Empire. If the hunts had a function, perhaps to clarify this mess, why were they so erratically spaced? Waves of burnings occurred in 1580–90 and again around 1630. Of course, the first and last of those years mark exactly the period of most ferocity across Germany as a whole.

Thus the Trier burnings must be seen first in a broader context of witchcraft accusations that had nothing to do with legitimacy, as in the stories of Ban de la Roche or Mora, Sweden. Second, in Trier and nearby areas, the accusation committees found victims and turned them over to higher authorities, certainly with their approval, or lynched them – an act that directly *defied* the authority of the courts. In 1591 and again in 1630 the archbishop-electors promulgated witchcraft legislation that attempted to rein in the committees and to subject them to the High Courts of Trier and Koblenz. However, 'neither of the witchcraft acts had any perceivable effect'[80] – bad instrumentalization, to say the least.

Partly because of the witch hunts, but even more because of the periodic fighting in the region during the Thirty Years War (1618–48), Trier became an area in which almost nothing could function regularly. When the Elector Karl Kaspar began a reform programme in 1652, he issued an edict *outlawing* witchcraft trials, seeing them 'as a serious menace to public order'.[81] For the time being, he had limited success, as trials continued in the region into the 1660s.

In all senses, the costs of the witch hunts were high. When public authority could be bolstered in thousands of less disruptive and expensive ways, there was no logic or need in the creation of committees, gallows or pyres. Other leaders deeply concerned with establishing a higher degree of social discipline and morality, as they defined it, made little or no use of witch hunts. Once more the search for some greater meaning for the executions, whether in undergirding a certain strain of feminist theory, the idea of state-building, or the purported universality of witches, is a failure. Sometimes fear is the key to history.

[*]

What emerges from the local studies presented here and from a mass of other detailed material is that in certain circumstances tensions among neighbours, as well as their long memories of death and misfortune in their midst and their willingness to see the devil at work in their community, helped to produce accusations of witchcraft. Whenever a person was tried on that charge in Europe or North America, it was no casual affair. Due to influences that can often be traced, a local elite and villagers became deeply frightened by the idea that a grave threat to their safety existed in their midst. The devil's helpers supposedly killed livestock and people. They selected the most helpless and innocent members of the community, babies, and murdered them for their master. They used the infants' bodies for the most repugnant purposes imaginable, or, it seems, so the common people and the educated strata believed for a time.

But it must be re-emphasized that witch trials were not the norm anywhere in Europe or North America. When they occurred, they grew out of unusually stressful situations, including the recent transmission of fear to the area. They had to have the approval and participation of the local elite, and in order to flourish they often depended on a judicial situation that deviated from the norm or was not supervised by a strong superior court.

At times courts in Salem, Ban de la Roche and across Europe did convict witches. Since children and animals continued to die in Europe and America for no discernible reason, and in some cases proof appeared sufficient to convict witches, why did the hunts end? The answer lies above all in the issue of evidence in witchcraft cases. The next chapter explores the long and bitter debate over this question.

NOTES

1. Richard Kieckhefer (1976) *European Witch Trials: Their Foundation in Popular and Learned Culture, 1300–1500* (Berkeley: University of California Press), p. 37.

2. Richard A. Horsley (1979) 'Who Were the Witches? The Social Roles of the Accused in the European Witch Trials', *Journal of Interdisciplinary History* 9 (4): 693.

3. Carlo Ginzburg (1992) *Ecstasies: Deciphering the Witches' Sabbath*, trans. Raymond Rosenthal (New York: Penguin Books), esp. pp. 89–110.

4. Carlo Ginzburg (1985) *The Night Battles: Witchcraft and Agrarian Cults in the Sixteenth and Seventeenth Centuries*, trans. John and Anne Tedeschi (Baltimore: Johns Hopkins University Press). Inquisitors eventually turned the peasants' tales of night battles into witchcraft.

5. Jonathan Lumby (2002) '"Those to Whom Evil is Done": Family Dynamics in the Pendle Witch Trials', in Robert Poole (ed.) *The Lancashire Witches: Histories and Stories* (Manchester: Manchester University Press), p. 67. And for a similar comment from 1621 by Robert Burton, a don at Christ Church, Oxford, see Richard Godbeer (1992) *The Devil's Dominion: Magic and Religion in Early New England* (Cambridge: Cambridge University Press), p. 24.

6. John Swain, 'Witchcraft, Economy and Society in the Forest of Pendle', in Poole, *Lancashire Witches*, p. 85.

7. Soili-Maria Olli, 'The Devil's Pact: A Male Strategy', in Owen Davies and William Blécourt, *Beyond the Witch Trials: Witchcraft and Magic in Enlightenment Europe* (Manchester: Manchester University Press).

8. Ibid., pp. 136 and xvii.

9. Elizabeth Reis (1997) *Damned Women: Sinners and Witches in Puritan New England* (Ithaca, NY: Cornell University Press), p. 153.

10. Jean Rott (1983) 'La Guerre des Paysans et ses suites en Basse-Alsace: Le cas de Huttgau' in Georges Bischoff et al. (eds) *Histoire de l'Alsace rurale* (Strasbourg: Librarie Istra), pp. 119–21.

11. Georges Bischoff, 'Les Paysans de Haute-Alsace en 1525', in Bischoff et al., *Histoire de l'Alsace rurale*, p. 131.

12. Robert Lutz (1969) 'Le Serment des Bourgeois du Ban de la Roche en 1598', Le Ban de la Roche, *Bulletin de la Société d'Histoire du Protestantisme du Ban de la Roche*, no. 2, pp. 3–4.

13. Wolfgang Schmitz (ed.) (1980) *Der Teufelsprozess vor dem Weltgericht. Nach Ulrich Tennglers 'Neuer Layenspiegel' von 1511 (Ausgabe von 1512)* (Cologne: Wienand Verlag), pp. 14–21, 44 and 50.

14. Johannes Geiler von Kaysersberg (1989) *Saemtliche Werke*, herausgeben von Gerhard Bauer (Berlin: Walter de Gruyter), vol. 1, pp. 109–38.

15. Johannes Geiler von Kaysersberg (1516) *Die Emeis* (Strasbourg: Johannes Brienninger), esp. p. XXXVI verso.

16. Ruth Mellinkoff (1993) *Outcasts: Signs of Otherness in Northern European Art of the Late Middle Ages*, vol. 1, text; vol. 2, illustrations (Berkeley: University of California Press).

17. Ruth Mellinkoff (1988) *The Devil at Isenheim: Reflections of Popular Belief in Grunewald's Altarpiece* (Berkeley: University of California Press).

18. Jean Bodin (1580) *De la Démonomanie des Sorciers* (Paris: Iacques du Puys), Book 4, p. 182.

19. Other editions appeared in Lyon in 1603 and 1608, and Rouen in 1606, for example.

20. Martin Antoine Del Rio (1611) *Les controuerses et recherches magiques de Martin Delrio . . . : diuisées en six liures, ausquels sont exactment & doctement confutées les sciences curieuses, les vanitez & superstitions de toute la magie: auecques la manière de proceder en iustice contre les magiciens & sorciers, accommodée a l'instruction des confesseurs*; traduit & abregé du latin par Andre du Chesne (Paris: Chez Iean Petit-pas); and Pierre de Lancre (1982) *Tableau de l'inconstance des mauvais anges et démons: où il est amplement traité des sorciers et de la sorcellerie*. Introduction critique et notes de Nicole Jacques-Chaquin (Paris: Aubier), originally 1612.

21. Nicolas Rémy (1930) *Demonolatry*, trans. E. A. Ashwin (ed.) and introduction and notes by Montague Summers (London: John Rodker), p. xxviii.

22. Ibid., p. 51.

23. 'La Sorcellerie en Alsace', *Bi Uns d'Heim* (88), no. 1, p. 21.

24. L. Schlaefli (1993) 'La Sorcellerie à Molsheim (1589–1697)', *Société d'histoire et d'archéologie de Molsheim et environs. Annuaire*, pp. 7–8.

25. Robin Briggs (1996) *Witches and Neighbors: the Social and Cultural Context of European Witchcraft* (New York: Viking), pp. 93, 178 and 417 n. 80; Marc Brignon (1983) 'La Sorcellerie dans le Pays de Salm aux XVIème et XVIIème siècles', *L'Essor* 53 (120).

26. 'Persin' was used as a name for the devil in St Marguerite in 1592, for example; Briggs, *Witches and Neighbors*, p. 417 n. 80.

27. H. C. Erik Midelfort (1972) *Witch Hunting in Southwestern Germany 1562–1684* (Stanford, Calif.: Stanford University Press), p. 71.

28. Steinthal ms., pp. 197–210.

29. Ibid., pp. 12v–22v.

30. Ibid., p. 107.

31. Schaefli, 'La Sorcellerie à Molsheim', pp. 8 and 18.

32. Steinthal ms., p. 17.

33. Ibid., pp. 19–29.

34. Walter Rummel (1991) *Bauern, Herren und Hexen: Studien zur Sozialgeschichte Sponheimischer und kurtrierischer Hexenprozesse 1574–1664* (Göttingen: Vandenhoeck & Ruprecht), p. 159.

35. Quoted in Rummel, *Bauern, Herren und Hexen*, p. 321.

36. Kai T. Erikson (1966) *Wayward Puritans: A Study in the Sociology of Deviance* (New York: John Wiley and Sons).

37. Carol F. Karlsen (1987) *The Devil in the Shape of a Woman* (New York: W. W. Norton).

38. Paul Boyer and Stephen Nissenbaum (1974) *Salem Possessed: the Social Origins of Witchcraft* (Cambridge, Mass.: Harvard University Press).

39. Mary Beth Norton (2002) *In the Devil's Snare: The Salem Witchcraft Crisis of 1692* (New York: Alfred A. Knopf).

40. Cotton Mather (1862) *The Wonders of the Invisible World. Being an Account of the Tryals of Several Witches Lately Executed in New-England* (London, John Russel Smith), pp. 167–8. Originally published in Boston in 1692. Bold type was used in the book where Mather wished to emphasize similarities between the Swedish and Salem cases.

41. John Putnam Demos (1982) *Entertaining Satan: Witchcraft and the Culture of Early New England* (New York: Oxford University Press), p. 11.

42. At least, so says every book except Norton, *In the Devil's Snare*, who reports that there is no contemporary evidence linking the girls to fortune telling; p. 23.

43. Boyer and Nissenbaum, *Salem Possessed*, p. 1.

44. Chadwick Hansen (1969) *Witchcraft at Salem* (New York: George Braziller), pp. 37–8.

45. Demos, *Entertaining Satan*, p. 384.

46. John Procter, executed for witchcraft in August 1692, charged in a letter written from prison to five members of the Boston clergy and

dated 23 July, that several young men had been tied neck and heels in the Salem jail to get them to confess; Hansen, *Witchcraft at Salem*, p. 133. And see Reis, *Damned Women*, pp. 158–60.

47. Devices and depictions of such punishment for deviance may be seen at the Mittelalterliches Kriminalmuseum, Rothenburg ob der Taube, Germany.

48. Leon Radzinowicz and Joan King (1977) *The Growth of Crime: the International Experience* (New York: Basic Books), pp. 105–6.

49. Henri Boguet (1602) *Discours des sorciers. Tiré de quelques procez, faicts de deux ans en ça à plusieurs de la même secte, en la terre de S. Oyan de Ioux, dicté de S. Claude au comte de Bourgogne. Avec une instruction pour une iuge, en faict de sorcellerie.* (Lyon: par Iean Pillehotte).

50. Corinna Schneider (2004) 'Markgrafschaftern Baden-Baden und Baden-Durlach,' in Sönke Lorenz and Jürgen Michael Schmidts (eds) *Wider alle Hexerei und Teufelswerk: Die europaische Hexenverfolgung und ihre Auswirkungen auf Suedwestdeutschland* (Ostfildern: Jan Thorbecke Verlag), p. 218.

51. Alan Macfarlane (1999) *Witchcraft in Tudor and Stuart England: A Regional and Comparative Study*, 2nd edn (London: Routledge and Kegan Paul), p. 161.

52. Lyndal Roper (1994) *Oedipus and the Devil: Witchcraft, Sexuality and Religion in Early Modern Europe* (London: Routledge), pp. 199–201, found that in mid-seventeenth century Augsburg lying-in maids were especially susceptible to charges of witchcraft.

53. Ibid., p. 188.

54. Ronald Füssel (2003) *Die Hexenverfolgungen im Thüringer Raum* (Veröffentlichungen des Arbeitskreises für historische Hexen- und Kriminalitätsforschung in Norddeutschland, 2) (Hamburg: DOBU Wissenschaftlicher Verlag Dokumentation), p. 220. And see his article 'Thuringia' (2006) in Richard Golden (ed.) *Encyclopedia of Witchcraft: The Western Tradition* (Santa Barbara, Calif.: ABC-CLIO), IV, pp. 1120–22.

55. Rita Voltmer and Günter Gehl (eds) (2003) *Alltagsleben und Magie in Hexenprozessen* (Weimar: Rita Dadder), p. 18.

56. Gerhard Schormann (1991) *Der Krieg gegen die Hexen: Das Ausrottungsprogramm des Kurfürsten von Köln* (Göttingen: Vandenhoeck & Ruprecht), p. 47.

57. Lyndal Roper (2004) *Witch craze: Terror and Fantasy in Baroque Germany* (New Haven: Yale University Press), p. 161.

58. Alison Rowlands (2006) 'Würzburg', in Golden, *Encyclopedia*, IV, p. 1230.

59. Sabine Schleichert (2004) 'Vorderöstereich: Elsass, Breisgau, Hagenau und Ortenau', in Lorenz and Schmidts, *Wider alle Hexerei und Teufelswerk*, pp. 259–60. In the Duchy of Flanders, 29.5 per cent of female victims whose status is known were widows and at least 44.7 per cent were married; 29.5 per cent were over age 50; Jos Monballyu (2002) 'Die Hexenprozesse in der Grafschaft Flandern (1495–1692)', in Herbert Eiden and Rita Voltmer (eds) *Hexenprozesse und Gerichtspraxis* (Trier: Paulinus), p. 288.

60. Alison Rowlands (2006) 'Age of Accused Witches', in Golden, *Encyclopedia*, I, p. 17.

61. William Monter (1997) 'Toads and Eucharists: the Male Witches of Normandy', *French Historical Studies* 20 (4) discusses the preponderance of males among witches in Normandy. In Estonia, 60 per cent of 193 known defendants were men: Maia Maidar, 'Estonia I: Werewolves and Poisoners', in Bengt Ankerloo and Gustav Henningsen (eds) (1993) *Early Modern European Witchcraft: Centres and Peripheries* (Oxford: Clarendon Press), p. 266; Antero Heikkinen and Tuno Kervinen, 'Finland: the Male Domination', in ibid., p. 319, find that males predominated there until the end of the sixteenth century. During all the hunts in Finland males comprised 49.3 per cent of known defendants. Kirsten Hastrup in 'Iceland: Sorcerers and Paganism', ibid., p. 398, found that Icelandic witches were men; the generic term for witch in Iceland is masculine. Russian witches were largely male; see Russell Zguta (1997) 'Witchcraft Trials in Seventeenth-Century Russia', *American Historical Review* 82 (2); and Valerie Kivelson (1991) 'Through the Prism of Witchcraft: Gender and Social Change in Seventeenth-Century Muscovy', in Barbara Evans Clements, Barbara Alpern Engel and Christine D. Worobec (eds) *Russia's Women: Accommodation, Resistance, Transformation* (Berkeley: University of California Press), p. 93.

62. Kivelson, 'Through the Prism of Witchcraft'.

63. It is difficult to know what to make of Valerie Kivelson's argument (2003) that 'in most spheres of Russian life male and female roles were

defined similarly', in 'Male Witches in Russia', *Comparative Studies in Society and History* 45(3) (July): 615. Perhaps this was true in a strictly theological sense, as 'sins of the flesh preoccupied [Eastern] Orthodox thinkers much less than in the West, and males and females both had to 'overcome gender in order to achieve sexless perfection': 615–17. But in practice huge differences between the roles accorded to men and women characterized Russian life; only males could become soldiers, government officials, priests, or independent merchants, for instance.

64. Heide Dienst (1987) 'Hexenprozesse auf dem Gebiet der heutigen Bundesländer Vorarlberg, Tirol (mit Südtirol), Salzburg, Nieder- und Oberösterreich sowie des Burgenlandes', in Helfried Valentinitsch (ed.) *Hexen und Zauberer: Die grosse Verfolgung–ein europäisches Phänomen in der Steiermark* (Graz: Leykam-Verlag), pp. 271–3.

65. R. Schulte (2000) *Hexenmeister. Die Verfolgung von Männern im Rahmen der Hexenverfolgung von 1530–1730 im Alten Reich* (Kieler Werkstücke. Reihe G: Beiträge zur Frühen Neuzeit 1) (Frankfurt: Lang), pp. 244–6; a chart of the accused by sex is on p. 246.

66. Monter, 'Toads and Eucharists': 563–94.

67. Boyer and Nissenbaum, *Salem Possessed*, p. 32. Midelfort, *Witch Hunting in Southwestern Germany*, pp. 2 and 79, argues that the breakdown of stereotype of old women as witches and a concomitant increase in the number of men occurred only during a large-scale craze. However, Christina Larner (1981) found the opposite in Scotland; *Enemies of God: the Witch-Hunt in Scotland* (Baltimore: Johns Hopkins University Press), p. 92.

68. Rita Voltmer (2002) 'Hexenprozesse und Hoch gerichte: Zur herrschaftlich-politischen Nutzung und Instrumentalisierung von Hexenverfolgungen,' in Eiden and Voltmer, *Hexenprozesse*, pp. 516, 520, 521 and 524–5.

69. Rita Voltmer and Herbert Eiden (2000) 'Rechtsnormen und Gerichtspraxis bei Hexereiverfahren in Lothringen, Luxemburg, Kurtrier und St. Maximin während des 16. und 17. Jahrhunderts', in Voltmer and Franz Irsigler (eds) *Incubi/Succubi: Hexen und Ihre Henker bis Heute. Ein historisches Lesebuch zur Ausstellung* (Luxembourg: Luxembourg City: Publications scientifiques du Musée de la Ville de Luxembourg, tome IV), p. 56.

70. Rita Voltmer (2000) 'Von der besonderen Alchimie, aus Menschenblut Gold zu machen oder von den Möglichkeiten, Hexenprozesse zu instrumentalisieren', in Voltmer and Irsigler, *Incubi Succubi*, p. 95.

71. Rainer Decker (2001) 'Entstehung und Verbreitung der Römischen Hexenprozessinstruktion', in Hubert Wolf (ed.) *Inquisition, Index, Zensur. Wissenskulturen der Neuzeit im Widerstreit* (Römische Inquisition und Indexkongregation, Bd. 1) (Paderborn: Schöningh), pp. 162–5.

72. Decker, 'Entstehung', p. 167.

73. Rita Voltmer, 'Ruwer und Eitelsbach in der Frühen Neuzeit', in Matthias Kordel (2003) *Ruwer und Eitelsbach: Zwei Dörfer im Spiegel ihrer Geschichte* (Trier: Kliomedia), 114–15.

74. Alison Rowlands (2003) *Witchcraft narratives in Germany: Rothenburg 1561–1652* (Manchester: Manchester University Press), pp. 206–10.

75. Richard Godbeer (2005) *Escaping Salem: The Other Witch Hunt of 1692* (New York: Oxford University Press), pp. 9, 13–14, 61, 116 and 118.

76. Schormann, *Krieg*, p. 58.

77. Malcolm Gaskill (2005) *Witchfinders: A Seventeenth-Century English Tragedy* (Cambridge, Mass.: Harvard University Press), p. 178.

78. Schleichert, 'Vorderösterreich', p. 254.

79. Marianne Hester (2002) 'Patriarchal Reconstruction and Witch-Hunting', in Darren Oldridge, ed. *The Witchcraft Reader* (London: Routledge), p. 276.

80. Johannes Dillinger (2006) 'Trier, Electorate of', in Golden, *Encyclopedia*, IV, p. 1136.

81. Ibid.

CHAPTER FIVE

THE DECLINE AND END
OF THE HUNTS

The collection of documents on witch trials in Steinthal contains nothing for the period between 1630 and 1674. Then there is one final incident. Georges Berdot, the local pastor, wrote to the provost of Ban de la Roche in March 1674 with his suspicions that the area's forester, Hans Neuweiller, had caused the deaths of two young brothers through 'sorcery'. The provost, Johann Lipp, in turn wrote to Count Ludwig Leopold Veldenz to inform him of the suspicions and ask what he wanted done. On the next day, the count replied to Lipp that he should personally investigate the affair. The provost quickly began an inquiry and found several villagers who said that Neuweiller had threatened the two boys, had somehow stopped up their digestive tracts, and had been able to suspend objects in smoke in the air. Meanwhile the forester had been arrested. He reportedly possessed a 'little book', and his father had been burned in Steinthal as a witch. On the other hand, several people stated that they had never known Neuweiller to practise sorcery.

In early August the count directed his provost to take the investigation further by interviewing more villagers. After another exchange of letters, the seigneur offered his opinion that probably no one was 'hexed', but 'rather it is much more believable' that a 'hereditary illness' was responsible for the brothers' deaths. Berdot had produced nothing that would 'serve as good evidence'. The pastor continued to write to the count about Neuweiller's evil acts into 1675, to no avail; in April of that year Veldenz ordered his provost to give a copy of Berdot's accusations to the forester in order to assist him in 'further [establishing] his innocence'.[1]

In Salem, the members of one jury that had found people guilty of witchcraft in 1692 reconsidered their judgments less than a year later. 'We confess,' wrote the jurymen,

that we ourselves were not capable to understand, nor able to withstand, the mysterious delusions of the powers of darkness, and prince of the air; but were, for want of knowledge in ourselves, and better information from others, prevailed with to take up with such evidence against the accused, as, on further consideration and better information, we justly fear was insufficient for the touching the lives of any.[2]

Just as their decisions in 1692 had reflected a widely held view in the colony that the accused witches were a dire threat to humanity and therefore had to die, the jury members' recantation in 1693 articulated a new predominant public opinion.

In these two case studies, attitudes toward witchcraft changed dramatically by the late seventeenth century. In Ban de la Roche perhaps only Count Veldenz particularly cared about finding 'good evidence' for witchcraft, but his was the decisive voice. Where his predecessor 50 years earlier would almost certainly have ordered the forester to be tortured, nothing of the sort happened in 1674. In Salem the broad change of heart in the community regarding proof of witchcraft is much clearer. But in both places the outcome was the same: there were no more witch trials.

Why did similar sceptical attitudes towards witch persecutions emerge near the end of the seventeenth century in two places so dissimilar in location, topography, culture and political structure?

The heart of the answer lies in the issue of evidence for witchcraft. Magistrates, clergy, the educated elite in general and ordinary citizens were deeply concerned throughout the witch hunts with the question of what constituted sufficient evidence of the crime. Allowing for the kinds of personal vendettas, prejudices and connections that have marred systems of justice in many lands, early modern courts convicted people primarily on the basis of the testimony and exhibits presented in trials. But largely because attitudes towards evidence varied, the incidence of witch persecutions, methods of investigation and rates of conviction all showed marked differences across Europe and North America.

Generalizations about why these variations occurred are not easy to make. The presence of even one strong-minded and influential person, whether for or against hunting witches, could make the difference between an outbreak of trials and their absence. However, it is possible to look carefully at the location of witch trials, in both the physical and social senses, and to reach some conclusions about which situations favoured their appearance and which did not. We will examine what can be called the geography or even the social geography of evidence.

This chapter also outlines the debate in Europe and Massachusetts surrounding proof of witchcraft and how the disagreement was finally resolved, albeit at different times in different areas, in the same direction. Since torture played a huge role in the witch hunts outside England and its colonies in North America, the first section will examine its role in continental and Scottish judicial procedure.

TORTURE

Judicial torture as a means of obtaining information about a case in progress appeared, or reappeared, in Europe somewhat before the first witch trials. Records mention torture by the early thirteenth century,[3] and it was widely used by the sixteenth century at the latest. Among prominent explanations for its resurgence, particularly but not exclusively as it pertained to the witch hunts, are that it served to instil discipline among the lower classes, that it had a punitive as well as an investigative purpose, and that it expressed a pornographic male interest in the female body.[4]

But, as the previous chapter showed for the Paris Parlement, torture was not the same across Europe. Exactly why it was used at all in continental judicial systems is often unclear in the literature on the witch persecutions. Torture in early modern Europe was usually a long process involving instruments designed for the job, the presence of a scribe and often of a doctor. Typically a specialist in the infliction of pain was brought in; after all, it would have served no purpose to kill the victim quickly without obtaining a confession. Given all this, it would have been quicker, easier and cheaper to execute people without torture, if the goal had been to eliminate troublesome types or to send the public a message about desired behaviour. As for a pornographic or sadistic interest in women's bodies, the serious arrangements of officials and equipment for torture make that motivation unlikely on a broad scale, although it cannot be ruled out entirely. But any prurient interest in such cases would have been unusual indeed, since women arrested on suspicion of witchcraft were often older and unattractive by the standards of the day.

When torture was employed, why execute the defendant after obtaining a confession?[5] If deviance was the initial problem, it would have been more logical to cause pain, link its infliction to some specifically proscribed behaviour, and then to release the victims back into society where their presence would have served as a living warning to others. This is the model presented in George Orwell's novel *1984*. Instead, defendants in continental witchcraft cases were tortured until they confessed to making a pact with the devil and committing *maleficia* on his orders. The victims were then executed for crimes against society.

It is pointless to refer to purported medieval superstition or backwardness as an explanation for the use of torture, which was not common in Western judicial procedure during most of the Middle

Ages.[6] In continental Europe and in Scotland, the application of torture expanded considerably toward the end of that period in connection with the widespread switch from 'feudal' or accusatorial legal procedure to inquisitorial practice. With the new approach, courts became much more active in gathering evidence; they no longer relied on what were supposed to be signs from God, as in the old trial by ordeal or combat, to determine guilt or innocence.[7] Witchcraft prosecutions were conducted in a new judicial system that insisted officials use their own powers of reason to find and weigh evidence.

In its early stages, from the eleventh to the eighteenth centuries, inquisitorial procedure required 'complete' proof for a conviction. This meant either the testimony of two eyewitnesses or a confession, the 'queen of proofs'. Therefore, substantial pressure arose in the courts to obtain confessions, which in turn opened the door to forcing them from suspects. Moreover, punishment of medium severity – that is, substantial periods of incarceration – was not yet available, so that sanctions tended to be either relatively mild, such as a day in the stocks; inflicted directly on the body in a one-time action, involving whipping, branding, or the like; or capital. Banishment was not always a possibility; what did it mean in any event to vagrants or habitual criminals? Allowing a person upon whom deep suspicion had fallen to walk away with, for example, a mark branded on the shoulder, did not seem enough punishment for a serious crime. But to execute someone required considerable evidence; on the Continent, as opposed to in English or North American tribunals, circumstantial connections alone were not enough. Hence the courts were led back to confessions and in turn to the use of torture to obtain them.

Edward Peters argues that it was impossible to use 'Romano-canonical procedure,' so called because it drew on traditions of Roman and church law, without employing torture; confessions required torture.[8] At the same time, the new procedure 'solved the problem of how to make the judgment of men', as opposed to that of God implied in the old system, acceptable to people. The new courts would make certain of the evidence by introducing confessions.[9] Even so, the German Carolina law code of 1532 required judges to investigate the details of all confessions and to reject those disproved by other materials.

In England the jury system precluded torture, because juries were allowed and encouraged to weigh exactly the kind of circumstantial material that continental courts found inadequate. Deprivation of sleep for several days, a highly effective torture, was used in England in 1645, but that was a decision of local officials operating at a time of fragmented central power. To this day, juries in countries whose judicial systems are based on English law can convict on less evidence than European continental tribunals will recognize. To make the point another way, on the Continent courts hesitated to order death unless they had 'complete' proof, which so often could rest only on a confession. In England less solid proof was required: 'beyond a reasonable doubt' does not mean 'complete'. Therefore juries in England or Massachusetts could and did convict witches without their confessions, on the basis of extensive testimony by witnesses to 'crimes'.

Wholehearted endorsement of torture's effectiveness in obtaining reliable evidence never existed in Europe. Legal commentators in Ancient Greece and Rome had expressed doubt on this point,[10] and beginning at least in the sixteenth century writers again questioned the results of physical methods in interrogation.[11] Jurists agreed that torture measured defendants' ability to withstand pain, which is far from the same thing as determining guilt or innocence. The most important continental law codes of the early modern period, the Carolina and the French Statute of Villers-Cotterets, issued in 1539, were deeply concerned with *limiting* torture. It was supposed to be applied only in capital cases, particularly in what were called *crimena excepta*, exceptional crimes. These included heresy, witchcraft, treason and, in the Holy Roman Empire, infanticide when the mother was suspected.

Torture was also supposed to be used only when there were already substantial indications (*indicia*) that a suspect was linked to a crime in some fashion. For example, if a body was discovered with deep stab wounds and a bloody knife was discovered in the room of the dead person's worst enemy, this would be an *indicium* that the person with the knife was involved in a crime. Indicia connecting a suspect to a crime had to be considerable – in France 'enormous' – before a judge could authorize physical torment.[12] If a judge should order torture without serious indicia, any confession 'shall not be believed nor shall anyone be condemned upon that basis'. People tortured in this 'illegal way' had to be compensated for their pain by the responsible authorities. Those who tortured in violation of the law would be punished, the Carolina promised.[13] It further forbade judges to accept abject, general confessions of guilt and admonished them to obtain details of a crime that 'no innocent person can know'.[14]

A reputation for any sort of unacceptable behaviour could serve as one of the indicia described in European continental law as demonstrating a possible connection between a person and a crime. When several serious indicia were present, a judge could order a suspect to be tortured.[15] But a bad reputation was never more than part of the material pointing to the appropriateness of torture, which itself might provide the proof of a confession. Even with a confession, as noted, the judge was supposed to continue the investigation and check for discrepancies. It could not have been often that such enquiries resulted in a finding of innocence once a defendant had confessed, but the possibility existed. On the other hand, people who withstood torture 'purged' the indicia against them and went free.

Contrary to a common assertion about how torture was regulated in Europe, the Carolina specifically permitted torment to be conducted 'much, often or seldom, hard or lenient'.[16] The law attempted simultaneously to make sure that torture was not used in the first place without extensive indicia and to allow judges wide latitude in its application once it had been approved.

Yet doubts about the efficacy of using pain to elicit the truth were expressed in the law codes and were built, in theory, into the process of torture. It was not supposed to be savage, to maim or to lead to death. A confession obtained under torture had to be repeated at another time, away from the torture chamber, as the best guarantee that it was sincere. Unfortunately, if suspects recanted at such a moment, they might well be returned to the torturer for another round of agony. Many torturers did in fact maim their victims; for example, bones were sometimes crushed in the 'boots' as ever more wedges were driven between metal collars attached around the legs and the limbs themselves. People treated in this way could never walk properly again.

A further major problem with the limitations on torture that the law codes urged is that local jurisdictions often ignored them. There was nothing legally wrong with such deviation in part of the core witchcraft zone; the Carolina, the law code of the loosely organized Holy Roman Empire, specifically stated that it did not override customary local procedures.[17]

It should already be apparent that gender had almost no place in early modern codes on legal procedure or in the discussion of how it should be carried out. Prosecution of witchcraft must be located in its context of highly developed European law. By the late Middle Ages, every part of every forest in the West was regulated, for example, and who was permitted to gather wood or hunt there was stipulated in law. Only members of authorized guilds could use certain materials or techniques in making products, mountain villages had the right to drive cattle to market along carefully described routes and so on. Even during panics about witches, courts followed established judicial procedures, which certainly dampened any temptation to use legal prosecutions to control unwanted types of people.

While jurists shared all the prejudices of their day and sometimes contributed to worsening them, they did not suggest that women deserved less than due process under the law. Rather, as we have seen, prominent jurists argued in the late sixteenth and early seventeenth centuries that in witchcraft cases magistrates needed to interpret indicia broadly for all suspects. Witchcraft was such a 'secret and execrable crime', as Jean Bodin put it,[18] that ordinary judicial standards did not have to be applied. Magistrates could proceed with 'corporal pain' in the absence of other indications of wrongdoing.[19] It was also common for zealots to argue, as Francesco Maria Guazzo did in 1608, that witches might not feel torture. They 'overcome all the pain by laughter or sleep or silence', he maintained.[20]

For Henri Boguet, witches were 'the greatest enemies that heaven has here below [on earth]'. To illustrate his view, he related a case from his personal experience dating from 1598. A 58-year-old woman, Françoise Secretain, was accused of sending five demons named Wolf, Cat, Dog, Joly and Griffon into the body of an 8-year-old girl. These spirits possessed and paralysed her. Secretain wore a small cross that was broken in one place; Boguet counted that as an indicium of crime. She could not cry, a trait supposedly common to witches. The judge did not say that her lack of tears was another indicium, for he considered other factors sufficient to establish Secretain's connection with the crime of inflicting possession on a person. These matters were the 8-year-old's strange behaviour, which began shortly after Secretain had visited her house, the broken cross and the woman's appearance – she was also called the 'fat Françoise'. Questioned at first without the use of torture, she would not confess. Boguet ordered her hair to be cut off, standard procedure in continental witchcraft investigations for men and women, and had her examined for a witch's mark. Nothing of the sort was found on Secretain, but by now she must have been terrified of what was to come. She began to confess, adding more and more of the standard tale of sex with the devil and harm inflicted at his command as her days in incarceration went by.[21] Boguet, an experienced and respected judge who wrote about the incident quite calmly, had been about to order the torture of a person on the slimmest of grounds. In doing so he would have violated the spirit, if not the letter, of continental legal codes. For him, the nature of witchcraft made such a course absolutely necessary. Still, he felt bound to operate with the law in mind at all times.

Boguet was a judge in Franche-Comté, located in eastern France along the Swiss border and just south of Alsace. Franche-Comté had changed hands between France, the Swiss Confederation, Spain and the Empire several times until France finally won it in the 1670s. Boguet was therefore free in 1598 to operate without the bothersome restraints of a superior court or, if he had so chosen, an overarching law code. Judges like De Lancre in the French Basque country or Remy in Lorraine also oversaw major witch hunts made possible in part because they occurred in borderlands where few constraints on the local judiciary existed.

The Carolina, the Statute of Villers-Cotterets, and other codes tried, though half-heartedly, to establish a centralized, standard set of procedures for all levels and aspects of judicial procedure in the regions they covered. Torture was supposed to be used only in certain circumstances, and it was to be distrusted. Local practice, unfortunately, often differed.

The same kind of contrast appeared regarding torture in witchcraft cases, as higher officials frequently adopted a sceptical position earlier than local magistrates did. In the part of France under the jurisdiction of the Parlement of Paris, permissible torture and punishments became less severe during the late sixteenth century. In 1624 the Parlement required an automatic appeal to it from lower courts for all witchcraft cases, which certainly indicated serious scepticism in the capital towards the charge. By the 1640s the Parisian magistrates rejected witch accusations altogether and even ordered punishment of lower court judges who had tortured prisoners in their care accused of witchcraft.[22] At roughly the same time, higher courts in Denmark, Sweden and Scotland also began to insist on reviewing lower tribunals' witch cases and to overturn many guilty verdicts.[23] As noted in the previous chapter, before 1692 New England magistrates reversed numerous convictions of witchcraft by lower courts. Outside of English jurisdictions, the cumulative effect of higher courts' actions in witch trials was to reduce employment of torture drastically during the seventeenth century.

The centralization and hierarchy of the Catholic Inquisition in Italy and Spain, for all its evil reputation in the popular mind, also helped dampen the use of torture. It could be applied only with the approval of the central Holy Office in either country, and (in theory) only after a conviction had been obtained. Torture was intended solely to clear up inconsistencies in the accused's testimony or to elicit details that the court supposed were missing. Inquisitors were discouraged from asking leading questions, the bane of trials elsewhere on the Continent, and were required to conduct rigorous cross-examinations of witnesses even for the prosecution. The inquisitors of Rome in particular insisted that testimony by suspected witches was of little value in prosecuting other defendants. Probably the Inquisition's long experience with the problems of testimony delivered under torture helped determine the cautious attitude of its highest officials towards the use of physical methods. By the 1530s the central office of the Spanish Inquisition, La Suprema, insisted on reviewing all convictions by inquisitorial courts for witchcraft or sorcery. Given its insistence on solid proof and its scepticism regarding hearsay, the Spanish Holy Office rejected many guilty verdicts. The Roman and Spanish Inquisitions 'prosecuted witchcraft and sorcery early and vigorously but were also the first courts to be sceptical of the evidence and mechanics of witchcraft charges'. These judicial bodies 'consistently offered the most leni-ent treatment' of accused witches.[24] Because torture was not widely used in witchcraft cases in Italy and Spain, where they usually went to inquisitorial courts, the more lurid kinds of statements about the witches' sabbat and other activities that so regularly appeared in continental courts further north were rarely heard there. The result was that the relatively few witch trials that did take place in south-ern Europe did not snowball into large-scale affairs.

The scepticism of the Holy Office in Rome helped to block inquisitorial courts from conducting major witch hunts.[25] During the early seventeenth century, a huge hunt threatened to erupt in the Basque country of northern Spain, but it was halted by a critical inquisitor who managed to convince La Suprema that the charges levelled against hundreds of villagers were illogical and contradict-ory.[26] In a less centrally regulated setting, as happened in nearby southern Franche-Comté at the same time, the hunt would prob-ably have continued, relied on torture and claimed many victims.

The history of torture in Europe from the thirteenth to the eighteenth centuries thus indicates that, in principle, officials saw it as an unfortunate but useful device, one which could be used only in carefully specified circumstances to probe for the truth. Euro-pean judicial torture was not designed or intended to be used to intimidate groups of people into acceptable behaviour. Indeed, the Inquisition began in the thirteenth century to replace the chaotic and bloody attacks on heretics by mobs, soldiers or lay authorities. In short, the new office aimed to replace lynching with regularized procedures. The inquisitors then tortured and burned relatively few people.[27] Inquisitors like Kramer, author of the *Malleus*, did turn from the pursuit of heretics to the prosecution of witches. But, as discussed earlier, Kramer quickly ran into difficulties in his invest-igations of the devil's aides. It is possible that the Inquisition limited early witch hunts more than it spurred them on; certainly that was the case throughout its history in Spain.

Torture was used in continental judicial procedures to establish 'complete' proof and because few middle-level punishments were available. Only in the late sixteenth century did other sanctions, in particular assignment to the galleys or incarceration in prisons, become available. These developments meant that a middle range of sanctions could be applied given a middle level of proof, something less than the old requirement of two eyewitnesses or confession. Circumstantial evidence could now play a much more important role than before in determining the outcome of a trial. As this happened, the courts' need for, and use of, torture decreased.[28]

The Enlightenment thinkers of the eighteenth century claimed for themselves the inflated title of *philosophe* and announced an Age of Reason in contrast to the benighted, superstitious times they said they had helped end. But European judicial procedure had never been a matter of whim or snap decisions; it had always been a search for the most reasonable assessment of evidence. In any event, when the Enlightenment made criticism of torture one of its key projects, it was knocking at a half-opened door, as torture had greatly declined in the courts a century or more earlier.

REASON, ENQUIRY AND WITCHES

The relatively slow spread of the witch trials after the first recorded, in 1324, is only one of several indications that there were serious doubts across Europe about the wisdom of the persecutions. Various authorities tried to restrain lynchings and prosecutions of witches in parts of Europe into the 1580s or even later. Then came the worst period, which lasted until roughly 1630.

During the relative calm before the last storm, one man in particular stood out as a strong spokesman against the witch hunts. This was the Dutch-German physician Johann Weyer, who published *De praestigiis daemonum* (On the deceptions of demons) in 1563. Five more editions in Latin quickly appeared, as well as three in German.[29] Again, we do not know why the book was so popular; republication does not necessarily mean that people widely accepted its theses.

Weyer did not object to the idea that the devil was hard at work in the world; rather, throughout the book he reiterated his belief in widespread demonic activity. Instead, he focused on problems in the stories told about witches' acts and accepted as proof of their vileness in many courts. He had been strongly influenced by his teacher, the famous doctor Cornelius Agrippa, who had expressed his own scepticism about witches' powers as early as 1510. As legal counsel for the city of Metz, Agrippa secured the acquittal of a woman charged with witchcraft in 1518, although his argument was more along procedural than evidentiary grounds.

Weyer worked at the ducal court of Jülich-Berg-Cleves. With its capital at Düsseldorf, Cleves was one of the few remaining centres in Europe where the Erasmian tradition of refusing to see religious doctrinal differences as heresies remained powerful. The Duke of Cleves was a committed Catholic, but he had no known differences with Weyer, whose writings approach Protestantism. In short, Weyer had been educated and later worked in an atmosphere of relative toleration, which in itself urged him to look into any issue on its merits. This approach can be contrasted to that of the *Malleus* and other witch finders' treatises, where the authors cite the ancients, the Bible and hearsay as proof of witches' capabilities and actions. Weyer too was not ready to break completely with ancient authorities; he revered much of ancient medicine, especially the Galenic theories of humours in the body that served as conventional wisdom for another hundred years or more. But he insisted at the same time on close observation of events, which emerged in the book as his preferred approach to judging any material.

Weyer wished to show that witch trials were cruel and inhumane procedures that could lead to the conviction of innocent people. Despite his respect for the ancients' ideas, he drew on his medical knowledge, observations and common sense in an effort to demon-strate that witchcraft was an impossible crime beyond human cap-abilities. He accepted the idea that demons carried out *maleficia* on earth, but mounted a multifaceted attack on the notion that the devil had to have human assistants in order to commit evil.

One part of this assault was on biblical, legal and logical grounds. Weyer insisted that the Bible said nothing about the demonic pact. If such an agreement were ever made between the devil and a human, it would have to be between a predator and its prey; thus it could have no legal, binding force and could not be regarded as a prosecutable crime.

The devil could do nothing that God did not permit and noth-ing that did not fit into His natural order; therefore witches could accomplish nothing beyond the strength of a normal human being. When some people appeared to be doing more than that, in fact the devil was creating illusions, to which the Bible often referred. Why believe that an ordinary human could command the devil, who had the powers of a rebellious angel? Satan hardly needed people's help, especially that of weak old people, to commit evil. Scripture does not speak of witches in the way that contemporary writers did, Weyer continued, and he argued that the Hebrew word used in Exodus for witch should be translated as 'poisoner'.

The other major prong of his attack on witch hunting consisted of observations about humans' physical and mental characteristics. Women who were said to vomit nails, for example, simply could not have done so; such objects would rip up the oesophagus on their way out, but no damage of this type was ever found. People could not change into wolves or other animals; this was contrary to 'nature and reason itself'. The crimes ascribed to witches were not verified by 'true and reliable witnesses'.

Weyer called for careful investigation of witchcraft accusations and argued repeatedly for reason, which will counter the 'usual atrocity connected with punishment'.[30] People required education and instruction to overcome their delusions, not torture. It was especially ridiculous to torment the typical 'witch', who was a woman 'usually old, melancholic by nature, feeble-minded, easily given to despondency, and with little trust in God'. The devil 'all the more gladly attaches himself' to such people in order to create illusions in their minds.[31]

Although Weyer was certainly against persecution, he was no feminist. He wrote, for instance, that women are weaker than men in 'spirit, mind, and natural disposition'. But to him, these were reasons why they should be punished less than men for the same offence.[32]

Weyer's work by no means demolished the established witch stereotype. Since he readily admitted that the devil was highly active on earth, other writers responded that it was a simple task for Satan to enlist human helpers. Jean Bodin in particular sought to undermine Weyer's arguments by reciting many cases of witchcraft that he knew personally or had supposedly heard from reliable witnesses. Nevertheless, Weyer had begun to raise doubts about the usual evidence introduced in witchcraft cases.

In 1588, Michel de Montaigne published his essay 'On the Lame', in which he attacked the heart of the witch persecutions. 'To kill people, it is necessary to have a luminous and sharp clarity; and our life is too real and essential to warrant [belief in] these supernatural and fantastic accidents', often seen as witches' acts. Montaigne agreed with Weyer that witches could not perform the feats mentioned repeatedly in trials. He asked, 'How much more natural is it that our understanding is moved out of place by the volubility of our defective spirit, than that one of us is carried away on a broom, along the shaft of the chimney, flesh and bone, by a strange spirit?' Such scenes were illusions, but not ones caused from without; they were 'domestic and our own'. It was entirely wrong to execute people on the basis of testimony that they had flown to a sabbat and committed *maleficia*. 'After all,' Montaigne continued, 'it is placing a very high value on one's conjectures to burn a man alive because of them.'[33]

At the time that Weyer and Montaigne wrote about witchcraft, European thought was still dominated by the idea that supernatural forces, either good or evil, were the cause of a vast array of phenomena in the universe. These two writers in particular were at the forefront of a shift to the idea that most events had some natural cause. Montaigne argued for 'verification by a non-marvellous way', by which he meant that the factors determining most events could be understood through the use of reason. For him the binary oppositions used to describe the world into his time were becoming inadequate to explain reality.

In effect, writers such as Montaigne and Weyer wished to bring the discussion of witchcraft down to earth and to observable, verifiable phenomena. They claimed that a whole range of connections and causative factors could account for what others called supernatural acts.[34] People had long understood some behaviour and activity, whether by humans or not, to be natural and to follow certain laws of the physical world. Sexual intercourse would, in certain circumstances, lead to pregnancy, even if the necessary conditions were, and still are, imperfectly understood. God might allow the pregnancy or not, but nevertheless the appearance, development and birth of a new human being followed predictable patterns that to a fair extent people could know. If they did not comprehend all the properties of a natural occurrence at any point in time, they expected to learn more about them; this was especially true as experimental science and observation began to gain ground in the late Middle Ages. If people had not accepted the principle that they could understand some physical laws, they would not have practised medicine or converted iron ore into metal, for example.

When something went wrong in the natural order of things, as people thought of it in the early modern period, the cause was often assigned to a supernatural realm of evil. Comparing attitudes towards the birth of a healthy female child and towards a deformed baby of either sex may help clarify the point. Ancient and medieval thought considered girl babies the result of a problem with the father at the time of conception: he may have been especially old, sick, weak or tired. Thus the birth of a female was seen as the result of natural actions and conditions, not of supernatural intervention. However, a baby of either sex with serious birth defects was termed a monster, 'marvel' or 'wonder', as opposed to a miracle, which could only come from God and could therefore not be evil. A wonder also represented something far from the norm, but in an ugly or distinctly unpleasant form, pointing to its evil origins.

Weyer, Montaigne and others took a stand against overestimating supernatural agency and using that judgement to convict human beings of crimes. Both writers were especially appalled by the unwarranted leap in logic that tied people with bad reputations to intervention in the world by the devil. Weyer wrote much about demons at work on earth, but he inclined even more towards finding the natural causes of events. The quality of evidence used to convict witches was poor, both men maintained. Montaigne once had the opportunity extended to him by a 'sovereign prince' to examine ten or twelve accused witches. Although some had confessed, supposedly freely, Montaigne remained absolutely unconvinced that he was looking at truly guilty people. He believed them deranged and remarked that 'justice has its proper corrections for such maladies'.[35] Malady was hardly the same as demonic intervention.

The bipolar view of the world, with its great stress on the role of the supernatural, was beginning to break down. Yet Weyer evoked passionate rebuttals, and at the time Montaigne wrote, his logic could not deter the certainty of many judges who accepted the confessions of suspects brought to torture. Even Christian Thomasius, professor of law at the Universities of Leipzig and then Halle, who became an ardent opponent of torture in the early eighteenth century, was still in favour of witch trials and the use of torture in them as late as 1694. When in that year the first witch-craft case he had ever encountered came to his department for an opinion, he read widely on the subject, particularly in Bodin, Del Rio and the *Malleus*. Armed with the views of the worst witch hunters, he came to a faculty meeting prepared to vote yes to the trial and torture. To his surprise, all of his colleagues held the opposite opinion. Only then did Thomasius realize that he had accepted 'inadequate' reasoning from the witch persecutors.[36] As bright and well educated as Thomasius was, it took this shock from his colleagues to make him re-examine the basis of his thoughts on witches. Much the same could be said about Cotton Mather in Massachusetts.

It seems that no logical argument could stop the witch hunts; the sordid experiences of the persecutions themselves had to give rise to definitive objections. However, that outcome depended to a large degree and for a long time on where the hunts took place.

THE SOCIAL GEOGRAPHY OF EVIDENCE

Chapter 1 described the formation of Christian solidarity and a persecuting society in Europe. The good Christians became accus-tomed to looking for enemies within. But it does not follow that the Christian community then identified deviants with such foes; indeed, lepers, homosexuals, agents of Eastern Orthodoxy or Jews were depicted as arch criminals.

Emile Durkheim, the father of modern sociology, offered an argument on the connections between social solidarity and perse-cution of criminals that remains intriguing. Various sociologists have drawn on Durkheim's views in an effort to explain witch trials. For example, Kai Erikson's *Wayward Puritans*,[37] which con-centrates on the Salem trials, relies on Durkheim's theory that all societies establish norms of behaviour. Societies label conduct which does not conform to those standards as deviance. In turn deviance is often made a crime. Societies follow these unwritten processes in order to define acceptable behavioural boundaries. Durkheim's concern was with crime in general, which he deemed 'normal': every society needs it to enable people to readily understand what is permitted and what is not.[38] Crime is the mirror in which normality can be seen.

Some accounts of the witch hunts, like numerous works on the Soviet Terror, argue that the elite created and then persecuted the deviants it needed in Durkheimian terms, so that acceptable behaviour would be clearer to all; this is a 'functional sociological explanation of punishment'.[39] But Durkheim's notions of crime and deviance do not fit the witch persecutions well. They may, as discussed in the previous chapter, obscure the point that witches were charged with serious, 'core' crimes. In addition, witch hunts, like lynching of African Americans, were largely a phenomenon of rural and small town life; they occurred in the principality of Nassau but not neighbouring Frankfurt, in Salem Village but rarely in Boston, widely in Franche-Comté but in small numbers in Besançon, and so on.[40] Villages are largely face-to-face communities, and in such settings a person's cumulative bad reputation could lead to an accusation of witchcraft if circumstances linked her to unfortunate events.[41] That is, reputation, as the law codes emphasized, served as an *indicium* of guilt or innocence. Durkheim himself suggested that his theory of the social creation of crime applied 'particularly in a small town'.[42] As Wolfgang Behringer has noted, 'tiny jurisdictions faced greater danger of prosecutions being more dependent on the whims of their rulers and the mood of the populace'.[43] To this one might add that tiny rural jurisdictions faced this problem most of all.

In a town of any size the population was much more fluid, which meant that general reputation could not count for as much as it did in a village. A cohesive community that could give a generally accepted opinion about the character of a defendant was much easier to find in rural milieus than in towns. On the other hand, municipal officials were much more used to relying on documents than on tradition and reputation. This approach to records and the fact that in towns not just a few people but hundreds, perhaps thousands, had been near babies when they died, for example, meant that urban courts needed a different kind of evidence to convict than did village tribunals. Town magistrates needed to hear from eyewitnesses who said they had seen the accused commit a crime, as opposed to people who reported the circumstance that 20 years earlier piglets had died after the defendant was in the farmyard. How could the fact that a crime of witchcraft had occurred even be established in a city, where proximity to a misfortune could involve hundreds of unknown residents or visitors? If no one can be found to blame for a 'crime', perhaps there is no crime.

In addition, urban settings are built environments in which people have created their surroundings. Social structure is also much more fluid and dependent on activity, not birth, than it is in the countryside. Therefore in towns people are more inclined to adopt the view that human actions, not supernatural ones of any variety, are responsible for events.

For these reasons, municipal judges tended to keep witchcraft defendants in jail longer, to take more care investigating their cases, and to acquit more of the accused than did village magistrates.[44] Conviction rates for accused witches were much lower in Geneva, for example, than in nearby rural areas. In the period between the beginning of the Reformation (1517) and the last known witch trial in the city, held in 1681, the conviction rate there was only about 30 per cent. Subtracting the panics connected with episodes of the plague, in which people charged with spreading the disease were tried as witches, brings the conviction rate in the remaining witchcraft cases down to 21 per cent.[45] Moreover, during the period of the witch prosecutions, Geneva was a republic with a hinterland. Most guilty verdicts in Genevan courts were returned against rural inhabitants of the republic, not against residents of the city itself,[46] which suggests that once more the dynamics of village social interaction influenced the standards of evidence.

It cannot be mere coincidence that one of the most urbanized parts of Europe, the northern Netherlands, had few trials of diabolically inclined malefactors and stopped using the death penalty for them quite early. During the sixteenth century, Amsterdam replaced nearby Antwerp as the centre of world trade and finance. Rotterdam, Haarlem, Utrecht and other cities of the Dutch northern provinces lay close together and made up a relatively dense urban network. The volume of international business transacted in the Netherlands was huge for its day, and it relied at bottom on written documents. The whole atmosphere of the region was as different as could be found in the early modern period from the intimate world of village witches and their accusers.

An extreme but telling example of urban authorities' approaches to witchcraft comes from the city of Frankfurt. While hundreds of witches were executed in surrounding principalities during the sixteenth and seventeenth centuries, no one was put to death on that charge in the city. Townspeople were occasionally arrested on suspicion of witchcraft, but Frankfurt's magistrates compiled a remarkable record as they investigated the accusations. A housewife, Endressen Krein, was arrested for witchcraft and sorcery in 1541. She confessed under torture but then retracted her statement, saying that she had admitted guilt only because of the pain. If she was a witch, she maintained, then all her neighbours were too. We can imagine what would have happened to her next in a village, but in Frankfurt she was kept in jail for three years while the magistrates decided what to do with her. Then in 1544, two preachers spoke to the city council on her behalf, saying that she placed all her hopes in God; she was freed.

In 1564 and again in 1573, suspects were jailed in Frankfurt for short periods on suspicion of committing witchcraft, but were quickly released. The second instance involved a woman and her husband who were tortured twice; however, they then withdrew their confessions. Torture in Frankfurt was certainly not nearly as ferocious as in Ban de la Roche, although both were Protestant jurisdictions.

Banishment of witches from Frankfurt did occur, in 1574 and 1585. Nothing regarding witchcraft is then recorded in the town until 1660, when a Pastor Waldschmidt gave a series of 16 sermons on witches along the lines of the *Malleus*. His talks and two books he published that year produced a 'very strong' impact on the populace. Even so, the next Frankfurt witch trial was not held until 1670. It dragged on for two years, producing a file of some 400 pages. Elisabeth Burgk, a widow of a respectable citizen of another town, was the defendant.

Philipp Jakob Spener, the senior pastor in Frankfurt, took a direct role in the case, while the city prosecutor was a doctor of law. Even though several of Burgk's natural offspring and step-children testified that she had forced them to attend a sabbat and had killed her husband, she was acquitted. The city's attorney pointed to contradictions in the children's testimony – one said something happened in daytime, another at night, for example. The perplexed city council sent the trial materials to the Universities of Speyer and Strasbourg for opinions, but these did not offer unequivocal advice. Under further questioning, the children then retracted their testimony. At this point Spener, having interrogated the children, said there were no grounds for proceeding with the case. Again the city council members spoke with the children, who now admitted their great dislike of their stepmother. Finally Burgk was freed and completely 'rehabilitated, without any kind of damages', presumably other than the gross inconvenience of being in jail and undergoing a trial that lasted some two years. This was the final witch trial in the city.[47]

In all of the Frankfurt cases, especially the last, it is clear that the urban authorities took great care to make sure that the charges of witchcraft before them were thoroughly investigated. No one in the municipal administration was in a hurry to convict. Suspects recanted their confessions after torture and were allowed to do so. In villages gripped by witch fear, this would have been a rare occurrence.

Known witch trials in Poland follow the same pattern: 3 per cent of them took place in large towns, 16 per cent in small towns, and 81 per cent in villages.[48] Even though the Polish defendants were almost always charged with the old sorcery, not the new witchcraft, these figures say much about the social geography of accusations of *maleficia*.

To some extent, the town/country difference in witch trials found so often across Europe is a replication of the divide between 'shame' and 'guilt' cultures. People know each other and the history of local families in small venues. In those settings a more rigid social hierarchy is likely to be in place than would be the case in a town. These circumstances tend to produce a culture of shame. That is, people's sense of worth comes from outside, from the community, because position in the community is not easily altered. Individual and familial conduct are taken as known quantities. Hans Neuweiller's father was a witch, so perhaps he is one, too. Shame, honour and reputation are bundled together in this kind of culture, although 'honour' is a term usually attached to those of higher social standing. In such a context it is difficult to change a reputation once it is established, and anyone with a good reputation reacts quickly when it is threatened.

Urban life involves less face-to-face knowledge of others and hence less reliance on reputation or honour. Town life depends much more on guilt culture, in which one's sense of worth comes from within. This orientation is more appropriate where neighbours, level of wealth, occupation and residence change more rapidly than in a village. Documents, not family history and traditional place in the social hierarchy, establish who one is. Such differences could be seen clearly in nineteenth-century America, for example; the northern states, much more urbanized and mobile in their populations, may be characterized as a guilt society. The southern states, still overwhelmingly rural, operated largely as an honour society.[49]

Considerations of evidence regarding crime in the two regions tended to diverge along these same lines. In early modern Europe a similar pattern characterized witchcraft accusations. On the whole they were investigated more carefully in towns than in villages, and acquittal rates were higher in the former. The same pattern pertains to higher courts compared to lower ones. In effect, the farther removed a set of magistrates was from the actual scene of purported witchcraft, the more attention had to be devoted to the cold documents at hand, and the less the immediate emotions of anger and fear raging on the local level mattered. If Jeanne was near a bull when it suddenly died and ten years later happened to pass by a house where a baby died the next day, those 'facts' had much greater resonance among her neighbours than they did to a judge sitting hundreds of kilometres away who had to look at evidence on a great many matters. Nor did the remote judge have to live among the villagers who blamed Jeanne for their troubles.

Of course no absolute division between village and town existed in regard to witch hunts. Often in cities strong voices supported witch trials, even if they took place largely in rural areas. Sharp debates went on in some areas, and finally across Europe, between members of the elite who thought that witches presented an immense danger and had to be hunted down ruthlessly and those who argued against broad hunts.

PRO- AND ANTI-PERSECUTION FORCES

Wolfgang Behringer has called the two sides in the witch debate the pro- and anti-persecution forces. The story of their differences is one of men struggling to preserve their own positions and authority as well as to seek the truth. What does not emerge from the contest are indications that members of the sixteenth- or seventeenth-century Western elite sought to frighten women or deviants through witch trials. Rather, they spent their time and ink on assessment of how serious the threat from witches was and how it should be combated.

Behringer's work on south-eastern Germany, more or less present-day Bavaria, shows that early in the history of witch persecutions, important figures in the region disdained both the new view of witches as horribly dangerous creatures, which was in full flower by the late fifteenth century, and the use of torture to convict them. The Diet of Tyrol in 1487 protested against excesses in the application of torture. In the whole of southern Germany, Geiler von Kaysersberg, preaching and writing in Strasbourg in the early sixteenth century, was one of the few major spokesmen to endorse the views of the *Malleus*. Into the middle of the century, more people laid charges before Bavarian courts that they had been slandered as witches than were indicted for witchcraft. Most slander cases ended in punishment of the defamer.

The new stereotype of witches did not take hold in Bavaria, and indeed seemed to be losing ground there, before about 1520. From then until roughly 1560 the elite rejected charges of witchcraft in the court system – which had been, not coincidentally, heavily centralized in the Duchy of Bavaria since the late Middle Ages. Even when an entire village accused a woman of witchcraft at Kempten in 1549, the governor of the prince-abbacy dismissed the charge and forbade the villagers to spread further slanders.

However, if the *Malleus* and similar works fell into disuse and were not republished in the mid-sixteenth century, the adherents of persecution continued to make their views known. In 1562 Georg Pictorius, a professor at the University of Freiburg, a Catholic institution in south-western Germany, expressed his deep concern on the issue. He wrote that, 'If the witches are not burned, the number of these furies swells up in such an immense sea that no one could live safe from their spells and charms.'[50]

Nevertheless, it seemed to require a new level of anxiety in south Germany, resulting from crop failures and rises in the price of food, before magistrates responded favourably to witchcraft accusations. The first execution of a witch in Munich occurred in 1578. Another round of crises in 1586–89, involving agricultural and commercial difficulties and the plague, appears to have sparked an outbreak of witch hunts that became severe in places. Yet witch persecutions did not affect more than about one-third of south-east Germany's cities, and in some towns the authorities held back from convictions. Eight women put on trial in Augsburg in 1590 were all acquitted, but at the same time, 'almost all authorities of the region argued for ruthless persecution of witches'; this might provide a quick escape from the 'plagues'.[51] The single worst hunt in the area occurred in 1590 in Ellingen, then a largely autonomous district administered by the Order of Teutonic Knights. At least 72 people were burned.

Witch persecutions were extremely erratic in south-east Germany, with a great concentration in the years immediately after 1590; of the fourteen witch hunts with more than twenty victims in the region, ten occurred in this period. The steady stream of trials to be expected if they were meant to control a particular kind of person is missing. Instead, the Bavarian hunts represented panicked responses to local difficulties, during which women and finally men of high status were accused and executed.

But together with the flames rose criticism of the hunts and the tactics used to obtain confessions. The University of Ingolstadt in 1592 proffered an official opinion that torture should not be 'applied on too little or very slight circumstantial evidence'. Innocent people might be induced to confess; however, the opinion hedged by saying that the 'really guilty' should be tortured and burned. In Munich local judges spoke out against unusual torture. The town of Weissenburg broke off its trials on advice from the city council of Nuremberg; Kaufbeuren also stopped its prosecutions after seeking the views of a doctor of law in Augsburg. The city pastor of Nördlingen denounced persecutions, and many priests and pastors in the religiously mixed area agreed. In the cities of Ingolstadt and Munich in the 1590s, ducal courts took cases away from local judges who were reluctant to try witches, but a number of citizens protested 'vigorously' against the ducal trials in 1590 and urged restriction of torture. Critical voices grew louder in Bavaria during the year.

Initially, major objections were to certain kinds of torture, for example putting a tight-fitting iron mask on the victim's face for long periods. When tortures returned to their 'normal' usage, confessions ceased and the hunts collapsed. Of course, the opposition continued to urge extreme tortures, following the recommendations of the *Malleus* and the work of Bodin.

Still, Duke Maximilian of Bavaria could not make up his mind to stop the trials completely, and autonomous zealots such as the one who headed the little prince-provostship of Ellwangen followed their own lead, burning dozens from 1611–14. Even after the severe torture and execution of a family of beggars brought to Munich in 1600 raised a heavy wave of criticism, the duke would not end prosecutions. The argument among theologians and doctors of law continued in the city, with some figures repeating the claim that witchcraft was the ultimate *crimen exceptum* and as such had to be fought with extraordinary weapons. Finally, the ducal authorities sought opinions from five universities and specialists as far away as Trier and Baden, much further north in Germany. By 1604, once the replies had been studied, it became clear that in most of the areas that responded torture was no longer being used against people accused of witchcraft on the basis of denunciations alone. The anti-persecution party appeared to have won a serious victory.

Nevertheless, the zealots were so well entrenched in the city that torture and prosecution continued into 1630. Early the next year, the Elector Maximilian (the duchy had been elevated to an electorate in 1623, meaning that its ruler voted in elections for the emperor) promised clemency to those who confessed to witchcraft. This was on the surface a slight gesture, but was enough to turn the tide in Bavaria against further trials. In 1631 Friedrich von Spee published his *Cautio Criminalis* in Germany. It sharply blasted witch trials, in which there were unjust acts against 'countless innocents daily'. Anyone could be made to confess; torture had been 'all powerful'.[52] The bitter complaints about excesses in Trier, Bamberg and Würzburg that arose in 1630 and led high Bavarian and imperial officials to condemn the hunts there became known across Germany. Another voice in the same key came from France in 1621. Bernard de la Roche Flavin, a long-time member of the Toulouse Parlement, proclaimed torture 'a dangerous invention'. He asked, 'What would people not say or do to avoid such great pain?'[53] It is highly likely that such publicity had an impact on the Veldenz family in Ban de la Roche, where trials are not recorded after 1630.

Women screamed from the burning pyres that they were guiltless and had been tortured especially grotesquely, their husbands added their objections, and learned members of the elite continued to attack torture. This was important pressure on the authorities to at least modify the hunts, but ultimately 'blind persecuting zeal' was 'discredited by the persecutions themselves'. It became apparent that unusual or severe torture had produced false confessions that resulted in the deaths of innocent persons. This problem compromised the authorities, who could not distinguish the guilty from the innocent,[54] and when this outcome became obvious, the witch trials in south-east Germany ended. They had collapsed over the issue of evidence.

Spee and other critics of how trials were conducted, for example Adam Tanner, writing in 1629, were in all other respects orthodox spokesmen for the reality of the witch stereotype. Tanner took special care to argue against Weyer's view that flight to the sabbat and other acts ascribed to witches were illusions produced by the devil. Tanner emphatically proclaimed them real. What Tanner, Spee, Flavin and several others protested against in the same period was the use of torture to obtain evidence. Spee and his contemporary Johann Meyfart agreed that torture was an invention of the devil. Spee even argued that some German magistrates who had persecuted witches with great energy must be agents of the devil; they brought the innocent into court and spared the real witches.[55]

The large German trials of the period from 1590 to the 1630s had raised the problem of proof. When it became clear that anyone could be convicted with the help of especially brutal torture, no one was safe from the charge of witchcraft and from the flames. In 1585 the magistrates at Rottenburg, Germany, after burning more than 20 females since 1578, remarked that at that rate there would soon be no women left in the town.[56] A 70-year-old French woman condemned to be strangled and then burned for witchcraft exclaimed in 1601, 'What is this, they say that every woman is a witch!'[57]

The most notorious and deadly witch hunt in England raised similar issues. In 1645 an obscure country gentleman, Matthew Hopkins, decided that a group of women were gathering near his home to conduct diabolical rites. He began to style himself the 'Witchfinder General' and to claim that he could identify witches. At first he searched for them in villages of north-east Essex, where, as mentioned earlier, a tradition of persecuting witches already existed. However, witch fear soon spread to neighbouring counties as well.

Hopkins persuaded a number of villages to allow him and his partner, John Stearne, to identify suspects and to torture them. According to Hopkins, the pair quickly began to receive requests for help from villages that believed they were besieged by witches. The investigators would arrive in a place and, listening to the local people vent their grievances and accusations, would choose likely suspects. The witch finders developed a set of procedures that produced numerous confessions: first they deprived the accused (overwhelmingly women) of sleep and food for days. The investigators pricked their victims all over with needles in an effort to find the devil's mark, and they tied suspects in uncomfortable positions to stools or tables for long periods of time. Hopkins and his followers would then watch to see if some 'imp', any kind of animal or insect, came into the room where the defendant was bound.[58]

In what might be called a witch panic, some 250 people from the surrounding area had to appear before local authorities on suspicion of witchcraft. Of these, 200 were investigated in the second half of 1645. More than 87 per cent of the 184 suspects known to have been tried were females. Probably at least 100 people were executed before the scare began to die down.[59]

Whether Hopkins furthered the hunt to make money is not clear; he protested at the time that he earned little from his work. It does seem that his services were in great demand for a while from some villages, which paid substantial sums to Hopkins, his assistants and a hangman.

A number of unusual circumstances made Hopkins's efforts possible in the first place. The English Civil War had disrupted the regular administration of justice, so that assize (circuit) judges were not in place in the early stages of the hunt. When Hopkins began his campaign, there was also a gap in authority at his home town, Manningtree, where the lord of the manor had died a few years earlier and left his estate, with its formal and informal authority, to his daughters. Finally, there was no local clergyman in Manningtree in 1645. Just as in Salem a few years later, the hunt occurred at a moment of disruption in political and judicial authority, and several influences that might have acted to restrain the persecution were missing.

However popular Hopkins's activities may have been at first, they quickly evoked objections. In 1646 the Reverend John Gaule, vicar of Great Staughton, preached a sermon denouncing the hunt. Although there is no record of exactly what he said, in the same year he published his views in a book. He charged that the witch finders:

conclude peremptorily (not from reason but from indiscretion) that witches not only are, but are in every place and Parish with them, every old woman with a wrinkled face, a furr'd brow, a hairy lip, a gobber tooth, a squint eye, a squeaking voice, or a scolding tongue, having a rugged coat on her back, a skull-cap on her head, a spindle in her hand, and a Dog or Cat by her side; is not only suspected but pronounced for a witch.

Every disease or accident, every strange motion by a cow or hog, is immediately 'reckoned and rumoured for bewitched' by Hopkins. Men who are 'conscientious or judicious' must regard such judgements as highly dubious.[60]

Gaule invited Hopkins to come to Great Staughton. Hopkins replied in a letter to one of the vicar's parishioners that he would soon visit the village, though he never did. It may be that Gaule's sermon reached the assize judges in Norfolk; in any event, they sent sharp enquiries to the Witchfinder about his methods. The magistrates in 1646 forbade the practices of starving, watching and depriving suspects of sleep. Within a year Hopkins was dead of tuberculosis, and after 14 months of intense activity, the hunt was over.[61]

John Gaule maintained even years later that witches existed and could do harm. He insisted that women were far more likely than men to become the devil's auxiliaries.[62] In short, he was much in the mould of Johann Weyer, Friedrich von Spee and others who accepted the existence of witches on earth but strongly questioned the kinds of procedures used to wring 'evidence' of *maleficia* from them.

Gaule went somewhat further than these other critics of the hunts, however, by pointing to the problem that anyone with a slightly strange appearance or bad reputation could be termed a witch and, in the hands of people using strong methods, be made to confess. H. C. Erik Midelfort argued in his study of south-west Germany that 'witch hunters stopped because they no longer knew how to find witches'.[63] But it would be better to say that the hunters were stopped, by members of the elite and sometimes by popular sentiment. Critics realized that since the witch finders could 'prove' that anyone was a witch, in reality they could not prove that anyone was a witch. However, this lesson did not come quickly or easily to people, particularly in small communities that had been badly frightened by the alleged presence of witches. It seemed to take a large hunt to drive home the point not that there were no witches, but that there was no reasonable test to discover them. The anti-persecution forces, who had been trying to make their case all along, were finally heeded.

One of the leading voices for persecution in Massachusetts was Cotton Mather. He had played a major role in engendering the mood of fear that helped produce a hunt after interfering in a case of 'witchcraft' in Boston in 1688. The next year he published an account of the affair in *Memorable Providences*, where he argued at length that the devil and his helpers presented a great threat to Massachusetts. He detailed the agonies that an Irish washerwoman, one Glover, had supposedly inflicted on the Goodwins, a respectable Christian family. He insisted that the spectre of Glover or other witches had attacked the Goodwin children. Prefiguring and undoubtedly contributing to the 'possession' of the girls at Salem Village, the afflicted Goodwins had 'fits' in which 'sometimes they would be *Deaf*, sometimes *Dumb*, and sometimes *Blind*, and often, *all this* at once'. Glover was executed, but Mather claimed she had said that others like her were still at large.[64]

Cotton Mather's views apparently appealed to many in Salem Village by early 1692, yet by no means resolved the subject of witchcraft in Massachusetts. Instead, the trials of that year ignited a new discussion. The pro- and anti-persecution parties then compressed much of their debate into the span of a few months, almost the period of the hunt itself. As the trials began, important voices in Massachusetts started to express dissatisfaction with the Oyer and Terminer Court, its conceptions of valid evidence and the spread of accusations. Ironically, Mather was among a group of ministers who quickly questioned the court's activities. They announced on 15 June that spectral evidence or 'Alterations made in the Sufferers, by a Look or Touch of the Accused' could not be considered 'infallible Evidence of Guilt'. Despite their dislike of such proof, admitted in Salem and the decisive factor in a number of convictions, the ministers hedged by calling for the 'speedy and vigorous Prosecution of such as have rendered themselves obnoxious'.[65]

Meanwhile, another influential minister, Samuel Willard, preached caution to his congregation in Boston. In late September he defied the governor's order not to write about the trials and published, under a pseudonym, a strong critique of the proceedings. Conviction by mere suspicion, he said, was 'contrary to the mind of God . . . besides, reason tells us, that the more horrid the crime is, the more cautious we ought to be in making any guilty of it'. The judges did not have matters of fact 'evidently done and clearly proved'.[66]

In a letter to a member of the governor's council dated 17 August, Cotton Mather appeared to agree. Spectral evidence alone is not enough to convict, he declared, but it should be used as presumptive evidence which would lead the court to investigate further. Mather suggested that the devil might impersonate good persons, perhaps even himself. He hinted at the possibility that innocent people may have been convicted; if so, they should be reprieved. But he also endorsed the judges' 'great work' thus far.[67] Two days later he appeared at the Salem gallows and urged the spectators to approve the hanging of George Burroughs. Standing with a noose around his neck, Burroughs had caused a sensation by reciting the

Lord's Prayer correctly, something a disciple of the devil was not supposed to be able to do. Mather nevertheless persuaded the crowd to let the execution proceed. By this time he was mired in profound contradictions about the evidence against the accused.

In October 1692, Mather published *The Wonders of the Invisible World*. Drawing on a book by the Englishman William Perkins, Mather listed a number of 'presumptions' that should spark an investigation of witchcraft. These included notoriety as a witch and the death of someone following cursing by the suspect. Yet these were not 'just and sufficient proofs'. A confession would be sufficient, but it had to follow 'due Examination'. He maintained that 'sufficient' testimony for a guilty verdict would also be two witnesses who said they had seen a defendant make a pact with the devil; Mather had now arrived at the continental, not the English, standard for conviction. Proof could also be that the witch had a 'familiar spirit', usually a small animal, that was in fact a demon assigned by the devil for the comfort and aid of the witch. Here Mather says nothing about how a court could be certain that an animal was more than it appeared to be. Finally, witnesses might state that a suspect carried out an act, a wonder, that could occur only with the help of witchcraft, for example raising a storm. Again, Mather does not make clear how the court was to determine that the witch had actually caused the storm. *Wonders* also ignores the question of spectral evidence. Several witnesses testified that it was the 'shape' of Bridget Bishop which pinched and tormented them, for example, even though Bishop herself was elsewhere at the time.

At this point, Cotton Mather's father Increase intervened in the whole affair. In early October he gave a sermon on witchcraft to a group of ministers gathered in Boston especially to hear him, then quickly published a book on the subject.[68] The elder Mather asserted that the devil may appear in the shape of an innocent and pious person as well as in the form of the wicked. This point alone attacked much of the testimony accepted by the Oyer and Terminer

Court, for the devil might assume the guise of an honest person and give testimony to destroy another upright resident. Noting that 'the Devils have of late accused some eminent Persons', Increase Mather found that the testimony of 'possessed' people should not be taken as proof of witchcraft, for then 'no Person whatsoever can be in safety'. What the bewitched say has happened to other people 'is not to be taken as evidence'. Scripture gives not the 'least Intimation' that it is proof of a diabolical connection when a possessed person falls into a fit under the glance of another individual.

Increase Mather concluded that 'the Evidence in this Crime ought to be as clear' as for any other capital offence. 'The Oath of a distracted . . . or of a possessed Person' was not accepted in accusations of murder, theft and so forth, and therefore could not be accepted regarding witchcraft. Finally, 'it were better that ten suspected witches should escape, than that one innocent Person should be Condemned'.[69] This was the strong voice of scepticism, not regarding the existence of witches, but about evidence for their *maleficia*. It was also a suggestion that innocent people had suffered.

The elder Mather was trying to allay the sense of panic about witches that had fallen upon the court and the community. In a statement entitled 'The Christian Reader' that prefaced his book, 14 ministers added their view that 'the more execrable the Crime is, the more critical care is to be used' in judging it.[70] Together, the men holding these views comprised a strong anti-persecution party in Massachusetts, which had developed in reaction to the witch hunt. In that same month of October 1692, they prevailed upon Governor Phips to halt the trials.

Although he allowed another special court to convene briefly in early 1693, there were no more executions. In May Phips pardoned and released the remaining prisoners. There followed the recantation of the Salem jurors, with its emphasis on the inadequacy of the evidence used to convict witches just a year before. It had at least required much less time and bloodshed in Massachusetts to resolve the issue that in Bavaria had dragged on for decades.

LEARNED CULTURE, POPULAR CULTURE AND THE TAMING OF THE WITCH

As the witch pyres began to go out, it was logical that a new or renewed positive image of women would emerge in Europe. Beginning at the latest in the middle of the sixteenth century, more beneficent pictures of women began to appear in western European art. Instead of figuring as the devil's followers engaged in repulsive acts, women in the new paintings carried out respectable tasks in a disciplined manner. Unlike medieval illustrations, in which women were often shown in prayer or as peasants without discernible individual traits doing menial labour, the new pictures gave females distinct personalities.[71]

An early example is *A Woman Weighing Gold (Die Goldwagerin)*, about 1530, ascribed to Jan Sandersran Messen. This attractive and clearly capable woman is taking care of business. There is a hint of greed in her face, but it is presented as an everyday human characteristic. Pieter Aertsen's *Market Woman at a Vegetable Stand*, 1567, depicts a clear-eyed, plainly but tastefully dressed woman who looks directly at the viewer. Perhaps her eyes convey a taste for innocent mischief, but there is nothing malevolent about her. Agostino Carraci's portrait *Anna Parolini Guicciardini*, 1598, depicts a respectable, serious woman holding a book. It would require a great leap of imagination to connect her with the insatiably lusty chatterers of the *Malleus*.

The goddess Diana now returns to her rightful place in Roman mythology, leaving the Furious Horde nowhere to be seen. In a large canvas by Jan Tilens (1589–1630), *A Mountain Valley with Diana and her Nymphs*, peace reigns. Diana would not be Diana without her bow and arrows, but she seems beyond a doubt to be after wild game, not souls. By the time Jan Vermeer (1632–75) was at the peak of his creativity, delightfully peaceful women carry on conversations or the business of daily life with a calm dignity that the viewer can hardly avoid sensing.

Although there were many reasons why Dutch painters led the way in depicting respectable women, one is certainly that the witch hunts ended relatively early in the Netherlands, clearing the ground for representations of females as serious, productive, but also fully human. By the early 1600s at the latest, it seems, Dutch artists reflected the fact that their society had better roles in mind for women than witches had afforded.

In England, theatre began to illustrate changes in the attitudes that had facilitated the witch hunts. Shakespeare created a host of spirits who might be good, bad or indifferent in plays like *A Midsummer Night's Dream* (probably 1595) and *The Tempest* (about 1610). These supernatural creatures could make mischief but did so largely to play upon humans' vanities and weaknesses. Ben Jonson spoofed the whole idea that humans could control supernatural forces in *The Alchemist* (1610). Thomas Middleton's *The Witch*, a comedy written between 1613 and 1615, presents witches as funny, rather harmless figures involved in antics that mimic courtiers' foibles.[72]

In the country's theatre of the early seventeenth century, the figure of the witch 'divided modernity from the rural past and scientific skill from supernatural and providential narrations'.[73] In other words, the witch began to be depicted as something that uneducated bumpkins believed in; educated people knew better. Witches became creatures from a faraway place or the distant past, for example the early Scotland of *Macbeth* (first performed about 1606), where in any event the hags can only see the future, not alter it. English culture was beginning to tame the witch and to depict the spirit world as not always purely good or purely evil.

Surely this trend both affected and reflected the thinking of English magistrates and juries, for the percentage of acquittals (other than during the great exception to all such patterns in 1645–46) rose 'enormously after 1620'. And after Matthew Hopkins and his hunt came to their ends, the minor gentry who comprised grand juries were increasingly reluctant to indict on the charge of witchcraft. Petty juries were more loath to convict when trials did occur.[74] James Sharpe remarks that after the Hopkins episode, witch hunting became associated with 'extreme sectarian Protestantism' and the instability of the 1640s and 1650s;[75] this was a time and an outlook that most people wished to leave behind. The educated strata of England were turning away from the sense, never deeply established in much of the country to begin with, that witches presented serious danger to society.

The French lagged behind a little and took a different direction in deflating the maleficence of spirits, but by the 1680s and 1690s had moved forward a great deal. Gallic minds now turned considerable talent and attention not to high culture, not to low culture, but to a blend of the two in the seemingly modest form of the fairy tale. Yet the importance of these stories can scarcely be overestimated when it comes to the witch persecutions. Witches, fairies, goblins and many another supernatural creature were now allotted a middle position in the grand scheme of things. That is, a witch or the devil himself could appear in stories but be conquered or outwitted; fairies might be kind and helpful. As Marina Warner puts it, 'this was the in-betweenness of a fairy land where phenomena took place that were not the result of maleficium, where supernatural beings who were not of the party of the Devil were believed to exist'. By 1685 Parisian women of high social standing told each other fairy tales and dressed up to play the parts. In the 1690s fairy tales began to appear in French; especially important and enduring was the collection by Charles Perrault entitled *Tales of My Mother*

Goose. The frontispiece to the book depicts an old woman – a kindly, intelligent woman telling harmless stories to children listening with rapt attention.[76] Mother Goose herself, of course, is usually shown as an attractive, benign older woman.

Across the West, the view that the spirit world was entirely good, entirely evil or even especially powerful was to disappear. Two small children could trick a witch and cook her in 'Hansel and Gretel'. By the 1960s and 1970s, endless rock songs touted the 'witchy woman' or similar types as intriguing and desirable, while the Rolling Stones even demanded sympathy for the devil. In a popular American country song, a young man could beat the devil in a fiddling contest. Such an outcome, indeed the contest itself, was inconceivable in the early modern period.

[*]

In the northern Netherlands the witch trials, if they may even be accorded that name, were largely over by the late 1500s; except for one area still under Spanish control, no executions took place there after 1600. This date is far too early for any impact of the 'scientific revolution' to have been present. The German critics of the witch hunts in the late 1620s and early 1630s were, judging by their writings, firm believers in the witch stereotype. They found fault only with the way trials were conducted, especially with the use of torture. René Descartes, who argued that the material universe was completely separate from the spiritual one, was 4 years old when the Dutch trials ceased and had not yet published his major philosophical treatise, the *Discourse on Method* (1637), when Friederich von Spee and other Germans scorned the practices of the trials. Isaac Newton was born in 1642 and did not begin to acquire wide renown until the publication of his *Principia Mathematicae* in 1686.

Thus it is not possible to chart a simple connection between the new science of the sixteenth and seventeenth centuries and the end of the witch hunts. In the 1560s Johann Weyer could simultaneously oppose the hunts, call for reliance on observed phenomena and reason, denigrate women, and indicate a deep faith that witches existed. About 130 years later, Cotton Mather performed scientific experiments and read avidly about the new science but also strongly promoted the Salem trials. Newton described several basic laws of the universe, which to 'modern' minds tend to exclude interventions by witches and the devil. Certainly that was the reputation attached to Newton's work by the *philosophes* of the Enlightenment. Yet Newton was deeply drawn to what would now be called magic or even gibberish; he 'devoted more of his time to alchemy in the early 1690s than he did to everything else put together'.[77] Several leading members of the Royal Society in the mid- to late seventeenth century, among them Henry More and Joseph Glanville, attacked scepticism toward witchcraft, partly out of a concern that eliminating a fear of the devil would in turn lead to atheism.[78] In these and many other cases down to the present, science has proved to be less than completely scientific. Those who practise science are human and do not relinquish their cherished beliefs, hopes, fears or paradigms lightly.

Yet certainly in the arguments of Montaigne, Weyer, Spee and others a more 'modern' approach to natural phenomena is emerging. They maintain that more and more can be understood in terms of the interaction of ordinary substances and forces, even if those things themselves cannot be fully comprehended. Courts should admit only evidence that could be confirmed by observation, not forced from helpless people through torture. On the whole the momentum of such thought was to ascribe ever less importance to evil, supernatural forces that could supposedly alter basic patterns of existence – raise a storm when all had been calm, possess a young girl, kill a healthy baby.

As the stories of the English theatre and the French society ladies acting out fairy tales suggest, it became increasingly fashionable during the seventeenth century to discard credulity about witchcraft. The social geography of evidence, favouring a more sceptical view in cities, enhanced this trend. Those educated people who opposed scepticism found themselves fighting a losing battle, especially because they often relied on fear of atheism, not on carefully reasoned arguments about the nature of the universe.

The Thirty Years War raged across central Europe, devastating parts of Germany and other lands numerous times, between 1618 and 1648. Both the coming of the war and its departure from a given area contributed to the decline of the witch hunts. When fighting reached any place, it became the inhabitants' overwhelming concern. Rather than torture and execute each other, they had to stick together as much as possible to avoid death at the hands of the contending armies. Even forces nominally friendly to the people of a region could turn on them in large and small ways, as ill-disciplined or hungry troops often pillaged and raped. With the end of the war, many of the old, small German political districts were amalgamated or absorbed into larger units. As this happened local princes and other rulers were able to assert more authority over their realms. In the Saar, for example, the princes now exercised more power over the villages; during the next few decades the rulers hampered and then halted the witch hunts that had been propelled from below. Royal authority expanded in France, and in 1682 Louis XIV issued an edict in which he spoke of the 'pretended crime of sorcery'. His law did not erase witchcraft from the statutes as a crime, but it did reflect the new and increasingly widely held view among the educated strata that witches did not commit real crimes.

By this time, the attitude of central authorities in most parts of the West had turned sharply against the idea that witch trials had any merit. Perhaps an entire era of heightened fear had closed; Jean Delumeau has remarked that by the middle of the seventeenth century, 'the generalized offensive of the Enemy [Satan], prelude to the end of days, had not come to pass, and no one could say any more when it would. A Christianity that had believed it was being cruelly besieged [now] demobilized itself.'[79]

Above all, however, the excesses of the witch persecutions themselves, in regard to both torture and the scale of many hunts, brought the whole nature of the proceedings into question. As it became clear that innocent people had been convicted on the basis of inadequate or absurd evidence, the trials collapsed, and subsequently (or well before this according to Montaigne) the way was opened for a more critical stance towards evidence of any kind, including the ways of the natural world.

The appalling features of the witch hunts made them unfashionable and repellent to many members of the elite. The questions raised about evidence encouraged educated people to be more open to further scientific enquiry. In these ways the end of the witch hunts encouraged the already developing scientific revolution to a much greater degree than developments in the scientific world contributed to the conclusion of the witch hunts.

NOTES

1. Steinthal ms., pp. 270–94.
2. 'The Recantation of the Salem Jurors, 1693', in Alan Charles Kors and Edward Peters, eds; revised by Edward Peters (2001) *Witchcraft in Europe 400–1700: A Documentary History*, 2nd edn (Philadelphia: University of Pennsylvania Press), p. 437.
3. Edward Peters (1985) *Torture* (New York: Basil Blackwell), p. 49.
4. See, respectively, Michael R. Weisser (1979) *Crime and Punishment in Early Modern Europe* (Atlantic Highlands, NJ: Humanities Press), pp. 131–2; Michel Foucault (1979) *Discipline and Punish: the Birth of the Prison*, trans. Alan Sheridan (New York: Vintage Books), p. 42; and Anne Barstow (1994) *Witchcraze: A New History of the European Witch Hunts* (San Francisco: Harper).

5. Note that in Salem those who confessed were not executed; this was most certainly not the continental practice.

6. Peters, *Torture*, pp. 3–50.

7. The best treatment is John Langbein (1977) *Torture and the Law of Proof: Europe and England in the Ancien Régime* (Chicago: University of Chicago Press).

8. Peters, *Torture*, p. 69.

9. Langbein, *Torture and the Law of Proof*, p. 6.

10. Peters, *Torture*, p. 33. In 866, Pope Nicholas I denounced forced confessions; Malise Ruthven (1978) *Torture: the Grand Conspiracy* (London: Weidenfeld and Nicolson), p. 43.

11. H. C. Erik Midelfort (1972) *Witch Hunting in Southwestern Germany 1562–1684* (Stanford, Calif.: Stanford University Press), p. 27, records the objections made by Andreas Alciatus in 1515. Peter Burke reports criticism of torture by the Italian physician Girolamo Cardano in the mid-sixteenth century; confessions obtained through infliction of pain were not to be trusted; see Peter Burke (1978) *Popular Culture in Early Modern Europe* (New York: Harper), p. 75.

12. John H. Langbein (1974) *Prosecuting Crime in the Renaissance: England, Germany, France* (Cambridge, Mass.: Harvard University Press), p. 240. For the reasons just discussed, and because the witch hunts and the use of torture (or lack thereof) varied so greatly across Europe, Michel Foucault's *Discipline and Punish*, pp. 33–41, seems distorted. At the least, his arguments appear incorrect for the period from the thirteenth through to the seventeenth century at the higher levels of European judiciaries. In particular, the notions that punishment and investigation proceeded as two parts of the same judicial procedure and that the degree of pain inflicted matched the degree of suspicion attached to a defendant (p. 42) would have been rejected by early modern jurists. Torture was to elicit truth or clear up inconsistencies in testimony.

13. The law codes known as the Carolina (1532) and the Statute of Villers-Cotterets (1539) are translated in Langbein, *Torture and the Law of Proof*. On torture as a violation of the law in the Carolina, see p. 273.

14. Langbein, *Torture and the Law of Proof*, p. 5.

15. Ibid., pp. 272–73 and 310–12.

16. Ibid., p. 283.

17. Ibid., p. 267.

18. Jean Bodin (1580) *De la Démonomanie des sorciers (Paris: Iacques du Puys)*, Book 4, p. 185v.

19. Ibid., Book 4, pp. 185v and 182.

20. Francesco Maria Guazzo (1988) *Compendium Maleficarum*. The Montague Summers edition, trans. E. A. Ashwin (New York: Dover), p. 56. Originally Milan (1608).

21. Henri Boguet (1602) *Discours des sorciers. Tiré de quelques procez, faicts de deux ans en ça à plusiers de la même secte, en la terre de S. Oyan de Loux, dicté de S. Claude au comte de Bourgogne. Avec une instruction pour une iuge, en faict de sorcellerie* (Lyon: par Iean Pillehotte), pp. A2v and 4.

22. Alfred Soman (1985) 'Criminal Jurisprudence in Ancien-Régime France: The Parlement of Paris in the Sixteenth and Seventeenth Centuries', in Louis A. Knafla (ed.) *Crime and Criminal Justice in Europe and Canada* (Waterloo, Canada: Wilfrid Laurier University Press), pp. 48–50.

23. See Soman, 'Criminal Jurisprudence'; Bengt Ankarloo (1993), 'Sweden: The Mass Burnings', in Bengt Ankarloo and Gustav Henningsen (eds) *Early Modern European Witchcraft: Centres and Peripheries* (Oxford: Clarendon Press), p. 290; and Christina Larner (1981) *Enemies of God: the Witch-Hunt in Scotland*, foreword by Norman Cohn (Baltimore: Johns Hopkins University Press), p. 75. Doubts at the highest level of government about the use of torture in Scotland can be documented as early as 1649; ibid., p. 109.

24. Edward Peters (1988) *Inquisition* (New York: The Free Press), pp. 101 and 111.

25. On the procedures of the Inquisition see John Tedeschi, 'Inquisitorial Law and the Witch', in Ankarloo and Henningsen, *Early Modern European Witchcraft: Centres and Peripheries*, pp. 83–95.

26. Gustav Henningsen (1980) *The Witches' Advocate: Basque Witchcraft and the Spanish Inquisition 1609–1640* (Reno: University of Nevada Press), esp. pp. 39–45.

27. Bernard Hamilton (1981) *The Medieval Inquisition* (New York: Holmes and Meier), pp. 30–2 and 52–3. Peters in *Inquisition*, pp. 54–5, agrees that 'unchecked fanaticism' was not an adequate response to heresy; the Church therefore created the Inquisition to establish more regular

procedures. That meant less, not more, violence against accused heretics. Peters finds (p. 84) that in Spain perhaps 3000 people were executed by the Inquisition between 1550 and 1800; however, few of those were witches.

28. The preceding argument is essentially taken from Langbein, *Torture and the Law of Proof*, pp. 1–61. Langbein specifically disdains the idea that the Enlightenment brought torture to an end on the Continent.

29. Johann Weyer (1998) *On Witchcraft. An abridged translation of Johann Weyer's De praestigiis daemonum*, Benjamin G. Kohl and H. C. Erik Midelfort (eds) (Asheville, NC: Pegasus Press).

30. Ibid., pp. 280 and 297.

31. Ibid., p. 268.

32. Ibid., p. 289.

33. Michel de Montaigne (1919) 'Des boyteux', *Les Essais de Michel de Montaigne* (Bordeaux: F. Pech), p. III, quotations on pp. 317 and 316.

34. Here the work of Reginald Scot (1964) *The Discoverie of Witchcraft* (Arundel: Centaur Press), pp. 118–20, 140, 241 and 388–90, first published in 1584 in England, should also be mentioned. Like Weyer, whom he cited with approval, Scot did not question the existence of witches and witchcraft, but rather found the powers ascribed to them unbelievable. Scot specifically attacks a number of cases mentioned by Bodin as ridiculous or the product of trickery. Scot also agreed with Weyer that old women were prone to 'melancholie' and delusions.

35. Montaigne, 'Des Boyteux', p. 317.

36. Franz Helbing (1926) *Die Torture: Geschichte der Folter im Kriminalverfahren aller Völker und Zeiten* (Berlin: P. Langenscheidt), pp. 136–7.

37. Kai T. Erikson (1966) *Wayward Puritans: A Study in the Sociology of Deviance* (New York: John Wiley and Sons).

38. A convenient collection of quotations from Durkheim on crime is George Simpson (1963) *Emile Durkheim* (New York: Thomas Y. Crowell), pp. 61–4.

39. Steven Lukes (1972) *Emile Durkheim: His Life and Work* (New York: Harper and Row), p. 162.

40. For the very small number of accusations and the low conviction rate of those accused in the city of Lübeck, see Rolf Schulte (2001)

Hexenverfolgung in Schleswig-Holstein vom 16.–18. Jahrhundert (Heide: Westholsteinische Verlangsanstalt Boyens), p. 67.

41. The issue of reputation figures repeatedly in the literature; see, for example, Robin Briggs (1996) *Witches and Neighbors: the Social and Cultural Context of European Witchcraft* (New York: Viking), p. 4; and Jim Sharpe (1996) 'The Devil in East Anglia: the Matthew Hopkins Trials Reconsidered', in Jonathan Barry, Marianne Hester and Gareth Roberts (eds) *Witchcraft in Early Modern Europe: Studies in Culture and Belief* (New York: Cambridge University Press), p. 244.

42. Emile Durkheim (1960) *The Division of Labor in Society*, trans. George Simpson (Glencoe, Ill.: The Free Press), quoted in Erikson, *Wayward Puritans*, p. 4.

43. Wolfgang Behringer (1996) 'Witchcraft Studies in Austria, Germany, and Switzerland', in Barry, Hester and Roberts, *Witchcraft in Early Modern Europe*, p. 79.

44. On Augsburg see Lyndal Roper (1994) *Oedipus and the Devil: Witchcraft, Sexuality and Religion in Early Modern Europe* (London: Routledge), pp. 199–201; and Wolfgang Behringer (1997) *Witchcraft Persecutions in Bavaria: Popular Magic, Religious Zealotry and Reason of State*, trans. J. C. Grayson and David Lederer (Cambridge: Cambridge University Press), p. 43, who notes that of 101 trials held there between 1581 and 1653, 64 ended in acquittal, 26 in banishment from the city, 8 in lighter penalties and only 3 in executions.

45. E. William Monter (1976) *Witchcraft in France and Switzerland: the Borderlands during the Reformation* (Ithaca, NY: Cornell University Press), pp. 47–9 and 101–6. The conviction rates are on p. 49.

46. Brian P. Levack (1992) 'Introduction', in Brian P. Levack (ed.) *Witch-Hunting in Continental Europe: Local and Regional Studies* (New York: Garland Press), p. x.

47. Walter Eschenroeder (1932) 'Hexenwahn und Hexenprozess in Frankfurt am Main', Inaugural-Dissertation, Johann Wolfgang Goethe Universität zu Frankfurt, pp. 13–52. And see Behringer, *Witchcraft Persecutions in Bavaria*, p. 42: in the cities of south-east Germany, no witches were burned until 1590, and even then, only 5 of 14 Imperial cities joined in the witch mania and executions. 'The majority of the

cities showed themselves apparently immune to the witch hunts in their hinterlands.'

48. Bohdan Baranowski (1952) *Procesy Czarownic w Polsce w XVII i XVIII Wieku* (Lodz: Lodzkie Towarzystwo Naukowe), p. 176.

49. Edward L. Ayers (1984) *Vengeance and Justice: Crime and Punishment in the Nineteenth-Century American South* (New York: Oxford University Press), pp. 1–50.

50. Quoted in Midelfort, *Witch Hunting*, p. 59.

51. Behringer, *Witchcraft Persecutions in Bavaria*, p. 121.

52. Behringer, *Witchcraft Persecutions in Bavaria*, p. 24; the second quotation is from Friedrich von Spee (1649) *Cautio Criminalis*, German edition (Frankfurt-am-Main, no publisher), p. 314.

53. Jonathan L. Pearl (1999) *The Crime of Crimes: Demonology and Politics in France, 1560–1620* (Waterloo, Ontario: Wilfrid Laurier University Press), p. 33.

54. Behringer, *Witchcraft Persecutions in Bavaria*, p. 206.

55. Hartmut Lehmann and Otto Ulbricht (1992) (eds) *Vom Unfug des Hexen-Processes: Gegner der Hexenverfolgungen von Johann Weyer bis Friedrich Spee* (Wiesbaden: Otto Harrassowitz), pp. 16–20.

56. Midelfort, *Witch Hunting*, p. 91.

57. Quoted in Robert Muchembled (1987) *Justice et Société aux 16e et 17e siècles* (Paris: Imago), p. 3.

58. See the Reverend John Gaule's description of coercion in C. L'Estrange Ewen (1929) *Witch Hunting and Witch Trials: the Indictments for Witchcraft from the Records of 1373 Assizes Held for the Home Circuit A.D. 1559–1736* (London: K. Paul, Trench, Trubner), p. 66.

59. J. A. Sharpe (1996) *Instruments of Darkness: Witchcraft in Early Modern England* (Philadelphia: University of Pennsylvania Press), pp. 128–30.

60. John Gaule (1646) *Select Cases of Conscience Touching Witches and Witchcraft* (London), quoted in Christina Hole (1957) *A Mirror of Witchcraft* (London: Chatto & Windus), pp. 142–3.

61. Hole, *A Mirror of Witchcraft*, p. 163, and Ewen, *Witch Hunting*, p. 66.

62. John Gaule (1657) *A Collection out of the Best Approved Authors* (London: Joshua Kirton), passim and esp. pp. 184–7, 208 and 214. For his views on women and the devil, see material quoted in Hole, *Mirror of Witchcraft*, p. 30.

63. Midelfort, *Witch Hunting*, p. 6.

64. Cotton Mather (1691) *Late Memorable Providences Relating to Witchcrafts and Possessions*, 2nd impression (London: Thomas Parkhurst) [originally 1688], esp. pp. 4–5 and 12–13.

65. 'The Return of several Ministers consulted by his Excellency [Governor Phips], and the Honourable Council, upon the present Witchcrafts in *Salem* Village'. Boston, 15 June 1692. Published as a postscript to Increase Mather (1693) *Cases of Conscience Concerning Evil Spirits Personating Men; Witchcrafts, Infallible Proofs of Guilt in such as are Accused with that Crime* (London: John Dunton), originally Boston (1693).

66. Samuel Willard, *Some Miscellany Observations*, cited in Peter Charles Hoffer (1997) *The Salem Witchcraft Trials: A Legal History* (Lawrence: University Press of Kansas), p. 129.

67. Chadwick Hansen (1969) *Witchcraft at Salem* (New York: George Braziller), pp. 141–3.

68. Mather, *Cases of Conscience*.

69. Mather, *Cases of Conscience*, p. 283.

70. 'The Christian Reader', in *Cases of Conscience*, p. 221.

71. Renaissance portraits did this for women but only in limited areas of Europe, especially Tuscany but also to some extent in Flanders; see Joanna Woods-Marsden (2001) 'Portrait of the Lady, 1430–1520', in David Alan Brown et al. (eds) *Virtue and Beauty: Leonardo's* Ginevra de' Benci *and Renaissance Portraits of Women* (Washington: National Gallery of Art and Princeton University Press).

72. John Swain (2002) 'Witchcraft, Economy and Society in the Forest of Pendle', in Robert Poole (ed.) *The Lancashire Witches: Histories and Stories* (Manchester: Manchester University Press), pp. 97–8.

73. Diane Purkiss (1996) *The Witch in History: Early Modern and Twentieth-Century Representations* (London: Routledge), p. 2.

74. Alan Macfarlane (1999) *Witchcraft in Tudor and Stuart England: A Regional and Comparative Study*, 2nd edn (London: Routledge and Kegan Paul), pp. 60 and 57.

75. Sharpe, *Instruments of Darkness*, p. 146.

76. Marina Warner (1995) *From the Beast to the Blonde: On Fairy Tales and their Tellers* (New York: Noonday Press), quote on p. 76; p. 285 on telling fairy tales; Perrault frontispiece on p. ii.

77. Richard Westfall (1993) *The Life of Isaac Newton* (Cambridge: Cambridge University Press), p. 210.
78. Sharpe, *Instruments of Darkness*, p. 245.
79. Jean Delumeau (1978) *La Peur en Occident (XIVe–XVIIIe siècles): Une cité assiégée* (Paris: Fayard), p. 415.

CONCLUSION

The approach to the witch hunts taken here has been to emphasize broad cultural patterns. New fears arose in Europe during the Middle Ages and became transformed into a matrix of ideas and images that helped to produce the persecution of women and men. Social and geographical location, judicial structures and decisions by individuals were the deciding factors in whether or not the general matrix would spawn witch trials.

The story of the witch persecutions in Europe and North America has to do with a profound shaking of people's confidence that their world could survive. Under attack repeatedly from the outside, and then under the blows of the Black Death, Western Christendom redefined itself and closed ranks. As part of that process, the elite described the 'good' people, to a large degree in contrast to others who allegedly engaged in repugnant, anti-human behaviour in the service of evil. Major figures in the Church identified the main conspirators by turns or simultaneously as heretics, Jews, lepers and finally witches. In many, though far from all parts of Europe and English-speaking North America, the idea that the big devil and his witch helpers were hard at work to destroy humanity became central to descriptions of reality.

Beginning in the eleventh century, the new trends found expression in the persecution of groups now deemed large and menacing to the good society. In the next several hundred years, charges of repulsive sexual acts and crimes against fertility were made against the designated enemies within. During the fourteenth century, the same images were applied to the potentially largest group of all – the witches. In contrast to the old sorcerers, who supposedly practised evil magic they possessed innately or had somehow acquired, the witches were seen as those who had made an explicit pact with the devil and become his followers, servants and sexual partners. Witches reputedly attended wild nocturnal gatherings, killed animals and people whenever they could, and flew instantaneously wherever they chose. The ability to fly made them particularly frightening, as they were said to be able to gather in large numbers in a moment; whether a region had previously been considered free of them did not matter.

Yet witch hunts did not automatically result from this confluence of ideas, even in the areas where the witch stereotype was most frequently and energetically promoted. For a hunt to develop, the following additional ingredients needed to be present:

- acceptance of the witch stereotype by the elite;
- the presence of ardent witch hunters who were convinced that witches constituted an immediate, grave danger to society and therefore needed to be discovered and eliminated;
- tensions among peasants – of the type that occur in every poor, rural milieu – that could erupt into charges of witchcraft once the elite had indicated its willingness to prosecute the accused;
- a readiness to accept the slightest indication, or merely the rumour, that someone had engaged in witchcraft as reason enough to proceed with a case. Torture was not an essential ingredient of witch trials, as its absence in most of the English cases and in Salem demonstrate; in those instances and in Denmark, juries were willing to convict on the basis of slim evidence indeed. Throughout the rest of Europe, tortured suspects provided the

names of other 'witches', sometimes arrested and tortured in their turn, producing in the worst instances a snowball effect.

Factors that were not essential for, but which often helped to facilitate the outbreak of a hunt, were:

- location on the periphery of a state or within a state, notably the Holy Roman Empire, where central authority was weak;
- the presence of a relatively tightly knit, face-to-face community in which each member had an established reputation; those with bad reputations, sometimes built up over a period of decades, were often brought before the courts as witches. In short, rural communities were much more likely to experience witch persecutions than were urban settings, where reputation counted for considerably less;
- the absence of review and appeals courts that oversaw the work of the original tribunals.

By now researchers have identified a number of regions of Europe in which men predominated among the victims or were only slightly less likely than women to be charged, enough so that it is necessary to be cautious about generalizing. Still, available data continues to suggest that 75 per cent or more of the victims were female. Age distribution of those killed will never be known in detail, but various studies now suggest that married women, not widows or marginalized females who found themselves alone, comprised the large majority of female victims.

But this does not mean that the hunts were an attack, intentional or otherwise, on women of any sort. It is necessary to look carefully at the dynamics of witchcraft accusations and trials in order to come closer to what they were all about. No author has shown a direct connection between the general misogyny of the period, which was embedded in Western culture long before and long after the witch hunts, and specific charges of witchcraft against women in any area. What was obviously a patriarchal society already had many mechanisms in place to control women, and no clear explanation has been given, nor can one be provided, for why men in some settings needed an even higher level of control. The question of why authorities would choose the particular accusation of witchcraft to achieve such control has also not been answered satisfactorily. Putting villagers on trial and then burning them at the stake was a drastic, lengthy and costly procedure; certainly some simpler means of increasing control could have been devised, had that been the goal. Arguments that witch hunting was woman hunting, or more specifically deviant woman hunting, continue to appear,[1] but they rely on the unsupportable implication that the persecutions were widespread and regular. In fact they were highly erratic.

The great 'demonologists' seem often to have been more concerned with personal or political problems than with denigrating women or catching witches. Negative images of women in such texts served to underscore the idea that the devil was physically present on earth. The extent to which the moderate, sceptical observers understood this aim in the witchcraft treatises is unclear, but the reluctance of officials in many places and times to promote hunts in western Europe, let alone in the eastern part of the Continent, indicates that the extreme view of women as the devil's natural assistants and lovers never dominated the scene. Since women were not so fundamentally smeared in the witch finders' manuals as an initial reading might suggest, females' image could improve as the persecutions declined.

The high incidence of women among the accused relates more to their sex-specific roles than to their sex per se or to any purported deviance. That is, women had certain capacities due to their biology – pregnancy, birth and nursing, to be precise – and other assignments that society deemed women's work. The second category included cooking, washing, agricultural tasks around the home, care of infants and preparation of the dead for burial. Men appear to have been mystified in the early modern period about how women did these things. God's will was accorded a place in some women's activities, especially in procreation, but the ability to transform materials could have a whiff of diabolical intervention about it as well. Women also commonly handled materials like menstrual blood, afterbirth or dead bodies, that men did not, and which therefore men could regard as more mysterious than the things they preferred to touch, like beer, ploughs and guns.

The issue of transforming materials requires a little more elaboration; after all, men grew edible plants from seeds, so that they too were intimately involved in the process of changing substances. Agriculture in Europe was of course discussed as part of God's beneficence. 'It is my Father who gives you the true bread from heaven,' Jesus said (John 6: 52), referring to both spiritual food and nourishment for the body. If seeds of plants and of good ideas are sown on good earth, they will grow. But sometimes 'the devil comes and takes away the word from their [people's] hearts', Jesus says in Luke 8: 11. Satan could presumably remove plants as well. Thus in early Christian thought, crops grow properly when natural conditions are favourable and the devil does not interfere.

In documents from the witch hunts, men do not sabotage the fields, which would have been the equivalent of a witch killing domestic animals or a person. The absence of such accusations was probably related to what could be observed in nature. Crops usually perished slowly, withering through lack of rain or warmth. Their expiration could be explained as natural, not supernatural, or if supernatural then a result of God's will. The devil was depicted as an active being who interfered to do something, not a creature who somehow caused the absence of rain or sunshine. To grant the devil such power would have been too direct an implication that he could alter basic natural processes, placing him on the same level as God. For any and all witch hunters, such a view would have been heresy. At the same time, crop failures might produce a higher level of general tension that could facilitate witch hunts, if the other necessary factors were in position.

Quick destruction – much more the devil's style – did come to cultivation at times in the form of hail, which in a few moments can completely ruin a young grain crop. 'Hail falls in narrow swaths and streaks, which makes it seem vindictive and personal. It can neatly slice off the corner of a wheat field, or ruin one farmer's entire crop and leave his neighbor's standing,' Jonathan Raban has written.[2] When the witch stereotype became firmly established in a region, it was easy to imagine that an acolyte of the devil had produced the hail as an act of malice against a particular person or community.

Men carried out most of the work involved in transforming seeds into crops, the first step in making food, and men were the millers who ground the harvest to make flour. Women took care of the subsequent steps in food preparation. In that part of the process, various herbs might be added – Europe was still poor indeed in spices – hence it was easier to think that vile ingredients had been introduced in cooking than to imagine that a male farmer, adding only water and humble manure to the soil, had somehow prepared a lethal harvest.

It is also worth keeping in mind that a creature that breathes and has blood in its veins dies in a different way than do plants, especially if the death is sudden. Animals and humans cry out, writhe and rasp for breath when they die, encouraging people to imagine that some malevolent force was intervening to end a life. Even in hailstorms, the demise of plants had less emotional impact than the death of a domesticated animal, let alone a baby, conveyed to a village.

Women were also around infants and household animals more often than were men, and when death came suddenly to tame or helpless creatures, suspicion fell on the persons close at hand. These various kinds of death and destruction need to be considered against the background of the age-old view in many cultures that women are weaker, more flighty, more gullible and even more sexually hungry than men; then the early modern idea that women were more likely to become the devil's followers makes a little more sense. Placed according to the thought of the period with a large group of negative characteristics, the feminine had long been associated with child murder and, by extension, other horrendous crimes. Yet what women did or the materials they handled were often more important in drawing the charge of witchcraft upon them than was the weight of characteristics assigned to them in the thinking of the age simply because they were female.

Large-scale witch persecutions did emerge from the belief system depicting weak and evil women, the devil and the practices of his followers, but the hunts represented a sharp departure from the usual means of social regulation. Sooner or later the trials, torture and executions severely disrupted the societies they touched – one of the major reasons they were halted by the elite. No activity can be deemed a control mechanism or part of state-building when it flares up extremely erratically, reaches into the dominant social strata as it spreads, and is finally rejected by the elite everywhere. Witch persecutions, which necessitated an expensive and time-consuming judicial apparatus, were far from the norm in western Europe and Massachusetts.

Partly for these reasons, the witch persecutions should not be described as a singular phenomenon; there were different kinds and scales of pursuit, so that it is necessary to speak of witch *hunts* in the plural. Likewise the word 'craze', which implies a loss of reason, will not serve. First, many jurisdictions never prosecuted witches. Elsewhere, the authorities did not lose sight of the possibility that many of the accused might be innocent, and investigated charges with some care. However, it is also clear that in various places officials and ordinary people succumbed to witch fear for a while, so that the accusation of witchcraft sufficed to put a judicial label on someone already convicted in the eyes of the community.

Although Hugh Trevor-Roper was wrong about several points when he published on the 'witch-craze' in the 1960s, he was correct in noting that 'when a "great fear" takes hold of society, that society looks naturally to the stereotype of the enemy in its midst'.[3] But such fear was always temporary.

The unusualness of hunts and their tendency to come in waves provided an opportunity to resist and criticize them. Above all, the witch hunts ended in a given area because a significant party of influential men – those apparently not crazed by anything – became convinced that innocent people were being executed. Although some European voices had long criticized the kinds of evidence commonly used to convict in witchcraft cases, it usually took a large hunt, on the order of dozens of accusations, before it occurred to a group within the elite that something had gone terribly wrong. It seemed that in place after place innocent people were being swept up in hunts and, on the Continent and in Scotland, tortured until they confessed to witchcraft. As any round-up of suspects expanded, the probability that guiltless people were being charged became more obvious. The anti-persecution group then made its objections to the hunts on the grounds that faulty evidence was being used to convict, which had nothing to do with the sexual composition of the defendants.

Challenges to the nature and quality of the evidence admitted in witch trials in turn encouraged rethinking of evidence on the natural world in general. Thus the end of the witch hunts contributed to the growth of the scientific revolution to a greater extent than the other way around.

As both cause and effect of the decline of the hunts in the West, a new and much more favourable image of women arose. And after a long period in which the devil, lesser demons and witches were seen as omnipresent and constantly threatening to the good society, by the late 1600s a whole middle world of supernatural creatures could be tamed in plays and stories. Mad Meg, a demented female unafraid to enter hell itself in search of treasure, yielded to Mother Goose.

For all of these reasons, no overarching social, anthropological, political or functional approach can explain the witch hunts. They were not:

- a bloody episode in a war waged by men against women. Direct evidence is lacking for this view, while logic and the irregular dynamics of the hunts argue against it;
- a campaign or concerted effort of any sort to control or frighten broad groups of the population, especially women, deviants or rural dwellers. In an extreme view, the persecutions are described as implementing a 'process of terror' designed to enforce social control. 'Violence and torture are components of the machinery for producing fear', the argument continues, which prevents any organized opposition from arising.[4] However, such machinery would have to be broad and regular; the witch hunts were neither. The elite would have had to give its full backing to such an effort, but that did not happen. Eventually the European elite everywhere rejected witch persecutions but did not lose its grip on society. The upper classes had long maintained and would continue to enforce their dominance by other means;
- a way of relieving social tensions by transferring aggression or guilt on to marginal individuals or scapegoats. Of course such transfers could have happened at times, but they cannot explain the scope, variety or legal procedures of the witch hunts. There is no correlation between European social change and witch hunts; the theory has been rejected by the foremost authority on Scottish hunts, for example, and repudiated by its originator for English persecutions;
- a response to cases of mass hallucinations produced by ergot poisoning. Ergot, a fungus that develops on stored grain under certain conditions, may poison humans who eat bread made from

the affected harvest. Hallucinations may occur as part of ergot poisoning. However, it is often accompanied by gangrene, convulsions and agonized death. There are no indications of serious physical illness or gangrene among people who were either 'possessed' or charged with witchcraft in Europe or Salem;

- a response to cases of hallucinations produced by handling certain types of toads or rubbing unguents made partly with atropines on to the body. Atropines, among them chemicals from the plant *bella donna*, may cause visions but can also produce horrible side-effects or death if taken in the wrong way or in too large a quantity. Again, there is no credible evidence of atropine poisoning in connection with alleged witches. Recipes for witches' unguents have survived from the sixteenth and seventeenth centuries, but most of them involve only inert ingredients such as dried bat's blood. Such substances cannot alter consciousness. Moreover, peasants did not usually mention flying or the sabbat until members of the elite put leading questions to them, typically sharpened by torture;

- an effort by male doctors to drive female midwives out of practice. This did not happen; in many areas of Europe, midwives continued to be the primary deliverers of babies into the nineteenth or even twentieth century;

- a drive by the authorities to stamp out a surviving fertility cult of people who actually gathered at night to celebrate their religion. No serious evidence for such a cult exists. Stories told across Europe and Asia feature people, or their spirits, who went out at night to battle evil forces or to journey to the land of the dead. But such myths and stories are not to be confused with what people actually did;

- a response by nervous religious and secular authorities to the spread of magic. The whole subject of magic is something of a red herring when it comes to the witch hunts. Witches were accused of worshipping the devil and becoming his servants, not practising magic by controlling him. Magic is not always clearly separated from religion, and indeed many, perhaps all religions, contain elements of magic. 'High' magic, referring to practices based on the use of books and depending on what passed for education in the conjuring arts, as opposed to 'low' or 'folk' magic, does appear to have increased in popularity during the late Middle Ages. Certainly the number of books on the subject grew. But when magicians tried to influence the course of events in the early modern period, they did not necessarily invoke the devil. In general neither high nor low magicians fell victim to the witch hunts, except during periods of heightened witch fear. Then traditional healers and conjurers, and especially people who possessed 'little books' of spells, might fall under suspicion. Sorcerers had long been prosecuted in Europe, and they continued to be at times during the witch hunts, but not simply because they were magicians. There had to be some evident negative results of their work in the eyes of the people who charged them with crime: a dead cow or baby, a hailstorm at harvest time and so forth. In Salem, Tituba and the 'possessed' girls started telling fortunes in 1691, according to some accounts; this 'low' magic would not have resulted in severe punishments, beyond whippings administered by masters and parents, if not for the deeply unsettled general atmosphere of the Massachusetts colony at the time;

- a result of a struggle between Catholics and Protestants in which each side, or the various sides, accused each other's adherents of being witches. Nor were the hunts part of a campaign begun with the Reformation and Catholic Counter-Reformation to instil new values into the rough and still partly pagan village population. That argument ignores the particular ways in which accusations of witchcraft typically arose within peasant communities, as members charged each other not with paganism, not with deviance in the sociological sense, but with committing acts considered crimes in any society.

Lynching in the American South; Soviet Terror; Nazi attempts to exterminate Jews, homosexuals, Romany, Sinti and other groups; and McCarthyism in America all basically relied on images of pure evil embodied in certain secretive, powerful beings who were out to destroy the good society. If the elite manufactured such images, they caught on in the imaginations of ordinary people. Finally the elite, seeing the disruption caused by the pursuit of the largely or wholly phantom enemy within, called a halt to the hunt, although this had to be done in Nazi Germany from the outside by force of arms.

As Elizabeth Reis has pointed out, one current parallel to the witch hunts, at least in America, is the pursuit of alleged child molesters.[5] Child molesters exist, while witches did not; but in both cases the charge itself has been terrifying and difficult to disprove, although a more careful attitude toward this issue appears to be on the rise. Surely society's deepest fears, that its children will be corrupted or destroyed, have surfaced once again. For some Americans, the idea that homosexuals lurk within the good society, are difficult to identify and are stealing children for their anti-human activities, remains frightening.

The witch herself lingers in our consciousness, for example in what appears to be a recurring need to render witches harmless every Hallowe'en and to defeat or convert them in countless films and television programmes. And we are aware of the Other in ways that relate directly to, in fact still are aspects of, the persecuting society. But now the Western elite ostensibly rejects the demonization of the Other, racism is not fashionable or is at least slightly disguised in references to the Middle Eastern terrorist, and fringe parties in Europe and America remain exactly that.

Still, the story of the witch hunts told here contains much that might continue to be pondered. Whatever 'modern' images dominate in Western society of minorities and the biggest group of all, women, can be tested against the pictures that fuelled the witch persecutions. Many males and females of the early modern period used their best understanding, their finest reason, to interpret misfortune as harm instigated by the devil and carried out by his human instruments, the witches. What seems reasonable and scientific in one era may be completely rejected in another. The Enlightenment, the 'Age of Reason', was not a breakthrough to a careful consideration of evidence in the natural world. As we have seen, that attitude was always a part of human endeavours to understand the world. Decades before even the earliest *philosophes* wrote, critics of the witch hunts – and for that matter their advocates – insisted that their views were reasonable. Finally, the Enlightenment produced totally unscientific modern racism, based often on the idea that one physical type was 'standard' and beautiful. It would be good not to take science too much on faith.

References in studies of the witch persecutions to a 'great social crisis' or to 'functional control of deviance' are reminiscent of older talk about other mysterious, disruptive forces: the approach of the Last Days, the hand of Satan, or 'Memorable Providences'. In trying to decipher the witch hunts, this study has instead emphasized individual decisions, the role of personality, the political setting and local conditions – all of which were conditioned by specific cultural trends that, if complex, need not be mysterious.

Representations of witches, or what is sometimes called the story of the story, are the most important aspect of the hunts to some writers. There is much justification for this focus, since the way a subject is produced and reproduced certainly bears deeply on its meaning, or becomes its meaning, in a culture. But this book has not been concerned nearly so much with 'the witch in history' as it has with particular human beings caught up in specific witch hunts.

[*]

I left Ban de la Roche, ending my walks through the villages, visits to the churches and the execution ground, and conversations with the descendants of witch hunt victims. Years later and a continent away, it is somehow easier than when I was there to imagine what happened in the Franco-German valleys above Strasbourg, or in many other European settings. Now, however briefly, I can picture a series of scenes: an action on the charge of witchcraft begins with a group of men, usually assembled in a village, trying to decide whether the accused persons have truly committed evil deeds in the devil's service. Especially at first, these men are uneasy about the whole affair. They do not know what to do. In some instances, the tribunal resolves not to proceed with a trial or to release some of those under arrest. But in many thousands of other incidents, the magistrates decide that enough accusations have arisen to warrant torturing a defendant. She is usually a terrified woman, less frequently a man or even a child, who is bound into devices operated by hirelings of the judges. The mechanisms, sometimes simple and sometimes intricate, cause extreme pain and may dislocate or shatter limbs. There is blood, screams of agony, smells beyond description. After a forced confession and a final appearance before the court, the convict is taken to the place of execution, where her neighbours have gathered. In England or Massachusetts she is hanged, often far from a quick and clean death. On the Continent or in Scotland she is strangled and her body burned, or she is burned alive.

Cross a jurisdictional line to a similar village, or go forward or backward several decades in time, and all of these scenes disappear. This book has sought to explain why such differences occurred.

NOTES

1. For example, in Julian Goodare (1998) 'Women and the Witch-hunt in Scotland', *Social History* 23 (3); and Katharine Park, 'Medicine and Magic: The Healing Arts', in Judith C. Brown and Robert C. Davis (eds) (1998) *Gender and Society in Renaissance Italy* (London: Longman), pp. 142–3.

2. Jonathan Raban (1997) *Bad Land: An American Romance* (New York: Vintage), p. 215. Raban was speaking of eastern Montana in the 1910s, but hail made the same impression centuries earlier in Europe.

3. Hugh Trevor-Roper (1969) *The European Witch-Craze of the Sixteenth and Seventeenth Centuries and Other Essays* (New York: Harper and Row), p. 190.

4. H. Sidky (1997) *Witchcraft, Lycanthropy, Drugs, and Disease: An Anthropological Study of the European Witch-Hunts* (New York: Peter Lang), p. 260.

5. Elizabeth Reis (1997) *Damned Women: Sinners and Witches in Puritan New England* (Ithaca, NY: Cornell University Press), p. 10.

CHRONOLOGY

*c.*155: birth of Tertullian (died 220)

354: birth of St Augustine (died 430)

6th century: first known depiction of the devil in the West

563: Church Council of Braga rejects view that Satan created the material universe

711: Islamic army enters Spain

787: Viking assaults begin on western Europe

906: *Canon Episcopi* calls night flying an illusion

11th century onwards: campaign for clerical celibacy

1022: first known execution of heretics in western Europe since the 4th century, Orléans

1047: Synod of Rome demands priestly celibacy

*c.*1048: Ralph Glaber, *Five Histories*

*c.*1049: expansion of papacy's claims to spiritual rule

1054: Schism between Western (Catholic) and Eastern (Orthodox) churches

1063: first slaughter of Jews, in Spain

1073–85: Pope Gregory VII strengthens the papacy

1084: first ghetto for Jews, Germany

1095: First Crusade. Murder of Jews in Germany by Crusaders

12th century: appearance of heresies – Cathars, Albigensians, Waldensians (Vaudois)

1143: first mention of the Bogomils, heretics from eastern Europe, in the West

1150: first charge of ritual murder by Jews, England

1179: Third Lateran Council legislates daily Christian life v homosexuality, lepers

1180: heretics in Besançon accused of making a pact with the devil

1182: expulsions of Jews begin, France

1204–61: occupation of Constantinople by Western Crusaders

1209: campaign against Cathar heresy begins in southern France

1215: Fourth Lateran Council. Trial by ordeal is rejected, torture becomes acceptable in ecclesiastical cases

1227 onwards: development of the Inquisition – acquires right to torture 1252

1231: the papal bull *Excommunicamus*, the fundamental document of the Inquisition

*c.*1237: Guillaume de Lorris begins the *Roman de la Rose*; completed by Jean de Meun around 1277

1240–42: Mongols conquer Russia

*c.*1250: priests begin to celebrate marriage in western Europe. Berthold of Regensburg preaches

1250s onwards: Western laws adopted v homosexual relations

1260s at the latest: appearance of vivid illustrations of the devil and hell, for instance in this decade in the Florence Baptistry

1274: death of St Thomas Aquinas

1275: trial of heretics in Toulouse, France, mentions sabbat of evil-doers with the devil

1290: expulsion of Jews from England

1291: Christians driven out of last stronghold in Middle East

1302: Roman Church declares it has right to determine salvation

1305–78: 'Avignon captivity' of the papacy; popes reside in Avignon, France

1306: major expulsion of Jews from France

1307–14: destruction of the Order of Knights Templar in France

1321 onwards: slaughter of lepers in France

1324: trial of Alice Kyteler for witchcraft, Ireland

1326: papal bull declares that many Christians make a covenant with hell

1327, 1358, and 1372: burnings of traditional magicians in Lorraine

1347–48: first wave of plague in western Europe. Burnings of Jews

1353: a trial of heretics in Toulouse mentions night gatherings and a witches' dance

1358: peasant rebellions (*jacqueries*) in France

1376: Nicholas Eymeric, inquisitor in Aragon and Avignon, *Directorium Inquisitorum*, describes heretics' gatherings with the devil

1381: Wat Tyler's peasant rebellion in England

1394–1406: trials of Waldensians and Jews for heresy in an area between Strasbourg, Basel, and Fribourg, Switzerland

1398: University of Paris condemns sorcery and calls it a heresy

1399–eighteenth century: the *Querelle des femmes*, dispute about women

1401: first English law calling for the execution of heretics

1405: Christine de Pizan, *The Book of the City of Ladies*, defends women

1419–24: trials of witches in Lucerne and Interlaken, Switzerland. First use of word *Hexerei* for witchcraft

1420s: Claude Tholosans tries more than 200 witches in Briançon, Dauphiné

1420s–1430s: Bernardino of Siena preaches in Italy

1431: Joan of Arc executed as a heretic

1431–49: Council of Basel; much concern with how to combat heresy

1435: *Errores Gazariorum*, first book to describe witches as a sect

1435–37: Johannes Nider writes *Formicarius*, pro and conwomen, linking them in some places to devil worship

1437: Purgatory becomes an article of faith for the Roman Church

1440–42: Martin Le Franc, *Le champion des dames*, continues the debate on women; also ties them to flight and demons

1453: fall of Constantinople to the Ottoman Turks

1456: Joan of Arc's second trial; her posthumous acquittal on the charge of heresy

1459: large witch trial in Arras

1485: failed witch hunt, organized by Heinrich Kramer, in Brixen, Austria

1486: publication of the *Malleus Maleficarum*, denouncing women and outlining how to try witches, by Heinrich Kramer

1489: Ulrich Molitor, *De lamiis et phitonicis mulieribus*, another important and widely read work of demonology

1492: Moors and Jews expelled from Spain

1508: Bamberger law code mentions only traditional sorcery, not witchcraft

1510: Cornelius Agrippa, famous physician and alchemist, expresses scepticism about witches' powers; he secures the acquittal of a woman charged with witchcraft in 1518

1511: Ulrich Tenngler's *Neuer Layenspiegel* (New Mirror for Lay Persons), another how-to manual for witch trials

1512–16: Isenheim Altarpiece by Matthias Grünewald

*c.*1516: Baldesar Castiglione begins *The Book of the Courtier*

1516–17: Johan Geiler von Kaysersberg, Strasbourg, *Die Emeis* (The Ants) warns of witchcraft

1517: Luther begins his protests against Catholic practices and doctrines; the Catholic Church excommunicates Luther in January 1521

1525–26: German peasant war

1526: Turkish victory at Mohács, Hungary, deepening the sense of threat to western Europe from outside forces

1530s: La Suprema, the central office of the Spanish Inquisition, requires that it review all witchcraft cases handled by inquisitors

1532: The Carolina law code of the Holy Roman Empire tries to specify the conditions in which torture may be used; does not mention witchcraft

1538: Spanish Inquisition cautions against believing the *Malleus*

1539: French law code of Villers-Cotterets tries to specify conditions for torture

1540s: The Fronde, nobles' revolt, in France

1560–1660: Little Ice Age

1562–1628: French Wars of Religion

1562: Georg Pictorius, professor at the University of Freiburg, expresses deep concern over the number and spread of witches

1563: Johann Weyer publishes book protesting treatment of 'witches'. Witchcraft laws in England and Scotland; English law repealed 1736

1571: Allied naval victory over the Turks at Lepanto

1580: Jean Bodin, *De la démonomanie des sorciers* (On the demonomania of sorcerers), a key treatise of demonology

1580s–1590s: first large wave of witch hunts around Trier, Germany

1581: Johann Fischart's *Vom Aussgelasnen Wuetigen Teuffelsheer* (On the Unleashed Furious Devil's Horde), Strasbourg, echoes Bodin and others

1584: Reginald Scot, *The Discoverie of Witchcraft*, a highly sceptical work

1588: Michel de Montaigne publishes his sceptical essay 'On the Lame'

1589: execution of Dr Dietrich Flade, Trier

1589–90: protest against Trier hunts by Cornelius Loos

1590: Christopher Marlowe, *Tamburlaine the Great*

1590–91: James VI, king of Scotland, brings witch hunts to his realm

1595: Nicholas Rémy, prosecutor-general of the Duchy of Lorraine, then part of the Holy Roman Empire, publishes

Daemonolatreia (Demonolatry) another argument on the danger of witches

1597: James VI publishes *Daemonologie*, a dire warning about witches

1602: Henri Boguet, *Discours des sorciers* (Discourse on sorcerers), another important work of demonology

1604: New English witchcraft statute adopted

1606: Shakespeare's *Macbeth* first performed

1607, 1620–22, 1629–30: witch hunts in Ban de la Roche

1611: King James Bible

Martin Antoine Del Rio, *Les controuerses et recherches magiques* (The controversies and researches on magic), another pro-persecution work

1612: Pierre De Lancre, *Tableau de l'inconstance des mauvais anges et démons: où il est amplement traité des sorciers et de la sorcellerie* (Table of the inconstance of evil angels and demons, with an ample treatment of sorcerers and sorcery), by a self-proclaimed great witch hunter

1618–48: Thirty Years War

1623: papal investigator Giulio Monterenzi writes an instruction to inquisitors expressing grave scepticism about proof of witchcraft

1624: the Paris Parlement requires automatic appeal from lower courts for all witchcraft cases

1628–30: witch hunts peak in Germany

1631: Friedrich von Spee publishes his protest v use of torture on accused witches

1634: Execution – for witchcraft – of Urbain Grandier, priest and confessor to 'possessed' nuns at Loudun, France

1636: Cardinal Francesco Albizzi travels through Germany; later expresses disgust at the witch burnings

1637: René Descartes, *Discourse on Method*, argues that the spiritual and material worlds are completely separate

1640s: Parlement of Paris begins to reject witchcraft cases

1642–46: English Civil War

1645: Matthew Hopkins conducts large witch hunt in Essex, England

1646: Reverend John Gaule, vicar of Great Staughton, England, begins to preach against improper use of evidence in the hunts

1670s: large hunts in Sweden involving children as accused and as witnesses

1682: edict of Louis XIV discouraging witchcraft trials

1683: defeat of Turks before Vienna

1686: Isaac Newton publishes *Principia Mathematicae*

1688: Glorious Revolution in England

1689: Cotton Mather publishes *Memorable Providences*, warning of the danger of witches, in Boston

1692: Cotton Mather publishes *The Wonders of the Invisible World*, another warning

1692–93: Salem, Massachusetts witch trials

1693: Recantation of the Salem jurors

1694: Christian Thomasius, professor of law at the Universities of Leipzig and then Halle, changes his mind about witchcraft; becomes an ardent opponent of trials

1697: Charles Perrault publishes *Tales of My Mother Goose* (in French)

1782: last known legal execution of a witch, Switzerland

WEBSITES

The following web addresses are just a few of the ones that present information, some accurate and some fanciful, about witchcraft and the witch hunts. Several of the sites have primary documents in English, German, French, Latin and occasionally other languages. A few of the addresses have interactive programs that can provide a bit of atmosphere for the hunts. Any web enthusiast will find many, perhaps endless links from these sites to others. Of course, the web changes every day, so any site listed below might not be there by the time one looks for it.

A place to start looking for materials, including illustrations related to the hunts, is the world's best collection on witchcraft, at Cornell University. The sources are partly accessible through http://historical.library.cornell.edu/witchcraft/about.html

It is possible to spend many days at the Library of Congress in Washington looking through the magnificent resources related to the witch hunts. A search for the word 'witchcraft' turns up entire collections within the library. http://www.loc.gov/index.html

Other useful sites are:

The Labyrinth: Resources for Medieval Studies, sponsored by Georgetown University: www.georgetown.edu/labyrinth/

Internet History Sourcebook Project, Paul Halsall, editor. Fordham University History Department Center for Medieval Studies. This site is rich in many kinds of documents, especially religious and legal material. http://www.fordham.edu/halsall/index.html

Philosophy Web Resources Hippias Search Engine, Brandeis University http://people.brandeis.edu/~teuber/hippias.html. Type in the name of any philosopher, widely defined, to find articles and original sources.

EuroDocs: Primary Historical Documents from Western Europe. Selected Transcripts, Facsimilies and Translations. Run by the Brigham Young University Library. www.lib.byu.edu/~rdh/eurodocs/

The Avalon Project at Yale Law School. Documents in Law, History and Diplomacy. www.yale.edu/lawweb/avalon/avalon.htm

A list of university courses taught in the United States and Britain on the witch hunts, with many useful links to syllabi and reading lists, is Brian A. Pavlac's http://departments.kings.edu/womens_history/witch/witchcourses.html

An important project on witch hunts in Scotland, produced at the University of Edinburgh by Julian Goodare, Lauren Martin, Joyce Miller and Louise Yeoman, is http://www.arts.ed.ac.uk/witches/

The major international group studying witchcraft, the hunts and related topics is the Arbeitskreis interdisziplinaere Hexenforschung, literally Working circle for interdisciplinary witch research. It has a home page in German but with a summary in English: http://www.uni-tuebingen.de/IfGL/akih/akih.htm

An important German website, only in that language, lists talks by scholars scheduled in Germany and new publications in various languages: http://www.hexenforschung.historicum.net/

And see also, in German, a site for early modern/modern history: http://www.geschichte.fb15.uni-dortmund.de/links/Fruehe_Neuzeit/

The witches' sabbat at Yuletide in Finland is the subject of a site created by a serious scholar, Rune Blix Hagen, at http://www.ub.uit.no/fag/historie/christma.htm

An amateur site with lots of documents and articles related to trials in Essex, England is www.hulford.co.uk/intro.html

On the lighter side, the following sites are gateways to museums and interactive sessions:

A witchcraft museum in Berry, France: http://www.musee-sorcellerie.fr/anglais/index.html

The National Geographic Society feature on Salem witchcraft. A bit sensationalistic, the site nevertheless strives to give visitors a feel for the hunt of 1692–93. www.nationalgeographic.com/features/97/salem/

A simulated witch hunt in Germany, 1628, is at http://departments.kings.edu/womens_history/witch/hunt/index.html

AFTERWORD AND
ACKNOWLEDGEMENTS

Until I wrote this book, I was a historian of Russia and the Soviet Union. But I also had the sometimes pleasant duty of teaching Western Civilization, a peculiarly American course that does in fact have its uses. When I first started to work on that class, it occurred to me that by making the first lecture on the witch hunts, I might find a good way to capture students' attention. That proved to be true, but I also caught my own attention in a serious fashion. Since that time, more than a few years ago, I have read steadily about the hunts. Finally it dawned on me, as I was writing a book about the Stalinist terror in the Soviet Union, that there were many useful comparisons between the witch hunts and Soviet mass repressions. To mention just two, the use of torture and reliance on denunciations were common in both. When I reached the point of writing this study, comparisons with Soviet history – and, for that matter, with another of my interests, lynching in the American South – provided, I think, a number of valuable perspectives on what happened to the witches.

Since this book is intended for a general audience – although I hope that scholars and students alike will also benefit from the overview of the witch hunts and several new ideas of my own provided here – I have not inserted an endnote for every point based on the existing literature. In any event, my greatest debt is to the hard-working people who have spent many years building up case studies of the hunts. Even if I have not always agreed with their conclusions, I have not ceased to be impressed by their ability to ferret out and use obscure sources often recorded in the first place in idiosyncratic language, sometimes in handwriting that can resemble chicken scratches.

I am aware of such problems in early modern materials because I used many of them for my own case study of Ban de la Roche/ Steinthal. By now I have also made my way through, I believe, a great many if not all the major works of demonology and of scepticism published in the sixteenth and seventeenth centuries, as well as the law codes and many other original documents. For assistance in that research I would like to thank the staff of the Carl A. Kroch Library, Cornell University, especially its curator, Mark Dimunation. In Strasbourg I worked in the friendly and patient confines of the Archives municipales and the Archives départmentales du Bas-Rhin. I wish to express my gratitude for help there, especially to Daniel Peter, *conservateur* at the departmental archives. The J. F. Oberlin Museum in Waltersbach, France, was a beautiful setting in which to spend a few days. I would like to thank Estelle Meri and Laurent Stauffer for assistance there.

At Miami University a number of institutions and individuals helped me a great deal. The Hampton Fund provided support that allowed me to make a preliminary trip to France to find out what sources were available for my research, while a Summer Research Grant and a Summer Salary award allowed me to do the work itself for the first edition. Two faculty improvement leaves gave me the time to work at Cornell and to complete the writing of this book. The Interlibrary Loan Office turned up many a rare or obscure work.

I am indebted to Bill Monter for conversations about witches. People who read and made highly useful comments on parts of the manuscript were Eric Ziolkowski, Carl Pletsch, and two colleagues in the Miami History Department, Renée Baernstein and Drew Cayton. I have also benefited greatly from discussions with my fellow historians at Miami, especially Charlotte Goldy, Wietse de Boer and Judith Zinsser. My wife, Margaret Ziolkowski, read the entire manuscript of the first edition and offered much sound advice. She has spent years listening to and discussing my ideas about the hunts, and she has continued to be the ideal intellectual partner. Together these people saved me from many an error.

BIBLIOGRAPHY AND
FURTHER READING

GENERAL TREATMENTS OF THE WITCH HUNTS

For those interested in further reading or in information about any particular aspect, personality, or region of the hunts, the best place to start is Richard Golden (ed.). *Encyclopedia of Witchcraft: The Western Tradition.* Santa Barbara, California: ABC-CLIO, 2006.

Other broad discussions of the witch persecutions are:

The Athlone History of Witchcraft and Magic in Europe, a multi-volume series edited by Bengt Ankarloo and Stuart Clark. London: Athlone, 1999–. Individual volumes cover periods from the ancient world into the eighteenth century.

BEHRINGER, WOLFGANG. *Witches and Witch Hunts: A Global History.* Cambridge: Polity, 2004.

LEVACK, BRIAN P. *The Witch-Hunt in Early Modern Europe,* 3rd edn. New York: Pearson/Longman, 2006.

MAXWELL-STUART, P. G. *Witchcraft in Europe and the New World, 1400–1800.* New York: Palgrave, 2001.

OLDRIDGE, DARREN (ed.). *The Witchcraft Reader.* London: Routledge, 2002. The volume contains a range of articles by leading scholars.

SCARRE, GEOFFREY AND JOHN CALLOW. *Witchcraft and Magic in Sixteenth and Seventeenth Century Europe.* London: Palgrave/MacMillan, 2001.

COLLECTIONS OF DOCUMENTS

BEHRINGER, WOLFGANG (ed.). *Hexen und Hexenprozesse in Deutschland*, 3rd edn. Munich: Deutscher Taschenbuch Verlag, 1995.

BOYER, PAUL AND STEPHEN NISSENBAUM (eds). *Salem Village Witchcraft: A Documentary Record of Local Conflict in Colonial New England*. Belmont, Calif.: Wadsworth, 1972.

DAVIDSON, L. S. AND J. O. WARD (eds). *The Sorcery Trial of Alice Kyteler: A Contemporary Account (1324) together with Related Documents in English Translation, with Introduction and Notes*. Binghamton, NY: Medieval and Renaissance Texts and Studies, 1993.

GIBSON, MARION, (ed.). *Witchcraft and Society in England and America, 1550–1750*. Ithaca, NY: Cornell University Press, 2003.

HANSEN, JOSEPH. *Quellen und Untersuchungen zur Geschichte des Hexenwahns und der Hexenverfolgung*. Bonn: C. Georgi, 1901.

Hexen. Analysen, Quellen, Dokumente (Digitale Bibliothek Bd. 93). Directmedia: Berlin 2003. Europäische Märchen und Sagen, hrsg. von Hans-Jörg-Uther (Digitale Bibliothek Bd. 110). Directmedia: Berlin 2004.

KORS, ALAN CHARLES, AND EDWARD PETERS (eds); revised by Edward Peters, *Witchcraft in Europe, 400–1700: a documentary history*. 2nd edn. Philadelphia: University of Pennsylvania Press, 2001.

LARNER, CHRISTINA, C. J. H. LEE AND H. V. MCLACHLAN. *A Source-Book of Scottish Witchcraft*. Glasgow: SSRC, 1977.

LEA, HENRY CHARLES (compiler). *Materials Toward a History of Witchcraft*, ed. Arthur C. Howland, introduction George Lincoln Burr, 3 vols. New York: Thomas Yoseloff, 1957.

LEVACK, BRIAN P. (ed.). *Witchcraft Sourcebook*. New York: Routledge, 2004.

SHARPE, JAMES, general editor. RICHARD GOLDEN, consulting editor. *English witchcraft, 1560–1736*. Six volumes of original materials from the sixteenth to the eighteenth centuries. London: Pickering & Chatto, 2003.

ORIGINAL SOURCES: DEMONOLOGY

BODIN, JEAN. *De la Démonomanie des sorciers*. Paris: Iacques du Puys, 1580.

BOGUET, HENRI. *Discours des sorciers. Tiré de quelques procez, faicts de deux ans en ça à plusieurs de la même secte, en la terre de S. Oyan de Loux, dicté de S. Claude au comte de Bourgogne. Avec une instruction pour une iuge, en faict de sorcellerie.* Lyon: par Iean Pillehotte, 1602.

CASTIGLIONE, BALDESAR. *The Book of the Courtier*, trans. and with an introduction by George Bull. New York: Penguin Books, 1967.

DE LANCRE, PIERRE. *Tableau de l'inconstance des mauvais anges et démons: où il est amplement traité des sorciers et de la sorcellerie.* Introduction critique et notes de Nicole Jacques-Chaquin. Paris: Aubier, 1982. Originally 1612.

DEL RIO, MARTIN ANTOINE. *Les controuerses et recherches magiques de Martin Delrio . . . : diuisées en six liures, ausquels sont exactment & doctement confutées les sciences curieuses, les vanitez & superstitions de toute la magie: auecques la manière de proceder en iustice contre les magiciens & sorciers, accommodée a l'instruction des confesseurs;* traduit & abregé du latin par Andre du Chesne. Paris: Chez Iean Petit-pas, 1611.

FISCHART, JOHANN. *Vom Aussgelasnen Wütigen Teuffelsheer.* Strassburg: Bernhart Jobin, 1581.

GAULE, JOHN. *A Collection out of the Best Approved Authors.* London: Joshua Kirton, 1657.

GEILER VON KAYSERSBERG, JOHANNES. *Die Emeis.* Strasbourg: Johannes Brienninger, 1516.

—— *Saemtliche Werke*, herausgeben von Gerhard Bauer. Berlin: Walter de Gruyter, 1989.

GUAZZO, FRANCESCO MARIA. *Compendium Maleficarum.* The Montague Summers edition, trans. E. A. Ashwin. New York: Dover, 1988.

INSTITORIS [HEINRICH KRAMER], HENRY AND JACQUES [JACOB] SPRENGER [it now appears that Kramer, also called Institoris, wrote the book alone]. *Le Marteau des Sorcières. Malleus Maleficarum. 1486*, trans. Amand Danet. Grenoble: Jerome Millon, 1990.

KRAMER, HEINRICH, AND JAMES [JACOB] SPRENGER. *The Malleus Maleficarum*, trans. Rev. Montague Summers. New York: Dover, 1969.

MATHER, COTTON. *Late Memorable Providences Relating to Witchcrafts and Possessions.* 2nd impression. London: Thomas Parkhurst, 1691.

—— *The Wonders of the Invisible World. Being an Account of the Tryals of Several Witches Lately Executed in New-England.* London, John Russel Smith, 1862. Originally Boston 1692.

NYDER [NIDER], JOHANNES. *Formicarius*. Introduction Hans Biedermann. Graz: Akademische Druck, 1971.

RÉMY, NICHOLAS. *Demonolatry*, trans. E. A. Ashwin (ed.) and with an introduction and notes by Montague Summers. London: John Rodker, 1930.

OTHER ORIGINAL SOURCES

ALIGHIERI, DANTE. *Inferno*, trans. and ed. Elio Zappulla. New York: Pantheon Books, 1998.

AUGUSTINE OF HIPPO, SAINT. *On Christian Teaching*, trans. with an introduction by R. P. H. Green. Oxford: Oxford University Press, 1997.

DE WALD, E. T. *The Illustrations of the Utrecht Psalter*. Princeton: Princeton University Press, 1932.

GLABER, RALPH (RODOLPHE). *L'An Mille*, trans. and ed. Edmond Pognon. Paris: Gallimard, 1947.

Holy Bible: The New Standard Revised Version. Nashville: Thomas Nelson, 1989.

KNIGHTON, HENRY. 'Chronicle', in *The Portable Medieval Reader*, ed. J. B. Ross and M. M. McLaughlin. New York: Viking, 1949.

MATHER, INCREASE. *Cases of Conscience Concerning Evil Spirits Personating Men; Witchcrafts, Infallible Proofs of Guilt in such as are Accused with that Crime*. London, John Dunton, 1693. Originally Boston 1693.

MONTAIGNE, MICHEL DE. 'Des boyteux', *Les Essais de Michel de Montaigne*. Bordeaux: F. Pech, 1919.

OBERLIN, J. F. 'Annales du Ban de la Roche surtout de la Paroisse de Valdersbach Commencées l'an 1770'. Manuscript, Oberlin Museum, Waltersbach, France.

'Originale Hexen-Protokolle aus dem Steinthal', Rare and Manuscript Collections, Carl A. Kroch Library, Cornell University.

'The Recantation of the Salem Jurors', 1693, in Kors and Peters (eds), *Witchcraft*.

'The Return of several Ministers consulted by his Excellency [Governor Phips], and the Honourable Council, upon the present Witchcrafts in

Salem Village.' Boston, 15 June 1692. Published as a postscript to Mather, *Cases of Conscience*.

SCOT, REGINALD. *The Discoverie of Witchcraft*. Arundel: Centaur Press, 1964. Originally 1584.

SPEE, FRIEDRICH VON. *Cautio Criminalis*, German edition. Frankfurt-am-Main, no publisher, 1649.

TERTULLIAN, 'De Culta Femina', in Rosemary Radford Reuther (ed.), *Religion and Sexism: Images of Woman in the Jewish and Christian Traditions*. New York: Simon and Schuster, 1974.

WEYER, JOHANN. *On Witchcraft. An abridged translation of Johann Weyer's De praestigiis daemonum*, ed. Benjamin G. Kohl and H. C. Erik Midelfort. Asheville, NC: Pegasus Press, 1998.

SECONDARY SOURCES AND CASE STUDIES

ANDERSON, BONNIE S. AND JUDITH P. ZINSSER. *A History of their Own: Women in Europe from Prehistory to the Present*, 2 vols, revised ed. New York: Oxford University Press, 2000.

ANKARLOO, BENGT. 'Sweden: The Mass Burnings', in Ankarloo and Henningsen (eds), *Early Modern European Witchcraft*.

ANKARLOO, BENGT AND GUSTAV HENNINGSEN (eds). *Early Modern European Witchcraft: Centres and Peripheries*. Oxford: Clarendon Press, 1993.

ASCHKENASY, NEHAMA. *Eve's Journey: Feminine Images in Hebraic Literary Tradition*. Philadelphia: University of Pennsylvania Press, 1986.

AVALOS, HECTOR IGNACIO. 'Satan', in Metzger and Coogan (eds), *Oxford Companion to the Bible*.

AYERS, EDWARD L. *Vengeance and Justice: Crime and Punishment in the Nineteenth-Century American South*. New York: Oxford University Press, 1984.

BAEYER-KATTE, WANDA VON. 'Die historischen Hexenprozesse: Der verbürokratisierte Massenwahn', in *Massenwahn in Geschichte und Gegenwart*, herausgegeben von Wilhelm Bitter. Stuttgart: Ernst Klett, 1965.

BAILEY, MICHAEL. *Battling Demons: Witchcraft, Heresy, and Reform in the Late Middle Ages*. University Park: Pennsylvania State University Press, 2003.

BARANOWSKI, BOHDAN. 'Posłowie' in Kurt Baschwitz, *Czarownice: Dzieje procesów o czary*. Warszawa: Pannstwowe Wydawnictwo naukowe, 1963.
—— *Procesy Czarownic w Polsce w XVII i XVIII Wieku*. Lodz: Lodzkie Towarzystwo Naukowe, 1952.

BARDELL, KIRSTEEN MACPHERSON. 'Beyond Pendle: The "Lost" Lancashire Witches', Poole (ed.). *Lancashire Witches*.

BAROJA, JULIO CARO. *The World of the Witches*, trans. O. N. V. Glendenning. Chicago: University of Chicago Press, 1964.

BARRY, JONATHAN, MARIANNE HESTER AND GARETH ROBERTS (eds). *Witchcraft in Early Modern Europe: Studies in Culture and Belief*. New York: Cambridge University Press, 1996.

BARSTOW, ANNE. *Witchcraze: A New History of the European Witch Hunts*. San Francisco: Harper, 1994.

BEATTIE, WILLIAM. *The Waldenses, or Protestant Valleys of Piedmont and Dauphine, and The Ban de la Roche*. London: George Virtue, 1838.

BEHRINGER, WOLFGANG. 'Malleus Maleficarum', in Golden (ed.), *Encyclopedia*.
—— *Hexen: Glaube, Verfolgung, Vermarktung*. Munich, Verlag C. H. Beck, 2000.
—— *Witchcraft Persecutions in Bavaria: Popular Magic, Religious Zealotry and Reason of State*, trans. J. C. Grayson and David Lederer. Cambridge: Cambridge University Press, 1997.
—— 'Witchcraft Studies in Austria, Germany, and Switzerland', in Barry, Hester and Roberts (eds), *Witchcraft in Early Modern Europe*.

BEN-YEHUDA, NACHMAN. 'The European Witch Craze of the 14th to 17th Centuries: A Sociologist's Perspective', *American Journal of Sociology*, 86 (1) (1980).

BERGESEN, ALBERT, *The Sacred and the Subversive: Political Witch-Hunts as National Rituals*. Storrs, Conn.: Society for the Scientific Study of Religion Monograph Series, 1984.
—— 'Social Control and Corporate Organization: A Durkheimian Perspective', in Donald Black (ed.). *Toward a General Theory of Social Control*, 2 vols. Cambridge, Mass.: Harvard University Press, 1984.

BETHENCOURT, FRANCISCO. 'Portugal: A Scrupulous Inqusition', in Ankarloo and Henningsen (eds), *Early Modern European Witchcraft*.

BILLER, PETER. 'The Common Woman in the Western Church in the Thirteenth and Early Fourteenth Centuries', *Studies in Church History*, 27. *Women in the Church*. Oxford: Basil Blackwell, 1990.

BISCHOFF, GEORGES. 'Les Paysans de Haute-Alsace en 1525', in Bischoff, Georges et al. (eds), *Histoire de l'Alsace rurale*. Strasbourg: Librarie Istra, 1983.

BLAUERT, ANDREAS. *Frühe Hexenverfolgungen: Ketzer-, Zauberei- und Hexenprozesse des 15. Jahrhunderts*. Hamburg: Junius Verlag, 1989.

BLÉCOURT, WILLEM DE. 'Witch Doctors, Soothsayers and Priests. On Cunning Folk in European Historiography and Tradition', *Social History* 19 (3) (1994).

BORDES, FRANÇOIS. *Sorciers et sorcières: procès de sorcellerie en Gascogne et Pays Basque*. Toulouse: Privat, 1999.

BOSSY, JOHN. 'Seven Sins into Ten Commandments', in Edmund Leites (ed.). *Conscience and Casuistry in Early Modern Europe*. Cambridge: Cambridge University Press, 1988.

BOYER, PAUL AND STEPHEN NISSENBAUM. *Salem Possessed: the Social Origins of Witchcraft*. Cambridge, Mass.: Harvard University Press, 1974.

BRAUNER, SIGRID. *Fearless Wives and Frightened Shrews: the Construction of the Witch in Early Modern Germany*. Amherst: University of Massachusetts Press, 1995.

BRIDENTHAL, RENATE, CLAUDIA KOONZ AND SUSAN STUARD (eds). *Becoming Visible: Women in European History*. Boston: Houghton Mifflin, 1987.

BRIGGS, ROBIN. *Witches and Neighbors: the Social and Cultural Context of European Witchcraft*. New York: Viking, 1996.

BRIGNON, MARC. 'La Sorcellerie dans le Pays de Salm aux XVIème et XVIIème siècles', *L'Essor* 53 (1983).

BULLOUGH, VERN L. 'Postscript: Heresy, Witchcraft, and Sexuality', in Vern L. Bullough and James Brundage, *Sexual Practices and the Medieval Church*. Buffalo: Prometheus Books, 1982.

BURKE, PETER. *Popular Culture in Early Modern Europe*. New York: Harper, 1978.

BYRNE, PATRICK F. *Witchcraft in Ireland*. Hatboro, Penn.: Folklore Association, 1967.

CAHILL, THOMAS. *How the Irish Saved Civilization: the Untold Story of Ireland's Heroic Role from the Fall of Rome to the Rise of Medieval Europe.* New York: Anchor Books, 1995.

CAMPBELL, COLIN. 'A Dubious Distinction: An Inquiry into the Value and Use of Merton's Concepts of Manifest and Latent Function', *American Sociological Review* 47 (1) (February 1982).

CLARK, STUART. 'Inversion, Misrule, and the Meaning of Witchcraft', *Past and Present* 87 (May, 1980).

—— *Thinking with Demons: the Idea of Witchcraft in Early Modern Europe.* New York: Oxford University Press, 1997.

—— 'Witchcraft and Magic in Early Modern Culture', in Jolly, Raudvere and Peters, *Witchcraft and Magic in Europe: The Period of the Witch Trials.*

CLEMENTS, BARBARA EVANS, BARBARA ALPERN ENGEL and CHRISTINE D. WOROBEC (eds). *Russia's Women: Accommodation, Resistance, Transformation.* Berkeley: University of California Press, 1991.

COHN, NORMAN. *Europe's Inner Demons: An Enquiry Inspired by the Great Witch-Hunt.* New York: New American Library, 1975.

COLE, R. L. 'Ban de la Roche: ein Beitrag zum Thema regionaler Hexenprozess im Elsass', *Alemannisches Jahrbuch*, Kondordia (1979/1980).

COULTON, C. G. (ed.). *Life in the Middle Ages.* New York: Macmillan, 1910.

CURTIN, PHILIP D. *The Atlantic Slave Trade: A Census.* Madison: University of Wisconsin Press, 1969.

—— 'Measuring the Atlantic Slave Trade Once Again', *Journal of African History* 17 (4) (1976).

DALY, MARY. *Gyn/Ecology: the Metaethics of Radical Feminism.* Boston: Beacon Press, 1978.

DARNTON, ROBERT. *The Great Cat Massacre and Other Episodes in French Cultural History.* New York: Basic Books, 1984.

DAVIDSON, L. S. 'Introduction', in Davidson and Ward (eds), *Sorcery Trial of Alice Kyteler.*

DAVIES, OWEN, and WILLEM DE BLÉCOURT (eds). *Beyond the Witch Trials: Witchcraft and Magic in Enlightenment Europe.* Manchester: Manchester University Press, 2004.

DAVIS, NATALIE ZEMON. 'Poor Relief, Humanism, and Heresy: the Case of Lyon', in *Studies in Medieval and Renaissance History*, vol. 5. Lincoln: University of Nebraska Press, 1968.

—— *The Return of Martin Guerre*. Cambridge, Mass.: Harvard University Press, 1983.

DE BLÉCOURT, WILLEM. 'Witch Doctors, Soothsayers and Priests. On Cunning Folk in European Historiography and Tradition', *Social History* 19 (3) (1994).

DECKER, RAINER. 'Entstehung und Verbreitung der Römischen Hexenprozessinstruktion', in Hubert Wolf, ed. *Inquisition, Index, Zensur. Wissenskulturen der Neuzeit im Widerstreit* (Römische Inquisition und Indexkongregation, Bd. 1). Paderborn: Schöningh, 2001.

—— 'Die Hexenverfolgungen in Herzogtum Westfalen', *Westfälische Zeitschrift* (1981–82).

DELUMEAU, JEAN. *La Peur en Occident (XIVe–XVIIIe siècles): Une cité assiégée*. Paris: Fayard, 1978.

DEMOS, JOHN PUTNAM. *Entertaining Satan: Witchcraft and the Culture of Early New England*. New York: Oxford University Press, 1982.

DIENST, HEIDE. 'Hexenprozesse auf dem Gebiet der heutigen Bundesländer Vorarlberg, Tirol (mit Südtirol), Salzburg, Nieder- und Oberösterreich sowie des Burgenlandes', in Valentinitsch (ed.), *Hexen und Zauberer*.

DILLINGER, JOHANNES. 'Trier, Electorate of', in Golden (ed.), *Encyclopedia*.

DOLLINGER, PHILIPPE et al., *Histoire de L'Alsace*. Toulouse, Eduard Privat, 1970.

DVAM, KRISTEN E., LINDA S. SCHEARING and VALARIE H. ZIEGLER (eds). *Eve and Adam: Jewish, Christian, and Muslim Readings on Genesis and Gender*. Bloomington: Indiana University Press, 1999.

DWORKIN, ANDREA. *Woman Hating*. New York: Dutton, 1974.

EIDEN, HERBERT and RITA VOLTMER (eds). *Hexenprozesse und Gerichtspraxis*. Trier: Paulinus, 2002.

ELLIOTT, DYAN. *Fallen Bodies: Pollution, Sexuality, and Demonology in the Middle Ages*. Philadelphia: University of Pennsylvania Press, 1999.

ELSTER, JON. 'Merton's Functionalism and the Unintended Consequences of Action', in *Robert K. Merton and Contemporary Sociology*, ed. Carlo Mongardini and Simonetta Tabboni. New Brunswick, NJ: Transaction Publishers, 1998.

ERASMUS, CHARLES J. 'Obviating the Functions of Functionalism', *Social Forces* 45 (3) (March 1967).

ERIKSON, KAI T. *Wayward Puritans: A Study in the Sociology of Deviance*. New York: John Wiley and Sons, 1966.

ESCHENROEDER, WALTER. 'Hexenwahn und Hexenprozess in Frankfurt am Main', Inaugural-Dissertation, Johann Wolfgang Goethe Universität zu Frankfurt (1932).

EVANS-PRITCHARD, E. E. *Witchcraft, Oracles and Magic among the Azande*. Oxford: Oxford University Press, 1937.

EWEN, C. L'ESTRANGE. *Witch Hunting and Witch Trials: the Indictments for Witchcraft from the Records of 1373 Assizes Held for the Home Circuit AD 1559–1736*. London: K. Paul, Trench, Trubner, 1929.

FOUCAULT, MICHEL. *Discipline and Punish: the Birth of the Prison*, trans. Alan Sheridan. New York: Vintage Books, 1979.

FÜSSEL, RONALD. *Die Hexenverfolgungen im Thüringer Raum* (Veröffentlichungen des Arbeitskreises für historische Hexen- und Kriminalitätsforschung in Norddeutschland, 2). Hamburg: DOBU Wissenschaftlicher Verlag Dokumentation, 2003.

—— 'Thuringia' in Golden (ed.), *Encyclopedia*.

GASKILL, MALCOLM. *Witchfinders: A Seventeenth-Century English Tragedy*. Cambridge, Mass.: Harvard University Press, 2005.

GIBSON, MARION. *Reading Witchcraft: Stories of Early English Witches*. London: Routledge, 1999.

GIELIS, MARCEL. 'The Netherlandic Theologians' Views of Witchcraft and the Devil's Pact', in Gijswijt-Hofstra and Frijhoff (eds), *Witchcraft in the Netherlands*.

GIJSWIJT-HOFSTRA, MARIJKE. 'Six Centuries of Witchcraft in the Netherlands: Themes, Outlines, and Interpretations', in Gijswijt-Hofstra and Frijhoff (eds), *Witchcraft in the Netherlands*.

GIJSWIJT-HOFSTRA, MARIJKE and WILLIAM FRIJHOFF (eds). *Witchcraft in the Netherlands from the Fourteenth to the Twentieth Century*, trans. R. M. J. van der Wilden-Fall. Rotterdam: Universitaire Pers, 1991.

GINZBURG, CARLO. *The Cheese and the Worms: the Cosmos of a Sixteenth-Century Miller*, trans. John and Anne Tedeschi. Baltimore: Johns Hopkins University Press, 1980.

—— *Ecstasies: Deciphering the Witches' Sabbath*, trans. Raymond Rosenthal. New York: Penguin Books, 1992.

—— *The Night Battles: Witchcraft and Agrarian Cults in the Sixteenth and Seventeenth Centuries*, trans. John and Anne Tedeschi. Baltimore: Johns Hopkins University Press, 1985.

GIRARD, RENÉ. *The Scapegoat*, trans. Yvonne Freccero. Baltimore: Johns Hopkins University Press, 1986.

GODBEER, RICHARD. *The Devil's Dominion: Magic and Religion in Early New England* Cambridge: Cambridge University Press, 1992.

—— *Escaping Salem: The Other Witch Hunt of 1692*. New York: Oxford University Press, 2005.

GOODARE, JULIAN. 'Women and the Witch-hunt in Scotland', *Social History* 23 (3) (1998).

GOODY, JACK. *The Development of the Family and Marriage in Europe*. Cambridge: Cambridge University Press, 1983.

HALL, DAVID O. *Witch-Hunting in Seventeenth-Century New England*, 2nd edn. Boston: Northeastern University Press, 1999.

HAMILTON, BERNARD. *The Medieval Inquisition*. New York: Holmes and Meier, 1981.

HANAWALT, BARBARA A. and DAVID WALLACE (eds). *Medieval Crime and Social Control*. Minneapolis: University of Minnesota Press, 1999.

HANSEN, CHADWICK. *Witchcraft at Salem*. New York: George Braziller, 1969.

HANSEN, JOSEPH. *Zauberwahn, Inquisition und Hexenprozess im Mittelalter*. Neudruck der Ausgabe München 1900. Aalen: Scientia Verlag, 1964.

HASTRUP, KIRSTEN. 'Iceland: Sorcerers and Paganism', in Ankarloo and Henningsen (eds), *Early Modern European Witchcraft*.

HEIKKINEN, ANTERO and TUNO KERVINEN. 'Finland: the Male Domination', in Ankarloo and Henningsen (eds), *Early Modern European Witchcraft*.

HELBING, FRANZ. *Die Torture: Geschichte der Folter im Kriminalverfahren aller Völker und Zeiten*. Berlin: P. Langenscheidt, 1926.

HENNINGSEN, GUSTAV. *The Witches' Advocate: Basque Witchcraft and the Spanish Inquisition 1609–1640*. Reno: University of Nevada Press, 1980.

HERLIHY, DAVID (ed.). *Women, Family, and Society in Medieval Europe: Historical Essays, 1978–1991*, introduction A. Molho. Providence, RI: Berghahn, 1995.

HESTER, MARIANNE. 'Patriarchal Reconstruction and Witch-Hunting', in Oldridge (ed.), *Witchcraft Reader*.

HOFFER, PETER CHARLES. *The Salem Witchcraft Trials: A Legal History*. Lawrence: University Press of Kansas, 1997.

HOLE, CHRISTINA. *A Mirror of Witchcraft*. London: Chatto & Windus, 1957.

HORSLEY, RICHARD A. 'Who Were the Witches? The Social Roles of the Accused in European Witch Trials', *Journal of Interdisciplinary History* 9 (4) (1979).

HSIA, R. PO-CHIA. *Social Discipline in the Reformation: Central Europe 1550–1750*. New York: Routledge, 1989.

HUFTON, OLWEN. *The Prospect Before Her: A History of Women in Western Europe*, 2 vols. Vol. 1: *1500–1800*. New York: HarperCollins, 1995.

HUPPERT, GEORGE. *After the Black Death: A Social History of Early Modern Europe*. Bloomington: Indiana University Press, 1986.

INIKORI, J. E. 'Introduction', in J. E. Inikori (ed.), *Forced Migration: the Impact of the Export Slave Trade on African Societies*. New York: Africana, 1982.

JAHODA, GUSTAV. *The Psychology of Superstition*. London: Allen Lane/Penguin, 1969.

JEROUSCHEK, GÜNTER. 'Kramer (Institoris), Heinrich (Ca. 1430–1505)', in Golden (ed.), *Encyclopedia*.

JOLLY, KAREN, CATHARINA RAUDVERE and EDWARD PETERS. *Witchcraft and Magic in Europe: The Middle Ages*, The Athlone History of Witchcraft and Magic in Europe, series eds Bengt Ankarloo and Stuart Clark. Philadelphia: University of Pennsylvania Press, 2002.

JOLLY, KAREN, CATHARINA RAUDVERE, and EDWARD PETERS, *Witchcraft and Magic in Europe: The Period of the Witch Trials*, The Athlone History of Witchcraft and Magic in Europe, series eds Bengt Ankarloo and Stuart Clark. Philadelphia, University of Pennsylvania Press, 2002.

KARLSEN, CAROL F. *The Devil in the Shape of a Woman*. New York: W. W. Norton, 1987.

KELLY, JOAN. *Women, History and Theory: The Essays of Joan Kelly*. Chicago: University of Chicago Press, 1984.

KENT, DALE. 'Women in Renaissance Florence,' in David Alan Brown et al. (eds). *Virtue and Beauty: Leonardo's* Ginevra de' Benci *and Renaissance*

Portraits of Women. Washington: National Gallery of Art and Princeton University Press, 2001.

KIECKHEFER, RICHARD. *European Witch Trials: their Foundation in Popular and Learned Culture, 1300–1500*. Berkeley: University of California Press, 1976.

KITTREDGE, GEORGE. *Witchcraft in Old and New England*. Cambridge, Mass.: Harvard University Press, 1929.

KIVELSON, VALERIE. 'Male Witches in Russia', *Comparative Studies in Society and History* 45 (3) (July 2003).

—— 'Through the Prism of Witchcraft: Gender and Social Change in Seventeenth-Century Muscovy', in Clements, Engel and Worobec (eds), *Russia's Women*.

KLAITS, JOSEPH. *Servants of Satan: the Age of the Witch Hunts*. Bloomington: Indiana University Press, 1985.

KLANICZAY, GABOR. 'Hungary: the Accusations and the Universe of Popular Magic', in Ankarloo and Henningsen (eds), *Early Modern European Witchcraft*.

—— *The Uses of Supernatural Power: the Transformation of Popular Religion in Medieval and Early-Modern Europe*, trans. Susan Singerman, ed. Karen Margolis. Princeton: Princeton University Press, 1990.

KLAPISCH-ZUBER, CHRISTIANE. *Women, Family and Ritual in Renaissance Italy*, trans. Lydia Cochrane. Chicago: University of Chicago Press, 1985.

KLÉLÉ, J. *Hexenwahn und Hexenprozesse in der ehemaligen Reichstadt und Landvogtei Hagenau*. Hagenau: F. Ruckstuhl, 1910.

KLUCKHOHN, CLYDE. *Navaho Witchcraft*. Papers of the Peabody Museum, XXII, no. 2. Cambridge, Mass.: 1944.

KNAFLA, LOUIS A. (ed.). *Crime and Criminal Justice in Europe and Canada*. Waterloo, Canada: Wilfrid Laurier University Press, 1985.

KORDEL, MATTHIAS. *Ruwer und Eitelsbach: Zwei Dörfer im Spiegel ihrer Geschichte*. Trier: Kliomedia, 2003.

LABOUVIE, EVA. *Zauberei und Hexenwerk: Ländlicher Hexenglaube in der frühen Neuzeit*. Frankfurt am Main: Fischer, 1991.

LANGBEIN, JOHN H. *Prosecuting Crime in the Renaissance: England, Germany, France*. Cambridge, Mass.: Harvard University Press, 1974.

—— *Torture and the Law of Proof: Europe and England in the Ancien Régime*. Chicago: University of Chicago Press, 1977.

LARNER, CHRISTINA. *Enemies of God: the Witch-Hunt in Scotland.* Foreword by Norman Cohn. Baltimore: Johns Hopkins University Press, 1981.

—— *Witchcraft and Religion: the Politics of Popular Belief.* London: Basil Blackwell, 1984.

LEHMANN, HARTMUT and OTTO ULBRICHT (eds). *Vom Unfug des Hexen-Processes: Gegner der Hexenverfolgungen von Johann Weyer bis Friedrich Spee.* Wiesbaden: Otto Harrassowitz, 1992.

LEHNER, ERNST and JOHANNA LEHNER (eds). *Picture Book of Devils, Demons, and Witchcraft.* New York: Dover, 1971.

LE ROY LADURIE, EMMANUEL. *Jasmin's Witch.* New York: Braziller, 1966.

—— *Montaillou: Cathars and Catholics in a French Village, 1294–1324,* trans. Barbara Bray. London: Scolar Press, 1978.

LEVACK, BRIAN P. 'Introduction', in Brian P. Levack (ed.), *Witch Hunting in Continental Europe: Local and Regional Studies,* 5 vols. Vol. 5: *Witchcraft, Magic and Demonology.* New York: Garland, 1992.

LIVET, GEORGES and FRANCIS RAPP (eds). *Histoire de Strasbourg des origines à nos jours.* Strasbourg: Éditions des Dernières nouvelles de Strasbourg, 1980.

LORENZ, SÖNKE and JÜRGEN MICHAEL SCHMIDTS (eds). *Wider alle Hexerei und Teufelswerk: Die europaische Hexenverfolgung und ihre Auswirkungen auf Suedwestdeutschland.* Ostfildern: Jan Thorbecke Verlag, 2004.

LUKES, STEVEN. *Emile Durkheim: His Life and Work.* New York: Harper and Row, 1972.

LUMBY, JONATHAN. '"Those to Whom Evil is Done": Family Dynamics in the Pendle Witch Trials', in Poole (ed.), *Lancashire Witches.*

LUTZ, ROBERT. 'Le Serment des Bourgeois du Ban de la Roche en 1598', *Le Ban de la Roche,* Bulletin de la Société d'Histoire du Protestantisme du Ban de la Roche (1969), no. 2.

MACFARLANE, ALAN. *Origins of English Individualism: the Family, Property and Social Transition.* Oxford: Oxford University Press, 1978.

—— *Witchcraft in Tudor and Stuart England: A Regional and Comparative Study.* London: Routledge and Kegan Paul, 1970.

—— *Witchcraft in Tudor and Stuart England: A Regional and Comparative Study,* 2nd edn. Introduction James Sharpe. London: Routledge, 1999.

MAIDAR, MAIA. 'Estonia I: Werewolves and Poisoners', in Ankarloo and Henningsen (eds), *Early Modern European Witchcraft.*

MANDROU, R. *Magistrats et Sorciers en France en XVIIe Siècle*. Paris: 1968.

MARTIN, RUTH. *Witchcraft and the Inqusition in Venice 1550–1650*. Oxford: Basil Blackwell, 1989.

MAXWELL-STUART, P. G. *Witchcraft in Europe and the New World, 1400–1800*. New York: Palgrave, 2001.

MELLINKOFF, RUTH. *The Devil at Isenheim: Reflections of Popular Belief in Gruenewald's Altarpiece*. Berkeley: University of California Press, 1988.

—— *Outcasts: Signs of Otherness in Northern European Art of the Late Middle Ages*, vol. 1, text; vol. 2, illustrations. Berkeley: University of California Press, 1993.

MERRITT, BERTHA (SUTERMEISTER). 'Witchcraft Trials in the Ban de la Roche'. [Masters] Thesis, Cornell University, 1926.

MERTON, ROBERT K. *Social Theory and Social Structure*, rev. and enlarged edn. Glencoe, ILL.: The Free Press, 1957.

METZGER, BRUCE M. and MICHAEL D. COOGAN (eds). *The Oxford Companion to the Bible*. New York: Oxford University Press, 1993.

MIDELFORT, H. C. ERIK. *Witch Hunting in Southwestern Germany 1562–1684*. Stanford, Calif.: Stanford University Press, 1972.

MONBALLYU, JOS. 'Die Hexenprozesse in der Grafschaft Flandern (1495–1692)', in Eiden and Voltmer (eds), *Hexenprozesse*.

MONTER, E. WILLIAM. *Calvin's Geneva*. New York: John Wiley and Sons, 1967.

—— *European Witchcraft*. New York: John Wiley, 1969.

—— 'Toads and Eucharists: the Male Witches of Normandy', *French Historical Studies* 20 (4) (1997).

—— *Witchcraft in France and Switzerland: the Borderlands during the Reformation*. Ithaca, NY: Cornell University Press, 1976.

—— 'Witch Trials in Continental Europe 1560–1660', in Jolly, Raudvere and Peters, *Witchcraft and Magic in Europe: The Period of the Witch Trials*.

MOORE, R. I. *The Formation of a Persecuting Society: Power and Deviance in Western Europe, 950–1250*. Oxford: Basil Blackwell, 1987.

MORMANDO, FRANCO. 'Bernardino of Siena, Popular Preacher and Witch-Hunter: a 1426 Witch Trial in Rome', *Fifteenth-Century Studies* 24 (1998).

MUCHEMBLED, ROBERT. *A History of the Devil: From the Middle Ages to the Present*, trans. Jean Birrell. Cambridge: Polity Press, 2003.

—— *Justice et Société aux 16e et 17e siècles*. Paris: Imago, 1987.

—— *La sorcière au village*. Paris: Plon, 1979.

MURRAY, MARGARET. *The Witch Cult in Western Europe*. Oxford: Oxford University Press, 1921.

NORTON, MARY BETH. *In the Devil's Snare: The Salem Witchcraft Crisis of 1692*. New York: Alfred A. Knopf, 2002.

OGEMBO, JUSTUS MOZART H'ACHACHI. 'The rise and decline of communal violence: an analysis of the 1992–94 witch-hunts in Gusli, southwestern Kenya', PhD dissertation, Anthropology, Harvard University, 1997.

OLDRIDGE, DARREN (ed.). *The Witchcraft Reader*. London: Routledge, 2002.

OLLI, SOILI-MARIA. 'The Devil's Pact: A Male Strategy', in Davies and Blécourt (eds), *Beyond the Witch Trials*.

PAGELS, ELAINE. *The Origin of Satan*. New York: Vintage Books, 1995.

PARK, KATHARINE. 'Medicine and Magic: The Healing Arts', in Judith C. Brown and Robert C. Davis (eds), *Gender and Society in Renaissance Italy*. London: Longman, 1998.

PEARL, JONATHAN L. *The Crime of Crimes: Demonology and Politics in France, 1560–1620*. Waterloo, Ontario: Wilfrid Laurier University Press, 1999.

PETERS, EDWARD. *Inquisition*. New York: The Free Press, 1988.

—— 'Introduction', in Jolly, Raudvere and Peters. *Witchcraft and Magic in Europe: The Middle Ages*.

—— 'Le Franc, Martin', in Golden (ed.), *Encyclopedia*.

—— 'The Medieval Church and State on Supersition, Magic and Witchcraft', in Jolly, Raudvere and Peters. *Witchcraft and Magic in Europe: The Middle Ages*.

—— *Torture*. New York: Basil Blackwell, 1985.

POCS, EVA. *Between the Living and the Dead: A Perspective on Witches and Seers in the Early Modern Age*, trans. Szilvia Redey and Michael Webb. Budapest: Central European University Press, 1999.

POOLE, ROBERT (ed.). *The Lancashire Witches: Histories and Stories*. Manchester: Manchester University Press, 2002.

PURKISS, DIANE. *The Witch in History: Early Modern and 20th-Century Representations*. New York: Routledge, 1996.

QUAIFE, G. R. *Godly Zeal and Furious Rage: the Witch in Early Modern Europe*. New York: St Martin's Press, 1987.

RABAN, JONATHAN. *Bad Land: An American Romance*. New York: Vintage Books, 1997.

RADZINOWICZ, LEON and JOAN KING. *The Growth of Crime: the International Experience*. New York: Basic Books, 1977.

REIS, ELIZABETH. *Damned Women: Sinners and Witches in Puritan New England*. Ithaca, NY: Cornell University Press, 1997.

The Return of Martin Guerre, film, directed by Daniel Vigne, 1983.

REUSS, RODOLPHE. *La Sorcellerie au seizième et au dix-septième siècle particulièrement en Alsace*. Steinbrunn-le-haut: Éditions du Rhin, 1987. First published 1871.

RIASANOVSKY, NICHOLAS V. *A History of Russia*, 6th edn. New York: Oxford University Press, 2000.

ROBBINS, ROSSELL HOPE. 'Introduction', in *Witchcraft: Catalogue of the Witchcraft Collection in Cornell University Library*. Millwood, NY: KTO Press, 1977.

ROCHELANDET, BRIGITTE. *Sorcières, diables et bûchers en Franch-Comté aux XVIe et XVIIe siècles*. Besançon: Éditions du Cètre, 1997.

ROPER, LYNDAL. *Oedipus and the Devil: Witchcraft, Sexuality and Religion in Early Modern Europe*. London: Routledge, 1994.

—— *Witch Craze: Terror and Fantasy in Baroque Germany*. New Haven: Yale University Press, 2004.

ROSEN, GEORGE. 'A Study of the Persecution of Witches in Europe as a Contribution to the Understanding of Mass Delusions and Psychic Epidemics', *Journal of Health and Human Behavior* 1 (1960).

ROTT, JEAN. 'La Guerre des Paysans et ses suites en Basse-Alsace: Le cas de Huttgau', in *Histoire de l'Alsace rurale*, ed. Georges Bischoff et al.

ROWLANDS, ALISON. 'Age of Accused Witches', in Golden, *Encyclopedia*.

—— *Witchcraft narratives in Germany: Rothenburg 1561–1652*. Manchester: Manchester University Press, 2003.

—— 'Würzburg', in Golden (ed.), *Encyclopedia*.

RUMMEL, WALTER. *Bauern, Herren und Hexen: Studien zur Sozialgeschichte sponheimischer und kurtrierischer Hexenprozesse 1574–1664*. Göttingen: Vandenhoeck & Ruprecht, 1991.

RUSSELL, JEFFREY. *Lucifer: the Devil in the Middle Ages*. Ithaca, NY: Cornell University Press, 1984.

—— *Satan: the Early Christian Tradition*. Ithaca, NY: Cornell University Press, 1981.

—— *Witchcraft in the Middle Ages*. Ithaca, NY: Cornell University Press, 1972.

RUTHVEN, MALISE. *Torture: the Grand Conspiracy*. London: Weidenfeld and Nicolson, 1978.

RYAN, W. F. 'The Witchcraft Hysteria in Early Modern Europe: Was Russia an Exception?' *The Slavonic and East European Review* 76 (1) (1998).

SABEAN, DAVID WARREN. *Power in the Blood: Popular Culture and Village Discourse in Early Modern Germany*. New York: Cambridge University Press, 1984.

SAID, EDWARD S. *Orientalism*. New York: Vintage Books, 1979.

SAWYER, RONALD C. '"Strangely Handled in All Her Lims": Witchcraft and Healing in Jacobean England', *Journal of Social History* 22 (3) (Spring 1989).

SCHLAEFLI, L. 'La Sorcellerie à Molsheim (1589–1697)', *Société d'histoire et d'archéologie de Molsheim et environs. Annuaire* (1993).

SCHLEICHERT, SABINE. 'Vorderösterreich: Elsass, Breisgau, Hagenau und Ortenau', in Lorenz and Schmidts (eds), *Wider alle Hexerei*.

SCHMITZ, WOLFGANG (ed.). *Der Teufelsprozess vor dem Weltgericht. Nach Ulrich Tennglers 'Neuer Layenspiegel' von 1511 (Ausgabe von 1512)*. Cologne: Wienand Verlag, 1980.

SCHNEIDER, CORINNA. 'Markgrafschaftern Baden-Baden und Baden-Durlach', in Lorenz and Schmidts (eds), *Wider alle Hexerei*.

SCHOLEM, GERSHOM. *Kabbalah*. New York: Quadrangle, 1974.

SCHORMANN, GERHARD. *Hexenprozesse in Nordwest-Deutschland*. Hildesheim: August Lax, 1977.

—— *Der Krieg gegen die Hexen: Das Ausrottungsprogramm des Kurfürsten von Köln*. Göttingen: Vandenhoeck & Ruprecht, 1991.

SCHULTE, ROLF. *Hexenmeister. Die Verfolgung von Männern im Rahmen der Hexenverfolgung von 1530–1730 im Alten Reich* (Kieler Werkstücke. Reihe G: Beiträge zur Frühen Neuzeit, 1). Frankfurt: Lang, 2000.

—— *Hexenverfolgung in Schleswig-Holstein vom 16.–18. Jahrhundert*. Heide: Westholsteinische Verlangsanstalt Boyens, 2001.

SETEL, DRORAH O'DONNELL. 'Witch', in Metzger and Coogan (eds), *The Oxford Companion to the Bible*.

SEYMOUR, ST JOHN D. *Irish Witchcraft and Demonology*. New York: Barnes and Noble, 1996.

SHARPE, J. A. 'The Devil in East Anglia: the Matthew Hopkins Trials Reconsidered', in Barry, Hester and Roberts, *Witchcraft in Early Modern Europe*.

—— *Instruments of Darkness: Witchcraft in Early Modern England*. Philadelphia: University of Pennsylvania Press, 1996.

—— 'Introduction', in Macfarlane, *Witchcraft in Tudor and Stuart England*, 2nd edn.

SIDKY, H. W. *Witchcraft, Lycanthropy, Drugs, and Disease: An Anthropological Study of the European Witch-Hunts*. New York: Peter Lang, 1997.

SIMPSON, GEORGE. *Emile Durkheim*. New York: Thomas Y. Crowell, 1963.

SOMAN, ALFRED. 'Criminal Jurisprudence in Ancien-Régime France: the Parlement of Paris in the Sixteenth and Seventeenth Centuries', in Knafla (ed.), *Crime and Criminal Justice*.

'La Sorcellerie en Alsace', *Bi Uns d'Heim* (88), no. 1.

STEPHENS, WALTER, *Demon lovers: Witchcraft, Sex, and the Crisis of Belief* Chicago: University of Chicago Press, 2002.

SULLIVAN, ANDREW. 'The He Hormone', *The New York Times Magazine*, 2 April 2000.

SURET-CANALE, J. 'La Senégambie à l'ère de la traite', *Revue Canadienne des études africaines/Canadian Journal of African Studies* 11 (1) (1977).

SWAIN, JOHN. 'Witchcraft, Economy and Society in the Forest of Pendle', in Poole (ed.), *Lancashire Witches*.

SWANSON, R. N. *Religion and Devotion in Europe, c.1215–c.1515*. Cambridge: Cambridge University Press, 1995.

TEDESCHI, JOHN. 'Inquisitorial Law and the Witch', in Ankarloo and Henningsen (eds), *Early Modern European Witchcraft*.

THOMAS, KEITH. *Religion and the Decline of Magic: Studies in Popular Beliefs in Sixteenth and Seventeenth Century England*. London: Weidenfeld and Nicolson, 1971.

THURSTON, ROBERT W. *Life and Terror in Stalin's Russia, 1934–1941*. New Haven: Yale University Press, 1996.

—— 'The Rise and Fall of Judicial Torture in the Witch Hunts and the Soviet Terror', *Human Rights Review* 1 (4) (2000).

TOIVO, RAISA MARIA. 'Marking (dis)order', in Davies and Blécourt (eds), *Beyond the Witch Trials*.

TOLNAY, STEWART E. and E. M. BECK. *A Festival of Violence: An Analysis of Southern Lynchings, 1882–1930*. Urbana: University of Illinois Press, 1995.

TREVOR-ROPER, H. R. *The European Witch-Craze of the Sixteenth and Seventeenth Centuries and Other Essays*. New York: Harper and Row, 1969.

TURNER, ALICE K. *The History of Hell*. San Diego: Harcourt Brace & Co., 1993.

VALENTINITSCH, HELFRIED (ed.). *Hexen und Zauberer: Die grosse Verfolgung – ein europäisches Phänomen in der Steiermark*. Graz: Leykam-Verlag, 1987.

VOLTMER, RITA. 'Die grossen Hexenverfolgungen in den Territorien zwischen Reich und Frankreich (16. und 17. Jahrhundert)', in Voltmer and Irsigler (eds), *Incubi/Succubi*.

—— 'Hexenprozesse und Hochgerichte: Zur herrschaftlich-politischen Nutzung und Instrumentalisierung von Hexenverfolgungen,' in Eiden and Voltmer (eds), *Hexenprozesse*.

—— 'Ruwer und Eitelsbach in der Frühen Neuzeit', in Kordel, *Ruwer und Eitelsbach: Zwei Dörfer im Spiegel ihrer Geschichte*.

—— 'Von der besonderen Alchimie, aus Menschenblut Gold zu machen oder von den Möglichkeiten, Hexenprozesse zu instrumentalisieren', in Voltmer and Irsigler (eds), *Incubi/Succubi*.

VOLTMER, RITA and HERBERT EIDEN. 'Rechtsnormen und Gerichtspraxis bei Hexereiverfahren in Lothringen, Luxemburg, Kurtrier und St. Maximin während des 16. und 17. Jahrhunderts', in Voltmer and Irsigler (eds), *Incubi/Succubi*.

VOLTMER, RITA and GÜNTER GEHL (eds). *Alltagsleben und Magie in Hexenprozessen*. Weimar: Rita Dadder, 2003.

VOLTMER, RITA and FRANZ IRSIGLER (eds). *Incubi/Succubi: Hexen und Ihre Henker bis Heute. Ein historisches Lesebuch zur Ausstellung*. Luxembourg: Luxembourg City: Publications scientifiques du Musée de la Ville de Luxembourg, tome IV, 2000.

WAITE, GARY K. *Heresy, Magic, and Witchcraft in Early Modern Europe*. New York: Palgrave Macmillan, 2003.

WALDREP, CHRISTOPHER. 'War of Words: The Controversy over the Definition of Lynching, 1899–1940', *The Journal of Southern History* 66 (1) (February 2000).

—— *The Many Faces of Judge Lynch: Extralegal Violence and Punishment in America*. New York: Palgrave Macmillan, 2002.

WARNER, MARINA. *From the Beast to the Blonde: On Fairy Tales and their Tellers*. New York: Noonday Press, 1995.

WEISSER, MICHAEL R. *Crime and Punishment in Early Modern Europe*. Atlantic Highlands, NJ: Humanities Press, 1979.

WESTFALL, RICHARD. *The Life of Isaac Newton*. Cambridge: Cambridge University Press, 1993.

WIESNER, MERRY E. *Working Women in Renaissance Germany*. New Brunswick, NJ: Rutgers University Press, 1986.

WIESNER-HANKS, MERRY (ed.). *Convents Confront the Reformation: Catholic and Protestant Nuns in Germany*, introduction Merry Wiesner-Hanks, trans. Joan Skocir and Merry Wiesner-Hanks. Milwaukee: Marquette University Press, 1996.

WILSON, ERIC. 'Institoris at Innsbruck: Heinrich Institoris, the *Summis Desiderantes* and the Brixen Witch-Trial of 1485,' in Bob Scribner and Trevor Johnson (eds), *Popular Religion in Germany and Central Europe, 1400–1800*. New York: St. Martin's Press, 1996.

WOODS-MARSDEN, JOANNA. 'Portrait of the Lady, 1430–1520', in David Alan Brown et al. (eds), *Virtue and Beauty: Leonardo's Ginevra de' Benci and Renaissance Portraits of Women*. Washington: National Gallery of Art and Princeton University Press, 2001.

WUNDERLI, RICHARD. *Peasant Fires: the Drummer of Niklashausen*. Bloomington: Indiana University Press, 1992.

ZGUTA, RUSSELL. 'Witchcraft Trials in Seventeenth-Century Russia', *American Historical Review* 82 (2) (1977).

ZIKA, CHARLES. *Exorcising our Demons. Magic, Witchcraft and Visual Culture in Early Modern Europe*. Leiden: Brill, 2003.

—— 'She-man: Visual Representations of Witchcraft and Sexuality in Sixteenth-Century Europe', in *Venus and Mars: Engendering Love and War in Medieval Early Modern Europe*, ed. Andrew Lynch and Philippa Maddern. Nedlands, Australia: University of Western Australia Press, 1995.

INDEX